Marie Anne

Marie Anne

The Frontier Adventures of Marie Anne Lagimodière

Grant MacEwan

Western Producer Prairie Books
Saskatoon, Saskatchewan

Cover design by Warren Clark, GDL
Cover illustration by Oni

Printed and bound in Canada by Modern Press ⸱⸱⸙⸱⸱ı
Saskatoon, Saskatchewan

The publisher acknowledges the support received for this publication from the
Canada Council.

Western Producer Prairie Books publications are produced and manufactured in
the middle of western Canada by a unique publishing venture owned by a group ⸱
of prairie farmers who are members of Saskatchewan Wheat Pool. From the first
book in 1954, a reprint of a serial originally carried in the weekly newspaper, *The
Western Producer*, to the book before you now, the tradition of providing
enjoyable and informative reading for all Canadians is continued.

Canadian Cataloguing in Publication Data

MacEwan, Grant, 1902-
    Marie Anne

Bibliography: p.
ISBN 0-88833-138-X

1. Lagimodière, Marie Anne, 1780-1875.
2. Northwest, Canadian — Biography. 3. Frontier
and pioneer life — Northwest, Canadian. I. Title.
FC3213.1.L33M32 1984   971.2′01′0924
F1060.8.L33M32 1984   C84-091352-4

Contents

Preface

Most of my writing experience has been in the area of western Canadian history, properly buttressed with footnote references. That was a matter of choice. There were also a few experimental ventures in pure fiction but none in fictionalized history, which I was inclined to view as an illegitimate union of two distinct forms. Now, to my surprise, I find myself engaged in fictionalizing history.

Marie Anne and Jean Baptiste Lagimodière were very real people on the western frontier. So were Miles Macdonell, Lord Selkirk, Lieutenant Governor Adams Archibald, Alexander Henry the Younger, Cuthbert Grant, Colin Robertson, Louis Riel, John Mac-Leod, Bouvier, Paquin, Belgrade, and others, although Patrick Potlatch might have to rate as a Saskatchewan River legend more than a proven personality. A serious effort was made to keep all these characters in their proper niches in history.

I had hoped to treat Marie Anne's story with all the accuracy and documentation befitting a good biography, but some parts of her life were found difficult or impossible to confirm. In order to make the best use of the indisputables and essentials in her career and present them for public reading, it was necessary to apply the brush of imagination where informational gaps were found to exist.

My interest in Marie Anne and Jean Baptiste Lagimodière goes back many years. I opened files bearing their names before 1946 and visited Maskinonge, Marie Anne's birthplace and scene of her childhood, in 1951. Exploring in the quaint and lovely old community west of Trois Rivières and three or four miles back from the St. Lawrence proved delightful as well as enlightening. From there the search shifted, naturally, to St. Boniface and other places where citizens bearing the family name would, hopefully, have some hand-me-down knowledge concerning the forebears. Most of those with whom I talked had little or nothing to offer, but their enthusiasm and good will were appreciated.

Some of the Marie Anne Lagimodière data collected were in conflict, but there was reason to conclude that the historical highlights in the lady's life were correctly established, thanks to the bits and pieces of information gathered from family sources, the Catholic Church records, and the personal efforts of Father Picton who received me from time to time at the Archbishop's House, St. Boniface, in 1951 and 1952. I am especially grateful for the resource information collected by the missionary-priest, Abbé G. Dugast, who spent twenty-two years at Red River and presented his findings in *La Première Canadienne du Nord-Ouest,* published by Cadieux and Derome, Montreal, in 1883.

The Dugast book, translated by Miss J. M. Morice, was presented before the Historical and Scientific Society of Manitoba as Transaction No. 62, on December 12, 1901. The paper was published a short time later on the pages of the *Manitoba Free Press.*

Still, there were gaps in the story, inviting a moderate degree of fictional treatment and dialogue. But there could be no question about Marie Anne's unequalled place in Canadian history and the high quality of her contributions to life on the frontier. The initial motivation for presenting the account in its present form, as accurate in all essentials as seemed possible, was simply to capture the story of this courageous and conscientious pioneer — the first woman of the white race to make her home in the Northwest. Secondly, I wished to make an account of her remarkable deeds available to all, young and old, who could enjoy it and derive inspiration from it.

Finally, I must offer my thanks to those who gave encouragement and help. Among these are the widely scattered members of the Lagimodière family or clan, Miss Marjorie Mercereau from Fredericton, New Brunswick, for her interest and assistance in the early stages of writing, prior to a twenty-six-year lull during which the incompleted manuscript gathered dust; the late Hector Coutu, great, great grandson of Marie Anne and Jean Baptiste Lagimodière, who farmed at Brosseau, Alberta, and prepared a useful family genealogy published under the title, *Lagimodière And Descendants 1635 - 1885;* and members of my own family who saw the manuscript in its later stages and offered helpful suggestions.

1

Louis'
grandmother

As November darkness came down upon the settlements at Red River, Marie Anne sat alone in her small room on the St. Vital side, humming an old French-Canadian paddling song and knitting furiously. She was always knitting, it seemed. Nieces said she could fall asleep in the old, roughcut rocking chair fashioned by her husband, Jean Baptiste Lagimodière, and continue rocking and knitting without a break in the rhythm of either.

The room's only light came from the blazing poplar wood in her open fireplace, but no more was needed. Her memories were more vivid when the lights were low. And even though the kindly wrinkles on her aging face showed as clearly as rills of erosion on an exposed hillside, the twilight shadows magnified rather than dimmed the marks of character, courage, and heroism.

Visitors might think the creaks from the venerable rocking chair made from native bur oak were warnings of total collapse at any minute. But the lady who knew most about it dismissed such fears, insisting with the brand of faith known only to elders that it would last as long as she needed it—although perhaps not a day longer.

The rocker's response to its occupant was like a good heartbeat, slow and steady. By coincidence or intent, the rhythm was the same as that of paddles in the strong, bony hands of the voyageurs who had brought her to the untamed fur country sixty-five years before—fifty strokes per minute.

Granny, as she was known affectionately up and down her side of the river, might have claimed more memories and distinctions than any westerner, man or woman, still living in 1871. As the first of her sex to settle in what was to become western Canada, and having

1

outlived her husband by sixteen years, she could have reported from memory on more important landmark events in early western history than anyone before or since.

She travelled hundreds of miles when a good canoe offered the nearest thing to Pullman luxury in transportation. She saw the coming of the Selkirk Settlers — the very first to come to the western fur country with an agricultural purpose — and helped those needy people who suffered hardship, persecution, fire, floods, and famine before savoring success. Indeed, she was an eyewitness to the awful conflict between the fur trade and settlement that reached its bloody climax in the Battle of Seven Oaks.

In later and somewhat better times, she travelled with members of her family on the annual buffalo hunt, upon which most residents depended for their "staff of life" known as pemmican. One of her distinctions was in rendering that blend of dried and pounded buffalo meat, melted tallow, and raw saskatoon berries much tastier than expected by consumers at her table.

There were other landmarks too. The lady growing old in the country of her adoption could recount the appearance of the first steamboats for river traffic, the first printing press in the West, the arrival of the first missionaries, the first surveyors, and the coming of the North West Mounted Police. She was a close observer of the Red River Insurrection in which her grandson was a leading figure and, more recently, witnessed the birth of the first western Canadian provinces. To each of these, Marie Anne Lagimodière could say, "I remember." Hers was a fine vantage point for the observation of western history.

On this particular night in November, 1871, she was expecting her usual Sunday evening visitor, her favorite grandson, Louis Riel. She was wearing her brightest homespun buffalo wool shawl to honor the hour.

"He's late tonight," she muttered to herself while listening for the familiar footsteps and knock at her door. "Poor boy; he's had so much on his mind! I don't know how he's carried it all. I hope he's all right."

With parental concern, she watched anxiously every event in Louis' life, especially his rapid rise to power and fame in the past two years. Success and trouble came together for him, particularly after October 11, just two years before, when surveyors working for the new Dominion of Canada arrived unannounced, with the purpose of marking the country in square sections. They appeared on the riverlot farm of André Nault, another of Marie Anne's grandsons and a cousin of Louis'.[1] They were there without permission or remorse. The easterners paid no attention to Nault's instructions to leave. Neighbors heard about the affront and came together carrying their guns. Louis Riel, who could speak English in a commanding manner and who had just returned after an absence of several years in educational pursuits at Montreal, emerged as spokesman. Although his leadership was untested, he performed like the man the Metis people had been seeking and quickly persuaded the easterners to leave and stay away.

For the often frustrated natives, this was the first clear demonstration of triumph over Anglo-Saxon arrogance and was sweet enough to bring rejoicing to all of Marie Anne's friends and relations.

A few days later, the same inspired Metis were effectively blocking the entry to Rupert's Land of the Honorable William McDougall, travelling on Canadian Government authority to become the first lieutenant governor in the West. His appointment, according to letters he was carrying, would take effect on the first day of December, the date set for the formal transfer of Rupert's Land from the Hudson's Bay Company to Canada.

The Red River Metis accused McDougall of ignoring the native people when workers were being hired for the construction of a government road being built westward from Lake of the Woods. They were additionally hostile when they learned that he was bringing sealed boxes containing guns. They met him at the boundary at Pembina and instructed him bluntly that he would not be permitted to cross, certainly not until there was a clear recognition of native rights and claims.

Riel's followers objected principally to the agreement to transfer Rupert's Land to Canada, made without even a word of consultation with the native people, who insisted that they held inherited claims to the country. The Metis anger was understandable and, having discovered a leader with all the essential characteristics, citizens of the mixed blood and their French friends became steadily bolder. Marie Anne admitted a wish to be younger so that she could carry Jean Baptiste's old buffalo gun and serve under her grandson.

"What's the latest news from Louis and his boys?" she asked with clocklike regularity, and appeared disappointed when there was nothing to report. Frequently, however, there was news.

On the second of November, Louis led 120 of his enthusiastic followers through the big gate at Fort Garry and seized the premises. It marked the birth of the New Nation and was accompanied by a proclamation promising friendship to all inhabitants. The document was signed by the tall and gentlemanly John Bruce and the young and more vigorous Louis Riel. By the same public notice, twelve representatives from the English speaking settlements were being invited to meet with twelve from the French and Metis communities to review the new political situation and consider measures that would unite all groups in one governing body.

There was opposition, of course—some of it violent—and the Government of Canada postponed the date for the official transfer of the country and sent Donald Smith—later Lord Strathcona—to mediate an acceptable basis for the takeover.

Events at Red River were reaching a critical stage and Marie Anne was receiving more rather than fewer evening calls from her grandson. The developments made her nervous but she had confidence in Louis and generally approved of his policies. She rejoiced to hear that he and his friends, who were the authors of a Bill of Rights, were appearing increasingly as reasonable people. Solution seemed to be within reach when one of the easterners who opposed the provisional government, a perpetual trouble-maker, Thomas Scott, was accused of assault and the attempted murder of a Fort Garry guard. Given a court-martial trial, the arrogant easterner and Orangeman was convicted and sentenced to be shot. Donald Smith made an ardent plea on Scott's behalf, but it was of no avail and the execution was carried out on March 4, 1870.

It was a grave error and some of Marie Anne's relatives believed it was the only major decision in the insurrection record that caused the wise grandmother to shudder and disapprove. Her intuition was good.

News of the precipitate punishment brought anger and turmoil in the East. Citizens of Quebec could understand Riel's reasons for refusing to halt the execution. Ontario's Anglo-Saxon and Protestant population, on the other hand, howled loudly for Scott's "murderers" to be brought to trial and punished appropriately.

Notwithstanding the Scott affair, however, the Manitoba Act, providing for the creation of the new province, was passed in the House of Commons on June 12 and Manitoba was given birth officially on July 15, 1870—a rare display of parliamentary haste.

But with the furor resulting from Scott's death, Prime Minister Sir John A. Macdonald knew he had to act firmly and quickly and moved to send a force of twelve hundred men under the command of Col. Garnet Wolseley to put an end to the alleged farce of a provisional government. The soldiers, after months of travel by slow and primitive means, arrived at Fort Garry amid mud and rain on August 24, 1870, to find the fort abandoned. Anticipating a fight and victory, they were disappointed and sought to give expression to their anger in other ways. There were some ugly scenes of mob violence, including a raid on the home of Julie Riel, Louis' widowed mother.[2] The soldiers wanted to find the local leader and his two most prominent lieutenants, Ambroise Lepine and W. B. O'Donoghue, but they had crossed the river and cut the ferry cable just minutes before the soldiers arrived.

In due course the eastern regiment departed, but the Red River region was left with division and ill feeling until October of the next year when a threat of trouble from the outside brought residents together. Fort Garry and the bigger river community were threatened with invasion by the disgruntled Irish known as Fenians. Unsuccessful in making effective strikes elsewhere to break British rule in Ireland, Fenian supporters were assembling in the vicinity of Pembina for an attack across the border.

"Does anybody know what those Fenian fellows want by attacking us?" Julie asked worriedly.

Her mother replied with more firmness in her voice: "They don't know what they want, except to attract attention and make trouble. When our Louis held Fort Garry, everybody didn't approve but everybody knew his purpose, exactly."

Julie had another concern: "They'll be pestering Louis to join them because they know the rest of the Metis people would follow him anywhere."

Marie Anne gazed pensively at a knothole in her roof, as if she expected the answer to pop out. "Everybody expects him to join," she said, "but I don't. I'll advise him to stay out of it or else get into it on the side of home defense. Now that we have a province, for which Louis can take most of the credit, he'd better be on the side of the defenders."

As if to confuse the Red River residents, W. B. O'Donoghue, the former teacher at St. Boniface College who had become Riel's principal colleague in the provisional government, was already with the Fenians and trying to persuade both Riel and Lepine to join. As if by Irish magic, O'Donoghue had suddenly appeared as "General O'Donoghue," but to his surprise, Riel, instead of joining the new rebel cause, was undertaking to recruit a troop of his own people to defend his province against any foe, just as his grandmother wanted him to do.

As it turned out, Riel and his volunteers were not needed. An American force, with the approval of Manitoba's lieutenant governor, Adams Archibald, crossed the boundary at Pembina on October 5 and promptly rounded up and arrested the intended attackers.

As one who tried to stay busy, Marie Anne was also one to keep herself well informed about local events. Most recently, there was the lieutenant governor's unexpected action in crossing the Red River to thank the volunteers for their loyalty at a moment of threatened danger, and Granny was eager to hear her grandson relate the circumstances in his own words.

"I'll see him tonight and get his story," she was saying to herself as rocker and knitting needles continued to work in harmony.

Snow was falling faster on this November evening and she was becoming slightly impatient as she waited. Then, suddenly, she heard the footsteps. The old rocking chair became motionless and a smile came over her face as she momentarily forgot her stiff joints and hastened to the door to greet her young hero.

"Bless you, Louis Riel," she said, "I knew you'd come but I always worry when you're late."

There was a hug and a kiss for Granny and then, removing his topcoat, Louis explained: "Yes, a little late; I called to see mother and helped her chink a few cracks between the logs of her house. The Indians say we'll have a long and cold winter."

"It's colder tonight, isn't it?" she asked.

"Yes, colder, and snow coming faster. It occurred to me on my way here that it was at this time of year and in this kind of weather that grandfather said 'farewell' to you and his kids and started away on foot to Montreal. I remember you telling me about that message from Colin Robertson to Lord Selkirk when the settlers needed help to ward off their enemies. I know you remember it well."

"I was thinking about that today," Granny replied. "That was fifty-six years ago, if you please. Jean Baptiste said he walked—or ran—every step of the way and he didn't get back for more than a year. We were sure your grandfather was dead. And while he was away, there was that awful Battle of Seven Oaks. The children and I were in the most unlikely place during the fighting—in the old chief's teepee. That good old Indian Peguis came to get us when the trouble started and we couldn't have been in a better place; but I heard every shot fired and kept wondering who was being killed. I knew the people on both sides. You're right; the weather was just like this when your grandfather picked up his gun, blankets, and snowshoes and started away.

"But now, my boy, sit close to me and tell me how you're getting along. So much happens in a week or two of your life! I was so glad you had a troop of your friends ready for home guard when those foolish Fenians were about to attack. You must tell me more about the lieutenant governor's visit to our side to thank you and shake your hand. Weren't you surprised? Tell me everything."

Even before Louis could answer, she was on her feet to get a comb with which to straighten his thick black hair, just as she would have done for the small boy of twenty years before. He accepted the motherly attention warmly, then slumped lower in his chair.

"Before we get into that," he said, "let me say again, grandmother, that these Sunday evening visits mean a lot to me. I wouldn't miss the benefits of your experience and judgment for anything.

And something else: if this is the sixth of November, 1871, then it's your birthday. You're eighty-nine and starting on your ninetieth. You look and sound as if you'll be around for a long time yet. I hope so. The Red River district needs you."

"Thank you, Louis boy. Now tell me about yourself."

"Yes," Louis responded with a shy smile, "there's been a lot of action for me in these weeks. It seems to be my lot to live with excitement—and danger."

"I know that," she interjected. "There's too much danger in your life. You really met the new lieutenant governor, didn't you? I think he's a good man—better than McDougall would have been. We might still be under the rule of old McDougall if you and your boys hadn't stopped him at Pembina. But tell me about Archibald."

"Well," Louis resumed, "I only saw him for a few minutes that day several weeks back, but I liked him. The fact that he wanted to cross the river to thank our Metis volunteers was a good sign. He's a big fellow and has a friendly way—like a good Frenchman—acts like he'd rather be your friend than your enemy. He asked most of my men for their names but didn't ask for mine. It makes me think he recognized me. If he did, he'd know there's a reward waiting for the person who captures me. He was careful about what he asked."

Granny dropped another piece of wood on the fire. "I'm going to make us a cup of tea, but you keep right on talking, Louis." This was what she wanted to hear, about Adams Archibald's apparent acceptance of her grandson.

"I didn't say anything to him," Louis continued, "until he completed the inspection and came back to me and shook my hand again. He said: 'You probably know more about this country than anybody else. I'm still a newcomer, you know. I've been here only a year but I like it, and your knowledge of the country, its history, and people, fills me with envy.' I enjoyed the short conversation," Louis went on, "and our men were pleased. But there are still those who are jealous or suspicious, you know."

Granny braced herself for a more caustic reply. Sitting stiffly and nursing a sour expression, she said, "I know the ones who would hate to see you getting the attention of the governor. I know what that schemer Dr. Schultz will be saying. Why wouldn't he keep quiet? He never was a friend of the native people and gave you lots of trouble when you were trying to set up a government that would serve everybody—not just the Company men and the English."

"Yes, I know what Schultz is saying — that it's a disgrace that the lieutenant governor would cross the river to shake hands with rebels like Riel and Lepine."[3]

With rising anger in her voice, the eighty-nine-year-old woman raised a fist and said, "Schultz forgets what you could have done to him when he was your prisoner. He'd like to forget that without the influence of the New Nation, there'd be no Province of Manitoba today. I'd like to ask him whose Bill of Rights formed the basis for last year's Manitoba Act!"

Louis was amused and offered no argument even when Granny added with frontier bluntness: "Except for letting Tom Scott be shot, you and your government didn't make any mistakes. But, Louis boy, I'm sorry I let my dislike for Schultz break your story. Go on."

"Well," said Louis, "there isn't much more to tell, except that Archibald was friendly and I got the impression he was inviting me to speak, so I did. When he said he envied the people who are familiar with the history of these parts, I told him about you. I said that if he wanted to meet the person who knew more about the Northwest than anybody, dead or alive, he had better meet Madame Lagimodière who is my natural grandmother and the adopted grandmother of half the people along the river. I told him you were the first white woman to come to this western country to stay—the very first.

"Well, it's getting late. I must be going but thanks again, grandmother, for your interest and your prayers. I'm not yet out of trouble; you know there are still those who'd be happy to see me dead. Your prayers have helped me greatly. I'll need them as much as ever."

"You know I'll be with you, my boy," she replied with emotion in her voice. "The members of your Metis race need you and so do I. I'll be praying."

"Just one thing more, Granny," Louis said, buttoning his coat. "If you meet the lieutenant governor and he asks about your experiences, please tell him the whole story starting right there at old Maskinonge. Please do. Good night."

2

A hint
of things to come

"What! Another drowning?" somebody shouted as neighbors rushed excitedly to the river's edge where the body of a little girl with bare feet, matted hair, and mud on her lifeless face was stretched out on the sand.

"God, yes, and it's Marie Anne," was the shocked response as villagers converged upon the spot and pressed forward to get a close view of the victim. "Oh, what a sweet child she was."

Marie Anne, fifth child in the family of Charles and Marie Gaboury, was eleven years old, small for her age, with blue eyes and black hair reaching to her shoulders. A winning smile made her a favorite up and down the Maskinonge River which emptied into the broad St. Lawrence about three or four miles to the south. Children in the habitant community were warned to stay away from the "big river" but allowed to play beside the smaller and slower one. On this day the little girl, wading too far from the shore, fell into a channel and was carried downstream until a boy, hearing her scream, plunged in and dragged her unconscious figure to the shore. In a matter of seconds the villagers were rushing with haste to the spot.

Nobody knew what to do to be helpful. Leaning over the sodden form of their child, Charles and his wife cried without restraint while friends and neighbors milled about breathing prayers for the dead. Life along the St. Lawrence and its tributaries was uncertain at the best of times; threats could come from torture-bent Indians, wild animals, or intruding Englishmen. More than once the Iroquois, considered the most ferocious of the eastern tribesmen, swooped down to plunder and kill. And among the friends standing nervously on the riverbank at this moment were men who had fought side by side with General Montcalm. They could tell in detail of that fateful day when many lives were lost, when the commanders of both French and English armies were mortally wounded, and North American domination was wrested from the French.

It was almost too much for the settlers, God-fearing family people whose oft-repeated prayers were for peace with freedom to pursue essential work on their seignorial riverlot farms and raise their children in the shadow of the church. Clearing land, making maple syrup, fishing, and hunting would keep them busy enough, if only disaster would stay away. "It's the second drowning in a month," a sobbing woman was saying.

Unnoticed among the sorrowing neighbors trying to bring comfort to the Gabourys was the friendly old Huron medicine man, Red Duck, standing tall, erect, and naked above the waist. He alone was calm as he stood with folded arms, his gaze fixed upon the girl.

"She is not dead," he began in deep monotones, showing scorn for the white man's unstable emotions. Settlers, with eyes buried in their hands to hide their tears, raised their faces and heard the wise man of the tribe repeat: "She is not dead. She will live long."

Stooping forward, he seized a sharp stone and began making marks in the sand. Moving his hands slowly as though in a trance, he sketched the clear outline of a canoe, pointing to the west. With all eyes upon him, the old man straightened, tossed his braids of coarse black hair over a shoulder and continued to speak, slowly: "Many times will her life be in danger, but her canoe will take her far toward the setting sun. She will live long and become the grandmother of many, this one with the good face of French girl and good heart of Huron."

At that moment the small girl's lips moved. "She's trying to breathe; she's not dead," her mother gasped while tightening an emotional grip on a handful of the child's wet clothes, and closing her eyes in prayer.

Charles Gaboury was now kneeling beside his wife, brushing traces of mud from his daughter's face and clothes. Sobs of sorrow turned quickly to cries of joy as friends moved closer to see for themselves and murmur, "Our dear Marie Anne is not dead! Blessed Mary!"

The girl sat up, coughed violently, and took a deeper breath, then rested her head on her father's arm. Charles Gaboury, still trembling from shock, stood and began gathering his daughter in his arms to carry her home. But as he leaned to lift her, a belated question flashed into his mind: "Who saved her? Who pulled my child from the river?"

For a moment there was no reply. Men and women who had been exercised only by the fear of another drowning, looked searchingly at each other. Then out of the silence came the squeaky voice of a youth with pubescent fuzz on his face: "Jean Baptiste Lagimodière did it. I saw him jump in and pull her out. He swims like a trout."

"Jean Baptiste! Well bless him," Gaboury replied while looking around for the young fellow whose father's farm was higher on the river. "Where is he?"

The fuzzy-faced youth spoke again, his eyes opening wider as he sensed the importance of his testimony. "He carried her here and then he ran home. You know, he's a bashful fellow. He's frightened of girls and he wouldn't want anybody to see him carrying one. He waited till you were here to look after her, then he ran like hell."

Marie Anne, her clothes still dripping river water, was carried tenderly to the log home on a farm fronting on the smaller river. While being carried, she heard her father's admiring observations about the Lagimodière boy who would face a bear but run from a conscious girl. He was not well known because he spent most of his time in the woods where hunting was at its best.

The girl wanted to walk the last part of the journey but her father insisted upon carrying her and placing her on her bed. The Gaboury home was neat and whitewashed but not pretentious like the great stone house of the seignior. It did very well in keeping the cold winds out and the warmth in. Outside was a stone bake-oven with nearby piles of wood cut in proper lengths. Inside were the essentials in homemade furniture, table and chairs, spinning wheel, and a rocking cradle ready for household duty at any time. On the walls hung the ever-ready musket and pictures of the favorite saints. Resting on the table was the principal source of light for evening hours, a shallow iron bowl containing tallow and wick, but people who retired early to beds didn't have much need for candlelight. The huge stone fireplace was an essential in every home, offering warmth and a degree of security that was too often snatched from colonists in this new land.

It was there under the sod-covered Gaboury roof that Marie Anne was born on August 15, 1780, and baptized the same day by the parish priest, Father M. Rinfret.[1] The little one, who inherited her mother's features and sweet disposition, was given her mother's names, Marie Anne.

The wee one took colic and played with her toes just like others in a community where babies came with the regularity of Easter. But when she was ten years old, the pattern of her life seemed to change and a propensity for adventure and trouble emerged. She fell out of a tree and broke an arm. Next, she was severely bitten when she intervened to save her pet engaged in a dog fight. There was the near drowning in the river, and being an outdoor girl who wanted to help the birds guard their nests and the squirrels to find sufficient food for winter stockpiles, she was frequently getting lost in the nearby woods. Henri was her favorite squirrel, a saucy fellow, but he could do nothing to spare her from troubles in the forests.

Perhaps it was a foreordained part of her education so she would be better able to take care of herself when beyond the range of home. Members of the Maskinonge community did not forget the time Marie Anne, a girl of ten, went to pick berries late one afternoon and failed to return. Delighting in the ripe raspberries she moved from bush to bush until she found herself in a strange part of the forest. Absorbed by the gay birds and the mossy floor, she had no thoughts of danger—not yet, anyway—and she wandered on. But when she turned to go home, she knew she had made a mistake. There on the woodland trail, to her horror, were more Indians than she had ever seen before. They were all men and dressed as if on a mission of war. With the upper parts of their bodies bare and painted, they appeared most frightening. Crouching low and remaining motionless and silent, she hoped they would soon pass on. But they did not; they made a fire that sent plumes of lazy smoke to dissipate above the tree tops, ate some meat, and squatted to smoke their pipes.

The little girl was frightened now as she recalled stories of St. Lawrence Valley children being carried away and never seen again by their families. She wanted to cry but knew it would be a mistake, so she muffled her sobs and tried to bury herself in leafmold to be more completely out of sight. Her longing for home was intense and to make matters worse, the Indians did not move on after their smoke. Instead, they made beds from spruce branches and settled down for the night.

Now what was a little girl trapped in the inky darkness to do? Should she venture through the night in the general direction of home, risking the danger of attracting sharp Indian eyes and ears? Possibly they were friendly, but there was an equal chance that they were hostile and cruel, with hatred for all members of the immigrant race. And could she find her way home if she did manage to escape unnoticed? In forest darkness, she could not be sure of directions.

And who could be certain that there were no bears prowling at night? She was afraid to stay and afraid to face the dark woods in an attempt to escape, so she just sobbed and shivered quietly in her cold nest of damp moss and finally went to sleep.

When Marie Anne awakened she was chilled through and damp from forest dew, but the sun was up. And the Indians? Where were they? Trembling with cold she peered cautiously about, but saw no one. They were gone; they had vanished and the forest was again quiet and peaceful.

Saying the briefest of morning prayers, the girl started for home as fast as she could run. The proper course was easy to find in the daylight, and she was soon at the clearing that marked the edge of her father's farm. She was spotted by searchers and her parents embraced her with tears of joy. Marie Anne cried and laughed alternately, clutching the dish of raspberries to ensure that it would not be upset.

"But why," Marie Anne's mother asked as she regained composure, "must it always be my little girl who has these unending brushes with danger?" Nobody could offer an answer. Fearlessness alone could not explain it. There was something here for which no one had a name. "An unusual child," Madame Gaboury said to her husband. "Could it be a hint of the quality of life ahead for her?"

Before long, the Gabourys had another reason for worry— Charles Gaboury's health. He had been a vigorous man. He could fell a tree faster than anybody in the parish. But Gaboury was failing and spending more and more hours on the big four-poster bed in his dirt-floored cabin. Neither French brandy, English bitters, nor Indian herbs improved his health, and just before Christmas in Marie Anne's thirteenth year, Charles Gaboury passed away, leaving his widow to provide for all but the eldest of ten children.[2] Gloom hung over the home for months. Never again would Mother Gaboury see her husband trudging home from a hunt with the carcass of a deer draped over his shoulders; never again would the children sit at their father's feet to hear his stories about the battle of the Plains of Abraham. Everything in French Canada dated from that fateful day. Gaboury had been one of the young habitants who, upon hearing of the capture of Louisbourg by the British in 1758, had bade farewell to his family and hastened away to offer himself for the defense of New France.

Time and again the plan of General Wolfe's attack had been scratched out with a stick on the dirt floor in the Gaboury home. Each time he told the story, there was some additional embellishment and Gaboury presented himself nearer the frontline in Montcalm's army. The children listened with unfailing attention. And with each telling, Wolfe, the English hero, became more the object of hatred.

Surrounded by death and confusion on that fateful occasion, Charles Gaboury made a vow to St. John the Baptist: "Let me survive this day and my life belongs to God." He tried earnestly to live accordingly. His years beside the St. Lawrence had been troubled but he acknowledged his blessings—a devoted wife, a big family, and a fertile farm extending a mile back from the little river. For what more could a man strive?

When the family rallied from its grief, it was clear that Marie Anne's help would be needed on the farm. There would be planting, reaping, spinning, milking, making butter and cheese, drying meat, boiling syrup, and caring for younger children. She accepted her share willingly, but there were many nights when she was so tired that she felt more like crying than going outside to play with other girls her age.

Altogether, the work was too much for immature muscles, and when an epidemic of summer fever struck the settlement, Marie Anne, weakened by fatigue, became a very sick girl. Neighbors sent for the blood-letter who came with lance and leeches, but he left her weaker rather than better. Days of fever were eating her flesh, and friends who came to see her shook their heads, fearful that this unusual child who escaped the river, the forest, and prowling Indians, would not recover this time. Only Red Duck, the medicine man, had other ideas and said again, "She will not die; she will make wigwam far away where the sun sets."

At a time of sorrow, it was good to be part of the community of Maskinonge. Marie Anne's mother saw neighbors coming and going, offering counsel and comfort and bringing gifts of currant jam and raspberry wine. And one early morning when the outside door was opened there was a bunch of blue forest flowers for Marie Anne. It was left anonymously during the night. Blue was Marie Anne's favorite color and though still sick, her eyes became big like mushrooms and her curiosity about the identity of the donor made her forget about her illness.

The priest called, as he had done with regularity, and suggested to the girl's mother: "If she recovers, she should not have to do that heavy outside work again. Let me find something easier for her."

She did get better and when sufficiently strong, was invited to take the position of assistant housekeeper at the priest's residence. She accepted with a smile and soon discovered a new independence and the pleasure of having an allowance. It was the first she was able to call her own. And, instructed by the teaching sisters, she learned to read and write. Color returned to her cheeks and lustre to her hair. She was a new person and for the first time in her life the boys were catching her special attention.

From her window in the church house she could see the villagers coming and going—ladies carrying vegetables and firewood, and men, including some gallant young ones, carrying guns, axes, and canthooks, or driving oxen. She had thoughts of romance and asked herself why she had never seen that Lagimodière boy who pulled her from the river when she was small. "I wonder what he looks like.

They say he's a wild young man but I'd like to see him. . . . I wish I knew who left the blue flowers when I was sick."

It was at one of the springtime gatherings in the sugar bush that she first saw Jean Baptiste Lagimodière. The warm days in early spring started the sap moving in the maples, and settlers took to the woods to tap the trees. Faintly sweet liquid dripped from the draining spouts into buckets which were hauled to the sugar houses. There, great vats were kept continuously hot to drive off the water and leave a thickened syrup. At this stage in the operation it was time for the people of the neighborhood to come together for the annual "sugaring off." Containers of thick syrup would be placed in snow to cool and the golden syrup became golden candy, inviting good chewing and good fellowship. Older people collected in knots to chew and converse; young men walked about briskly to see and be seen by the girls, who responded with flourishes of gaiety.

This season's sugaring off was in the Lagimodière bush, two or three miles above Maskinonge. Marie Anne had a secret wish to be present. And sure enough, the young man she would not have identified, Jean Baptiste, was pointed out. She allowed herself the reckless pleasure of a glance when he was nearby and was pleasantly shocked to see him staring at her. But he was still a bashful fellow and instantly turned away to place more wood on the fire under one of the kettles.

The girl Jean Baptiste had once pulled from the river was now nineteen years old, with sparkling eyes and braided dark hair. He was twenty-three, tall, with bold stride and brown hair that hadn't been trimmed since the last sheep-shearing. A blue feather in his wild hair suggested kinship with the native people, and his athletic bearing attracted everybody, especially the girls.

Again and again Marie Anne tried to get a clear view of this young man without disclosing her interest. She didn't know it but he was trying to hide exactly the same sort of interest until, with deceptive boldness, he came to offer a plate of choice sugarchew to the girls. Knowing she should not be the first to speak, Marie Anne nodded her thanks, blushed, and said nothing. The young man came again with sugar. Quite clearly he wanted to say something but couldn't manage it; he wanted to say something about a big party at the Manor House in May which he intended to attend. Although the words failed him again, Marie Anne seemed to get the message or, at least, understood that there was a message. Hearts, it seemed, could talk when other means of expression failed.

After returning to her place of residence that evening, the priest overheard her remark to the other housekeeper: "How I wish I had a nice blue dress."

A few days later the priest, an understanding person, asked:

"How would you like to drive to Trois Rivières, see the birthplace of La Verendrye who opened the way to the distant west? You'd see where many of the leaders in the early fur trade lived. And maybe you'd want to buy some things for yourself."

A girl of nineteen years could be pardoned for being unimpressed by history and its personalities, but she replied with emotion: "Father, I'd love to go. I've never been there. Would the stores have blue dresses? But how could we go? It's more than twenty miles."

"Ah," the priest replied, "I've arranged that. Monsieur Le Blanc and his daughter Cecile—you know them—are driving there tomorrow and they'll take you. You'll be away three days."

The girl jumped up and down in her glee and refrained with difficulty from embracing the priest. "Trois Rivières! A long drive! Perhaps a nice dress the color of a blue feather! Tell them I'll go. Oh yes, and thank you, Father."

The party of three riding in a springless carriage drawn by two hardy black horses set out early in the morning. The jolting journey would take many hours as the trail wound through forests and across unbridged streams. But the countryside was all new to both girls and it was wonderful, enough to make them forget the discomfort of the carriage. Late in the afternoon, Le Blanc pointed the cherry sapling he carried for a buggy whip and said: "There, that's Trois Rivières, where the best voyageurs come from. We'll sleep at my friend's house tonight and tomorrow you can see everything; I mean the stores."

For the two Maskinonge girls dressed in homespun, the big town brought surprises and thrills. The shops and the nice clothes overshadowed everything else, including the La Verendrye connections and the town's associations with Radisson and Groseilliers. Their visions of a fur trade had led to the organization of the Hudson's Bay Company, the English company that persisted longer than any other in the business. Marie Anne spent most of her savings on a blue muslin dress and a generous petticoat. With the bit she had left, she bought a small mirror bearing the name of Trois Rivières on its back. Priceless possessions, every one, and on the long and rough return to Maskinonge she fondled the packages as if they contained fragile gems. Each time she thought of that blue dress she smiled with joy and could scarcely wait to show it to her mother and Father Rinfret, and to wear it to the May Day party.

"Did you enjoy Trois Rivières?" her younger sister asked.

Marie Anne replied, "Yes, I'll show you the dress!"

But the daily routine following the trip brought a return of loneliness. Missing the warmth of her home environment, she wondered, at times, if the simplest course for her would be to take vows and become a nun, thereby turning her back upon all thoughts of husband and home. But just as often, she decided that the life of a nun was not for her, and she would retire to the seclusion of her room to inspect the blue dress and speculate how it would be received on that great evening of the party.

The May Day celebration at the Manor House had no rival in the social life of the entire year—unless it were the St. Martin's Day event in the autumn when tenants visited their seignior to pay rentals with fish, game, or farm produce. The customary procedure began when people assembled at midafternoon at the big stone house with its steep roof and high, peaked windows. It was the home of the seignior, that man of rank and wealth, who dominated the community and from whom the rent-paying settlers would seek the usual permission to "plant" or erect the May Pole in his honor. No seignior could refuse to accept this partially pruned and much decorated tree, around which the May Day guests would sing and drink his health. Nor could he decently refuse to furnish the food and beverage for the banquet and dance to follow in his house. Settlers did not hide their intention of recovering as much as possible of their rental payments to the master by eating and drinking well on May Day.

An evening of gaiety followed the banquet of fine food and boasting. It was the one to which Marie Anne had looked forward. Everybody for miles around was present. Cider and home-brewed ale were poured freely, and there was dancing to Trapper Fortin's fiddle. The very floors of the big house vibrated from merriment. Entire families attended; babies were tucked away in improvised beds on the floor; teenagers too young to dance and too shy to mix freely with the opposite sex, amused themselves by doing nothing in particular—and doing it awkwardly. Marie Anne in her blue muslin dress was as conspicuous as a pine in a grove of maples and, sure enough, Jean Baptiste was there with the familiar blue feather in his long hair. With his sister, he was learning to dance while he and everybody present knew he would be more at ease on a bear hunt or in a canoe race. But the truth was that Jean Baptiste did nothing badly, except facing a girl. Marie Anne, likewise an amateur at dancing, wished the man with the blue feather would be reckless enough to ask her to dance. Now and then their eyes met and she felt a friendship for this person whose voice she had never heard.

It seemed that the evening would pass with nothing more than childlike glances between them; but in the dying moments, Jean Baptiste came her way, removed the blue feather from his hair and placed it in hers, bowed awkwardly, and walked away. She accepted with a smile and by the time she thought of something to say, Jean Baptiste had fled.

Thereafter, Marie Anne found herself thinking of him as a long-time friend. She placed the feather in a book given to her by the priest and thought about her hero as she retired for the night and when she arose in the morning. She felt an involuntary concern about his food and she wanted to repair his leather clothes when stitches broke. It didn't make sense but she conducted imaginary conversations with him.

It was so nice to close her eyes and dream about him, but in sober moments she wondered if this was a forbidden relationship to be forever constrained by separation and silence. "He travels so far! What hope that I could ever have him to myself?"

But before long, a great secret sadness filled Marie Anne's heart; she heard that Jean Baptiste was to go west with the fur company's canoe brigade. In her distraction she sugared the venison instead of salting it and burned the fish for Friday's dinner. She was being silly, she told herself, because he would be far away and soon forget her. She now believed she should remove him from her thoughts. She would. She'd forget all boys.

But if she banished him from her mind, it was not for long. A few minutes after her bold resolution on that June morning, a young fellow appeared at the door of the priest's house, saying, "These violets are for Marie Anne Gaboury. Jean Baptiste, who left today to join the brigade, said to tell her to think about him every evening when the sun is setting and he will come back, some day."

Violets may have carried messages before but never had they spoken with warmer sentiment. They said exactly what the girl wanted them to say and she knew at once who had left the flowers when she was sick.

When the door closed, she dropped to her knees and breathed her plea: "Bring him back to me safely, and soon."

No spoken words had ever passed between them, but on that evening, as the sun sank below the horizon, two hearts spoke silently across the distance that separated them. Doubts took flight, for Marie Anne at least. She quickly rescinded her resolution to forget him. How could she consider such a thing? She saw him with her mind's eye, masculine, courageous, so completely her ideal.

Forget him? Never! He belonged to her. The violets said so.

3

Waiting
and dreaming

Adventure was something that Jean Baptiste Lagimodière craved the way a deer craves salt. From boyhood he heard tales about the vast fur empire far to the west, into which none but the most courageous white men had ventured. From boyhood it was his dream to join the North West Company's brigade of big freight canoes and paddle to that land of mystery and danger. He wanted to experience new customs, pit his wits against frontier hazards, live by his gun and, someday, return home to Maskinonge as a silent hero. Many times he flexed the muscles of his right arm to study its tough and powerful qualities and to assure himself that he was ready to take his place as a voyageur.

When the opportunity came, he seized it and was eager to be going—at least until the eve of departure when he was gripped by the depressing thought of separation from family and friends, certainly for months, perhaps for years, and possibly forever. Short absences from home, in the course of which he carried a roll of blankets and a long flintlock gun, were not uncommon in his life. But the necessity of squatting in a long Montreal canoe pointing into the unknown was something from which return would be difficult if not impossible.

On the day of departure from Lachine there was the final shout from spectators on the shore: "They're away!" At once the voyageurs broke into song, filling the valley with old French paddling tunes, to the strains of which their paddles moved in perfect orchestration. Well-wishing friends left the shore. The sound of singing became faint and, except for the almost noiseless ripples as paddles cut the water, silence reigned again on the river.

Jean Baptiste was not one to spend time analyzing his own feelings. Life was too full, too vibrant, for introspection. But departure, coupled with the steady rhythm of paddles and growing periods without as much as one word of speech, turned his thoughts inward to find the main cause of his sadness. Yes, it was that girl with whom he had never exchanged even a phrase of conversation. She was the first and only one to monopolize his thoughts. For a moment he forgot where he was; his paddle dropped motionless and he mumbled something almost audible: "What's the matter with me? Why couldn't I have said something to her? Fool! Why didn't I take those flowers to her house instead of sending young Pierre? I might have spoken to her and heard her say something in return."

The spell lasted only until the frowns and curses from other voyageurs brought him back to his duty. Caught in the act of dreaming, he heard the steersman shout, "What the devil you thinking about, young fellow?" Blushing, he resumed paddling.

With every passing hour, more miles came between Jean Baptiste and the girl. The realization stirred a loneliness he had never known before. He peered into the sunset, straight ahead, as if expecting to catch a glimpse of a pretty face. He wondered if Marie Anne were thinking too.

Back on the Maskinonge River, Jean Baptiste was recognized as a skillful canoeman, but here in the big and seasoned crew, he was inconspicuous unless he fell asleep or became lost in dreams. Old hands with paddles were suspicious of newcomers, at least until they demonstrated what they could do at the end of a fourteen-hour day, and how they would bear up on the portages where canoes and freight had to be taken from the water and carried overland, sometimes for miles. Freight was packaged in ninety-pound bales — an approved weight for carrying. But partly to impress or embarrass the novice, and partly to bolster his own ego, a seasoned voyageur would frequently carry two of the ninety-pound bales on a portage trip. Packing, however, was not really new to Jean Baptiste, and to surprise those who looked upon him as a fledgling, he, too, hoisted a second bale on top of the first and strode away to keep pace with the hardened, rum-drinking older canoemen.

Back at Maskinonge, Marie was indeed thinking but her thoughts were not on her work. Trying to guess the brigade's progress on a crude map in the priest's office was not very satisfactory. Wanting to know where Jean Baptiste would end each day and the appearance of the country through which he was travelling, she turned to François Barbeau, the old man who had made a score of trips over the route. Running to his cabin, she would plead, "François, tell me, please, where they will be travelling today. And what time will it be here when Jean Baptiste sees the sunset?"

Adventure was written in deep lines on the old man's face. He knew every portage on the long journey as thoroughly as he knew his way to church on Sunday morning. A listener for his stories was always welcome, and as he drew laboriously on his longstem pipe, he made sketches on the dirt floor when his old map proved inadequate. Each day she returned to ask the same question, listen intently, and then return to her room to pray.

Weeks passed, and months. Jean Baptiste remained with the canoe that paddled up Red River, past the mouth of the Assiniboine and as far as Pembina, where both the Hudson's Bay Company and the North West Company had trading posts. There, upon leaving the brigade, he adopted the independent life of a freeman, free to hunt and trap and argue with the old companies about the price for his furs.

Gradually, the new life engrossed him and with the adaptability of young manhood, he accepted the ways and customs of the frontier, even those that would have shocked the residents of Maskinonge. Conscience told him that the practice of taking Indian "wives" as a temporary convenience was wrong, but frontier friends assured him that it was practical. It did help to have someone to sew a man's clothing, cook his meals, take care of tent and bedding when travelling, and help to keep the bed warm at night. In accepting the fur country, he decided that he might as well accept its customs too. Thereafter, he was giving less and less thought to the girl at Maskinonge and his promise to return soon.

While his devotion waned, Marie Anne did not forget to watch for the sun to set. Popularity with other young people, especially the very eligible Louis Legrande, might have made it easy to forget Jean Baptiste. But she didn't. Although the violets were withered and dry, they retained a beauty for her. And the blue feather taken from his hair the last time she saw him remained pinned to her blue dress, a lasting reminder.

Everybody agreed that Louis Legrande would be a good catch. Young, decorous, proud and talkative, Louis was starting on a good farm and it appeared that all he had to do to win a girl in the area was to propose. Marie Anne liked him and enjoyed his company on the few occasions they were together, but refused to encourage him beyond the point of friendship.

Most people were expecting a marriage but when it didn't happen, the elderly gossips began to talk. "What's the matter with that girl?" one of them asked. "Twenty years old and not married yet! As far as I can find out, she isn't even trying to have a steady beau."

"You may be right about that," came the reply, "but I can tell you something that must have escaped your notice. For weeks after

Jean Baptiste — young rebel that he was — left to paddle away to the West, Marie Anne went every day to old François Barbeau's house to study his maps and ask questions about how far the canoes had gone. And François told me with his own tongue and made me promise I'd never breathe a word of it, that she left tear drops on his maps every time."

"Are you telling me that Marie Anne is in love with Jean Baptiste?" the listener asked. "Why, I heard her admit that she had never spoken a word to that boy."

"I don't care," came the reply. "Didn't he pull her out of the river and save her from drowning a few years ago? Even if she didn't fall in just to be rescued, a girl doesn't have to be talking to be in love with a boy. I think the Lagimodière boy is the one Marie Anne is waiting for and if he is, she'll be here when he comes back."

Marie Anne's mother, whether aware of her daughter's feelings for Jean Baptiste or not, reminded her that it was time she married, adding as subtly as she could, that Louis Legrande would provide a good home and be a generous husband and father. But the girl did not argue; she did not doubt that the slightly vain and boastful Louis would be a good provider and make a reliable husband and father. The highly domesticated fellow was the kind that most mothers would wish to have for sons-in-law, but Marie Anne made it clear that the choice of husband had to be her own.

Louis' solicitude was growing. Two years after Jean Baptiste went away, Louis proposed. "I can give you a good home and pretty clothes," he said with the confidence of one who believed that no girl in the parish would decline his proposal.

"Oh, Louis," she replied, "you've been kind to me. I do like you. I like being with you." She hesitated, searching for words. "I know it would make any other girl happy to have your proposal of marriage. Nobody will understand why I cannot accept. You've done me an honor, but I can't marry you and I can't tell you the reason why not. It would sound silly; you wouldn't understand."

Surprised but undaunted, he tried again. "Marie Anne, I really want you. If you refuse, then surely I have a right to know the reason. I must know, and I promise not to talk about it."

She knew she owed him that much. Her words tumbled out: "Louis, there is one man in my heart. There's no room for another."

Her hopes that he would not ask for more information were shortlived. "Who is he? Do I know him? Does he love you?"

"That's the ridiculous part," she said, wiping her eyes. "I don't know how he feels. It's two years since I saw him; we've never even spoken. See how foolish it sounds? But I can't forget and I love him now, whether he still thinks of me or not. Nobody will understand. I'm sure you don't. I wish I didn't have to talk about it."

Louis was astonished. He thought he had come to know the girl, even though she had never shown the relaxation and trust for which he hoped. There was always a barrier that puzzled and challenged him. But this most recent revelation was unbelievable.

"Do you mean you've waited two whole years for his return?"

"Yes," she answered.

"How much longer will you wait?"

"Louis, I just don't know. It sounds senseless but that's how it is."

"Don't you think it's possible that he's married by now, with children?"

"Possible, yes, but I don't believe it. If he is married, well, I have to get used to it before I'll make new decisions about my life."

"I don't understand it, Marie Anne," he said with a hint of anger. "I don't like it."

Her manner stiffened. "Of course you don't. You thought you could have any girl in Maskinonge, just by asking. It won't hurt you to find you can't. . . . But I'm sorry, Louis; I didn't mean to say that, even though you are used to getting what you want too easily."

Louis had a quick temper and he was not one to accept rebuke gracefully. This time he surprised the girl and answered mildly, "You may be right. It's funny how a man isn't interested in the fish that are easy to catch. Will you at least promise me that some day, perhaps, I may be permitted to ask you again?"

Yes, she would promise that much. They said good night and parted, each to spend hours in fruitless review of the evening's conversation. Before morning, Marie Anne was telling herself she had been a fool, throwing away the chance to marry the best young man along the river. And for what? Perhaps a dream, and proud Louis would not ask again.

In the morning, as the priest ate breakfast, he could see the pale, worried appearance of his helper. She tried to smile as usual but it was a poor attempt and the priest asked, "What is it my child? Something troubles you."

"Father," she replied, "I do want to talk with you. Can we talk now?"

"Certainly. My time and attention are yours."

She told him everything and the priest was sympathetic. He had known her from babyhood, knew her inherent strength of character, and her tale of strong, enduring devotion to a man she admired was no surprise. But how impractical was her dream: There was no place for dreamers in habitant society and it was his duty to discourage this flight of fancy.

"My child," he began, "the fondness for that man of your dreams gives but little hope of becoming reality in the form of marriage. Even if you were sure of his love, you cannot be sure of his return, and you would be making a mistake by discouraging a likely husband. Louis would be good to you. He'd give you a pleasant home, and Louis needs a wife. I must be honest with you and tell you that I think you made a mistake."

"Thank you," she replied. "I'm sure you're right. It wasn't my reason that kept me from accepting Louis, but my innermost feelings. I just can't help thinking that Jean Baptiste belongs to me and I to him, even though distance and the years of his absence separate us. If he would only come back so I could know how he feels about me!"

Months passed, and time and reason seemed to be working for Louis—if he was still interested. Marie Anne's mother kept reminding her that all the girls of her age were married or getting married. "What's to become of you?" she asked, then added soberly, "Of course, I never expected you to do just like other girls."

The girl was beginning to hope that Louis would propose again; next time, perhaps, she would feel differently about things. Sometimes they walked in the forest and their friendship was much as always, but Louis was unwilling to risk another rejection.

Spring came and with it the annual conjecture: Which of the hunters and voyageurs will return with the fur cargoes from the West? What tales of adventure? What news of disaster? When the first fleet of canoes drew up at the dock at Lachine, who should step ashore but Jean Baptiste Lagimodière. Looking more mature, more weather-beaten and more muscular, he was just as captivating as when he went away. Impatient to get home and learn what had happened in his long absence, he set out for his father's farm as soon as the routine discharge and wage settlements could be completed.

The members of his family greeted him with delight. They had hundreds of questions, and friends and neighbors flocked around with more. In record time the news passed throughout the river community: "Jean Baptiste is back."

When Marie Anne heard it she wanted to shout for joy. But feeling it was not seemly for one of her age, she restrained herself. In addition, she was suddenly afraid that he had forgotten her, that the four years of absence had erased the memory of violets and the sentiment they carried.

"Where will I see him?" she asked herself. "Will he be very changed? Will he remember me at all? Will he be as shy as ever?" Questions racked her mind and distracted the performance of her household duties.

There was a knock at the door, and for an instant she felt too dazed to respond. Her heart was beating rapidly. Mastering her emotions, she opened the door and there stood Louis. Recognizing her state of excitement, he stepped back and asked, "Are you all right?"

Receiving no reply he spoke again: "It's me, Louis; may I come in?"

Recovering her composure and trying to hide her embarrassment, she tried to laugh and said, "Of course, Louis! Did you think I wouldn't know you? Please come in."

Her unusual behavior started Louis thinking. Could it be that it was related to the return of Jean Baptiste? He would soon know.

"There's to be a party at the Manor House," he said. "It's to be a welcome for Jean Baptiste Lagimodière. Everybody wants to see him. I called to ask you to come with me."

Marie Anne paled and Louis believed he had the answer to his question of long ago; it was for Jean Baptiste that she waited. It must have been because of him that she had refused his offer of marriage. For a moment, he hated the voyageur and wished he had lost his scalp to prairie natives. But Louis was sensible enough to accept fate's decision. If Jean Baptiste could claim Marie Anne's lasting loyalty, he would have to forget her and look elsewhere for a wife. Whatever happened now, there would be no more indecision.

"Yes, yes, I will go to the party," Marie Anne said, wishing she did not have to meet the test of facing Jean Baptiste for the first time in years with all the Maskinonge eyes upon her. "Thank you, Louis, it was good of you to come this morning."

It seemed that everybody for miles around was at the Manor House reception, but for Marie Anne, one figure stood out alone. Jean Baptiste seemed to have changed a little; he was perhaps less bashful but still the man of her dreams. Suddenly, the moment for which she longed was upon her. Turning from his conversation at the center of the hall, he walked straight toward her and looked into her eyes. Her heart was beating madly.

"Marie Anne! You are Marie Anne! Did you get the violets?"

His voice was strong. She should have known it would be like that, hesitant but deep and warm. They were not strangers; they were old friends, and she answered him with new confidence. "Yes, Jean Baptiste, I am Marie Anne and I still have the violets. Their fragrance is still sweet."

For a moment they studied one another, each seeming to read the other's heart, before he was swept away to be greeted by new arrivals at the party. Marie Anne turned and found Louis at her side, Louis in fine woolen capote, elegant buckled shoes, and delicately brushed hair.

He spoke: "He's come back, Marie Anne. It was for him that you waited. He's a lucky man." Louis could be the gentleman.

"Yes, Louis, isn't he attractive? Perhaps he doesn't seem so to you, but for me there was nobody like him. No matter what happens, there never will be."

Louis repeated that he believed he could have made the girl happy, but added generously: "Jean Baptiste is an exciting fellow and you may have been right in your judgment. I hope everything will work out well and you'll be happy."

The evening passed, but not without a few more precious words between Marie and Jean Baptiste. "When will I see you again," he asked, "and where? It must be soon. I know now it's important. I hope you think so too."

"I know it is. Tomorrow would not be too soon."

"Tomorrow, I will come. Will you wear the blue dress?"

Tomorrow came and as the days went by the two young people were often together. It was like the working out of a well laid plan. Everybody, with the possible exception of Louis, was pleased with this revelation — a romance like a fire that had smoldered for years and then broken into a beautiful flame.

For the girl, it seemed too good to be true, but she was wise enough to know that disappointments can appear unexpectedly. What if he were to go away again with the canoe brigade? It was a sobering thought, but she wasn't going to allow fears about the future to mar the present happy relationship.

How glad she was that she waited! Life with Louis would have been secure, comfortable, and dull. Humans were given minds and imagination so that life might be an adventure. When she walked with Louis, she noted, they followed the well beaten paths; when with Jean Baptiste, they abandoned the old paths and made new ones. It was there in the forest stillness that Jean Baptiste found the courage to talk about marriage. His proposal was clumsy but it was earnest and Marie Anne's answer was yes.

She was in his arms, raising her face to his. It was for this that she had waited. They talked about the future. To her delight he had arranged for a farm not far from Maskinonge, a new farm with good soil and big trees to furnish logs for their house. He would start building at once and then, when the marriage bans had been announced three times, they would be married. They would live together, work together, and play together. There would be little ones and Heaven would be theirs.[1]

4

With face
to the west

When it became apparent that the new house being made from pine logs would not be ready for the newlyweds on their wedding day, April 21, 1806, Jean Baptiste arranged for the use of a cabin on an adjoining farm. The rented structure was not handsome, but it would break the wind and turn most of the rain for a few weeks. The setting was lovely — hills with the hue of a bluebird's feathers to the north, heavy maple trees to the east, and the Maskinonge River within a stone's throw to the west. Marie Anne's cup of happiness was running over and Jean Baptiste should have been busy enough with tasks on the new farm to ensure contentment. In addition to the completion of the house, there were logs to cut and split for rail fences, stumps to be demolished, plowing with a pair of black Normandy oxen borrowed from the seignior, and the preparation of a garden plot shaped to fit Marie Anne's precise specifications.

Jean Baptiste could be a good worker as long as he was interested, but he had a record of restlessness, and whether his wife recognized it or not, his love of adventure was quite capable of overruling his dedication to menial tasks. That characteristic could, and did, spell trouble for a new wife.

For anyone with wanderlust in their bones, the spring season presented the biggest temptations. Before the new house was completed, Marie Anne detected a change in her husband's manner, almost as clear as a rabbit's changing coat at the same season. He was talking more about the Northwest where he had lived for four years. He was thinking with visible nostalgia about buffalo hunts, gay times at Pembina, and friends among prairie Indians. Marie Anne liked to hear him relate his adventures in the fur country, but why this sudden preoccupation?

She didn't allow herself to think it was serious, but one evening after a heavy day with logs, her husband unburdened himself in his own blunt way. Blaming the spring months, he admitted he had been caught up by the unyielding spell of the Northwest. "You won't like this," he warned his worried wife, "but try to understand. My feeling for you, it's the same as ever, but I can't do anything to kill that urge to go back with the canoes. I've decided I can't live here — not for now anyway. I've got to go, but it means leaving you for awhile, maybe a year. Then I'll come back and we'll live on our farm and have a family, a big family. You'll be all right, I promise. You'll always be my wife. You can live with your mother or stay with my family on my father's farm."

It was the longest speech Jean Baptiste had ever made and almost as exhausting as lifting pine logs. And it was enough to strike the bride of a few short weeks with shock and pain. She buried her face in his buckskin jacket, still pungent with smoke from the tanning, and said nothing. But if he interpreted her silence as submission, he was totally wrong. Unwilling, yet, to trust herself with a reply to this cruel proposal, she kept her silence and went to bed, not to sleep but to weep and think.

By the time he retired to bed, her eyes were dry and she was ready to make her speech, a brief one, but carefully rehearsed. "Ba'tiste," she said with iron in her voice, "I didn't marry you to live alone. I married you to be with you. Now, you won't like this any better than I liked what you said to me, but I have to say it. If you go west, I go too."

Had he heard her correctly? The words stunned him as he hadn't been stunned since a drunken hunter held a knife over him at Pembina. Angry as much as shocked, the words came more easily now. "What damn nonsense, girl! Don't you know that no white woman has ever gone beyond Grand Portage or Fort William? You don't know what you'd be getting yourself into if you went out there. No girl raised here could stand the life there." With mounting impatience he repeated, "You don't know what you're talking about. Would you be able to live without a house, without a priest, and without friends?"

She nodded in the affirmative and smiled faintly to indicate that she was listening. And Jean Baptiste talked on. "You think you'd be ready to sleep on spruce branches beside the river and travel all day in wet clothes? And live on pemmican? Damn it, woman, you'd have to be crazy to think about it."

He stopped talking long enough for her to start again. She had no intention of inviting a long debate, but felt she should answer him and hope to have the last word.

"If you really believe you must go," she said firmly, "I give you a wife's consent to do so, but in case you didn't hear me correctly before, I repeat: If you go, I go too."

His opinion was unchanged. To take an attractive young wife to that uncivilized country would be sheer madness, but he knew now that his wife was not fooling. His choices were clear and limited; he could decide to settle down at Maskinonge where his life would be dull, or he could stoop to her foolishness and allow her to accompany him to the West. The former he could not do; the latter he did not want to do.

He thought of a way to resolve this problem in his own favor. He would sign on as a North West Company voyageur, then place the request to take Marie Anne along before William McGillivray, the head of the company. He would refuse to accept a woman passenger and Jean Baptiste's wife would be forced to remain behind.

Great idea, he thought. Of course McGillivray would not allow an idle woman to take up valuable space in a freight canoe. Jean Baptiste would go next day to Trois Rivières and put it to the company men there. Marie Anne prepared a package of food for his trip and Jean Baptiste set out on foot, just as he had embarked upon many long distance journeys before.

He met the North West Company men but was astonished and disappointed when they did not refuse the unusual request. Calmly, they told him: "Your wife can go but you will have to pay for the extra 150 pounds of freight. And you can't expect the voyageurs to change their ways because a woman wants to travel. You know how the canoemen eat and drink and swear. It would be a mistake for you to take her, but if you are that foolish, we'll let her travel."

The decision was made and there was no time to lose. Plans for the brigade were already well advanced and crews were being recruited and signed to contracts. Jean Baptiste signed as an experienced voyageur, and it was understood that the cost of his wife's passage would be charged against his wage account.

The news travelled like a grass fire at Maskinonge. "She's going too," people were saying in astonishment. "Even Jean Baptiste admits it's an awful mistake, but you know the will power of that girl."

The days that followed were frantically busy and by the middle of May, the Lagimodières were ready to leave with the brigade from Lachine. They took Marie Anne's forty pounds of personal luggage and Jean Baptiste's handcarved fiddle that he had carried on the previous trip to Pembina. After tearful farewells and many well-meaning warnings, the newlyweds were starting on what Marie Anne facetiously called their honeymoon. They went first to Montreal and then another nine miles to Lachine where the company canoes were being assembled.

Lachine buzzed with activity. Cargo was piled at the river's edge and voyageurs—each with a newly decorated paddle—were milling about, impatient to be going. And the gossip on every tongue was about the young woman who was going. "Imagine, she's going all the way to Red River—if she lasts that long."

"There she is," a man was saying, pointing his paddle in her direction. "Holy Joseph, she's pretty but she must be insane. What in hell are things coming to?"

"Why would the company allow her to go?" came the response. "It's not safe for her, and it's hardly respectable for a young woman to be travelling in that company. She'll know what I mean before she goes far."

Marie Anne tried to close her ears to the gossip because she knew very well she was going anyway, regardless of what anyone said. She might die en route but nothing would induce her to turn back. Glancing up at her husband, she wondered if he had heard the current whispers, but his whiskered face gave no clue to his thoughts. If he had heard them, he'd have probably said, "Let 'em talk. Nothing short of hellfire would stop her now."

"What big canoes!" she exclaimed in his presence and received no reply. "Ba'tiste, I said, what big canoes!"

"I told you they were big," he said without smiling, then hurriedly joined the men who were loading to get the maximum of freight into the limited space. He had told her about the size, but she had to see for herself to be impressed. Each of the so-called Montreal canoes was twelve paces long and each would require eight or ten paddlers. She had not thought of canoes being big enough to carry four tons of freight and another three-quarters of a ton of voyageurs. Nothing was the way she had imagined it, and the mounting confusion made her feel ill. For a moment she was afraid she could be persuaded to abandon the adventure and return alone to Maskinonge. She walked away from the scene and quickly recovered the confidence she needed.

She watched Jean Baptiste and his fellow workers toiling in the sun, fitting what seemed like big packages into small cavities, bundles of trade goods, food supplies, personal effects, kegs of rum, guns, hatchets, kettles, and a few tents, one of which was for her and Jean Baptiste if they wanted it. Indeed she did and would be grateful for the privacy it would provide.

Men talked in loud voices and as the time for departure drew near, excitement ran high. The men were jubilant as they sought to get acquainted with those with whom they would be sharing a canoe. The Lagimodières would be travelling in a brigade of four canoes. With ten men in each canoe and a woman in one, there would be forty-one people together at the camping hour. The men would have to co-operate; time alone would tell if the presence of a young woman would have an influence upon the rough and ready voyageurs. Ahead were two thousand miles and several months of travel, day after day of exposure to hot sun and driving rain, and an unchanging diet of corn meal and fat pork. Ultimately, there would be the triumphant arrival at Fort William, Red River, or whatever the chosen destination.

Taking her place in the center of the canoe, Marie Anne recognized another testing hardship — that of sitting in a cramped position day after day amid the bales of freight. She might have wished she could periodically get out and run behind as she had done many times when travelling by sleigh in winter seasons. There'd be no such freedom here.

She had no fear of being hungry, but suspected that the quality of the food and the manner of dispensing it would become monotonous, even nauseating. Her daily ration of one quart of cornmeal and an allowance of fat pork — same as that for the men — sounded unappetizing and dreary. But the loaded canoe, riding low in the water, gave proof that luxuries were out of the question, and she said again to herself: If Jean Baptiste can do it without complaining, I can too.

There was much waving and weeping at the moment of departure. Then, as if to ease the sorrow of separation, the voyageurs, responding to the bowsman's signal, broke into a favorite paddling song, matching its rhythm to the motions of their paddles:

Derrière chez nous il y a un étang,
En roulant ma boule,
Trois beaux canards s'en vont baignant,
Rouli roulant, ma boule roulant,
  En roulant, ma boule roulant,
  En roulant ma boule.

Le fils du roi s'en va chessant,
En roulant ma boule,
Avec son grand fusil d' argent,
Rouli roulant, ma boule roulant,
  En roulant, ma boule roulant,
  En roulant ma boule.

Marie Anne was calm but in no mood for singing. Regardless of her spirit, the uncertainty of the days ahead was awesome. Still, turning back was not in her thoughts. She would try to keep herself occupied, doing what she could to help or cheer the men in her canoe. Speaking for all to hear, she assured her own man that she would carry her own belongings over the portages. Amused smiles on ten male faces indicated doubt that she could do it. She, too, was slightly amused at their reaction, and repeated silently that she would show them that being a woman did not make her helpless.

For the first night, the brigade camped on the westerly end of Montreal Island where travellers paid their respects at the Shrine of St. Anne, the patron saint of Brittany. Marie Anne placed her offering in the gift box, the last she would see for months, maybe years. Then, facing the shrine and making the sign of the cross, she said a simple prayer for protection and peace: "Oh Mother of Jesus, keep us from the dangers of rivers and lakes and violent men. And watch over all at Maskinonge until Jean Baptiste and I return to that place. Amen."

Everybody slept on spruce boughs, the hardened voyageurs under overturned canoes, and the Lagimodières in their small tent. Marie Anne could not sleep, not even with the reassuring arm of Jean Baptiste around her. Spruce needles pierced her tender flesh, and she could not tear herself away from a review of the first day's events and the prospects for the shapeless days ahead. She heard the bowsman's call to rise and was glad the night of mounting physical discomfort was over. By the time the teapot hung over a campfire was hot, the canoes were reloaded, and minutes after sunrise, they were ready to move out against the strong current of the Utawa River.

The old hands warned the voyageur novices that because of portages and rough water, travel on this stream would be slow and heavy. But after an hour on the water, the bowsman would select an inviting riverside location and order a brief stop for part two of breakfast. Crewmen had their cup of tea before sunrise; now they would devour their cornmeal mush and fat pork, practically the same fare as at other meals. The only variation would consist of an occasional addition of fresh fish taken from the river.

With every halt for meals or portages, the bowsman was the first man to jump into the shallow water at the shoreline to steady the canoe as others disembarked. He was followed into the water by the steersman and then the paddlers. Marie Anne, the last to leave the boat, would be spared from a wetting by being carried on her husband's strong shoulders. Paddling on a river with many portages, the men's clothing was never dry before it was time to jump again into the water near the shore.

Voyageurs knew their days would be long and, with or without portages, they would be tiring. On a river, they complained about the portages, but on a lake where a day's paddling might be unbroken except for brief intermissions for a smoke, they might wish for the change of pace offered by a portage. No wonder their moods varied like March weather; they sang, complained, laughed, and cursed their occupation but remained intensely loyal to it.

Marie Anne had tried to prepare herself for work and danger, but the monotony of sitting at the exact center of the canoe, hour after hour, was something for which no preparation could be effective; and the cramped position caused her legs to ache cruelly. The tasks for which she could assume responsibility were limited. She won the gratitude of the men in her canoe by doing all the mending and the preparation and cooking of fresh fish when the men were engaged at a portage. These were useful chores but hardly satisfying for one accustomed to a much wider variety of activities.

More than once Jean Baptiste saw her eyes fill with tears and knew that she was thinking of dear old Maskinonge, or suffering from leg cramps. For good reason, he worried about her, and although he ceased to talk about it, he still believed that she should not have come.

Even as he thought about it, bullets whistled over the bow of the boat and the voyageurs crouched low and reached for their guns. "Indians!" they said with one voice. "Keep low, they'll likely shoot again." No native figure was in sight, but one of the men replied with a shot to remind anybody within range that canoemen can shoot too.

The men had neither the time nor the will to engage in a war with the tribesmen, but here was a convincing reminder of another hidden danger for which travellers should be prepared, and paddling resumed at a faster pace.

Lake Nipissing's blue water and green border offered the brigade their first lengthy spell of canoeing without the necessity of periodic portages, and the miles passed pleasantly. Lake water, of course, could be rough enough to toss loaded canoes like corks in a washtub and, wisely, the men chose to travel close to the shore to permit a fast retreat to some nearby cove in the event of a sudden squall. But Nipissing remained calm and the only squalls came from the cormorants.

On Rivière de Française, the current favored the canoes all the way, but presented five portages, all short ones. Then the party seemed to coast right into Lake Huron, the sight of which brought shouts of welcome from the men. The days on Huron passed without incident except for drenching rains from which there was no protection, forcing everybody to sleep in wet clothing.

Then there was Lake Superior, big and treacherous, with all the characteristics of an inland sea. The sun was setting when the brigade moved through the narrows and halted for a night camp on a stretch of white sand. The lake was peaceful and might have passed for the Sea of Galilee on a calm evening. As usual, Marie Anne gathered wood and started a campfire while the others joined in the routine of unloading, beaching the canoes, and making ready for the extra ration of rum that would honor Lake Superior.

Superior would be the last, long lap of the journey to Fort William, at the end of which there would be relaxation and celebration. It was a pleasant prospect. And despite tired muscles, the rum induced the men to sit longer at the fire to sing some French songs and exchange stories. Steersman Dorian, as always, had stories from earlier adventures on this route. He told about the swimming moose that upset his canoe on Lake Superior, and then about a big wind storm on the same lake — a typical Dorian exaggeration — so strong that it picked up his loaded canoe, carried it the full distance of a paddling day, and set it down without loss of either cargo or men.

Marie Anne joined in the laughter and Jean Baptiste said he was glad that she hadn't forgotten how to laugh. But there was one voice more sober than the others, that of the bowsman. He agreed that progress to date had been good, and there would now be the advantage of straight travel, without the time-consuming portages, all the way to Fort William. "But by Gar," he said as he eased himself off the sand to make his bed under an overturned canoe, "you know you can't trust this old lake. I've seen the damnedest storms on this water. Sometimes they came up so fast that nobody had time to pull a waterproof over his shoulders or get a boat to shore. I tell you, a storm can come up just like my old woman's temper."

Jean Baptiste had no stories to tell but when he and Marie Anne finally retired to bed, the rum was still having its effect and he was in a mood to talk.

"Good men in this crew," he said. "Best I've travelled with."

"They seem like good people," she replied. "I guess we've been lucky in getting along so well. Maybe a woman in the crowd can bring good luck. Think so, Ba'tiste?"

He snickered and said nothing. She tried him with a more important question: "Ba'tiste, are you glad I came, or do you still wish I had stayed home?"

He wasn't ready for that question, and stammering slightly, replied: "Sometimes. . . ." then held her more closely making additional words unnecessary.

Lake Superior in the morning light looked beautiful, calm, and innocent. Voyageur hearts were light and Marie Anne's voice mingled with the others as paddling songs—unusual at early morning hours—echoed across the water.

Suddenly, the big lake seemed to erupt in anger. With hurricane force, the wind assumed command, and men turned their canoes toward the shore and paddled furiously. Here, without warning, the travellers were caught in the dangerous test of which they had been warned. Boats rose and fell as waves broke over them. Marie Anne was frightened. Having no paddle with which to take action, she closed her eyes and prayed for deliverance for all those battling desperately against the driving wind and waves.

There were signs of panic among the men. That would only weaken their chance of survival, and Marie Anne found the strength to make a show of composure. Crouching low and clinging to Jean Baptiste's ankle, she shouted to the men that they were doing well and must keep it up. Her words may have been lost in the howl of the storm, but it helped to bolster her own spirits. A huge wave broke overhead and she struggled to bail water from the boat, praying silently for divine rescue.

Turning to see how her own canoemen were getting along, she caught a glimpse of one of the other canoes in trouble, and cried out: "Oh God, they need help over there." The other boat was almost swamped and the crew were throwing freight overboard, bailing water, and fighting with all their strength against the waves.

"Pray, Marie Anne, pray," she was saying to herself, but even as she said it, the other canoe tipped and disappeared under an enormous wave. Momentarily, all traces of the boat were erased and then it reappeared, bottom side up. The men from the overturned canoe went under, then came to the surface, struggling. Marie Anne could count eight of them in the water but knew they had no chance of swimming to the shore, and only a slight chance of being picked up by one of the three remaining canoes.

"Come this way," paddlers in Marie Anne's canoe bellowed, but the wind hurled the words back at them. Rescue seemed hopeless. It was all that men in the upright canoes could do to stay afloat, but the young lady could sit still no longer. Defying instructions to remain low and hold both sides of the canoe, she stood erect and shouted frantic words of encouragement to the strugglers in the water. It did no good, and a mountainous wave cut off her view. Only a tug from her husband's right arm pulled her down and prevented her from toppling overboard.

When visibility improved somewhat, she thought she could still see eight men in the water making perceptible progress. One of the men reached her canoe and was pulled over the side. A second man made it to one of the other canoes; then a third and a fourth were pulled from the water. Sad to say, two of the young men went under and did not reappear.

Marie Anne felt sick but knew this was no time to surrender her strength. The storm raged on and their lives remained in imminent danger; nobody was sure of surviving. She sank back into the squatting position and took a firmer grip on Jean Baptiste's ankle. The assurance that he was still there gave her fresh courage, and from the depths of her memory came the words of the old medicine man who spoke years earlier beside the little Maskinonge River: She will live long. Many times will her life be in danger but she will live long.

There was another reason why she must live: She thought of the child she believed she was carrying and of which she had not yet said anything; the thought seemed to rout her fears. Jean Baptiste must be told now, she decided. It would help him too.

"Ba'tiste," she called loudly as a splash of lake water struck her face. "Are you listening? We must live. Do you hear me? We must live for the child, your child, our child under my heart. We must live."

What a moment to reveal this personal information! But his eyes acknowledged that he heard. At the same instant, he heard the bowsman say, "The wind is dropping, boys. We're going to make it." Even the hardened old voyageur was moved to add: "Thank God."

All except the two men who were lost succeeded in reaching the lake's north shore. Exhausted and sad, they ate their corn meal and pork and wasted no time in preparing their beds. Even wet clothes and bedding would not prevent them from resting and catching snatches of sleep.

In the seclusion of their tent, the Lagimodières talked about the baby Marie Anne believed she was carrying. Jean Baptiste tried to say something of the joy his wife's words brought to him, but sharing what was in his heart was not something he did easily, and he did little more than mutter some indistinct phrases. But his wife understood and wondered if their child would be the first of its race to be born in the new country.

He thought it likely that it would be; then, speaking like her guardian, he said: "You must take care of yourself. I will try to help you. You have to stop taking risks. Our baby comes first." He tried to find adequate words to tell her how much the men had admired her readiness to wade ashore after the storm in order to spare them as fully as possible, and that they were grateful for the encouragement and strength her words brought to exhausted men still battling with their paddles.

Many times during the night, men quit their beds to throw more wood on the fire and hover close to the flames until some warmth penetrated their wet clothes. Morning dawned bright and clear as though nature was trying to atone for the cruel treatment of the previous day. Nothing, however, would blot out the memories of that struggle, and nothing would remove the sadness occasioned by the loss of two colleagues. The men could carry their sorrows with them but as they knew very well, they would be expected to reload and be on their way to Fort William.

With a delay of an hour or two, the brigade was again in motion, this time with three canoes, three-quarters of the freight, and thirty-eight men instead of the original forty. They paddled closer to the shore line, thereby taking less chance of being caught in another storm. But in the remaining days of the journey to Fort William, paddling conditions were ideal and morale returned slowly but surely.

A young easterner making his first trip to the West found the lake to be distressingly big and asked why people didn't call it Superior Ocean. He was a happy fellow when he heard Dorian call out, "Cheer up! Tomorrow we'll see Fort William."

5

Fort William

Fort William was wrapped in a soft summer mist and Mount McKay, standing like a faithful sentinel a short distance to the southwest, was barely able to tell canoemen where to change courses to strike the entrance to Kaministikwia River and the fort.

"I see it," Marie Anne exclaimed with the enthusiasm of one who had just discovered a new star in the firmament. "Fort William! Doesn't that mean that we're more than halfway to Pembina—or wherever we're going? It's not very high but it's huge the other way."

Big and solidly built Fort William was still new, and the odor of curing pine logs was pronounced and pleasant. When Jean Baptiste made his first trip to the West five years earlier, Grand Portage, farther west on the same lakeshore, was the North West Company's midcontinental rendezvous. There, the arrogant Simon McTavish, who made his home at Montreal, moved about with the air of a commanding officer. In the meantime, it was discovered that Grand Portage was on the American side of the international boundary and the Company leaders set about to build a replacement. In selecting the site at the mouth of the Kaministikwia—often called the Kam—the fur trade route between Montreal and the Northwest was given a northerly bend at this point. Now, in 1806, Simon McTavish was dead and the new fort was christened William, honoring McTavish's successor, William McGillivray.

The fort, with a stout stockade, contained just about everything needed to service the fur traders' empire—living quarters, packing houses, blacksmith shops, carpenter shops, a canoe yard, stone storage houses, and a jail in which obstreperous voyageurs could be held. Above the stockade loomed the great central hall where wintering partners, together for the annual meetings in June, conducted their business and plotted hopefully for the ruination of the opposing company. There, too, they banqueted as lavishly as the remote location would allow.

On this day the wintering partners and voyageurs from east and west rallied at the riverbank to welcome the most recent brigade and hear about fortunes and misfortunes on the route. At the same time, the recent arrivals would be offered advice about placing their canoes at a river's edge already cluttered by scores of the big Montreal canoes and scores of the not-quite-so-big North canoes from as far west as the Athabasca.

Remembering the wild revelry at Grand Portage where the corn and lard eating canoemen from the St. Lawrence met to change cargoes with the equally robust pemmican eating men from the fur country westward, Jean Baptiste was worried. His fears were for his wife, but he was not inclined to disturb her, perhaps needlessly, by telling her about the brutal scenes and vulgarity to which she might be exposed.

Unconscious of the dangers lurking there, she stared gleefully at the pine and spruce log structures. "It's good to realize that we're more than halfway to Pembina. It'll be good to rest here," she said.

"Yes, more than halfway," he answered, making no comment about a rest.

Having made their canoes secure, the travel-weary voyageurs set out to inspect the Company's principal post and share in the carefree excitement of all except Jean Baptiste. At first Marie Anne could not understand why he was more quiet than usual, but suddenly she had a clue and a feeling of horror.

"Those men!" she gasped, walking more closely to her husband's side. "They stare at me like brutes."

It was as Jean Baptiste had feared. Many of the men from the west had not seen a white woman in years and now, face to face with one who was not only white but young and pretty, they leered with delighted surprise and undisguised lust.

"This is horrible! You must not leave me, Ba'tiste, not even for a minute."

With his hand protectively on her arm, she felt relieved. There was noise everywhere, loud and coarse laughter, quarreling, fighting, and vile oaths in both English and French. It was extremely disturbing and she took a new position with her back to the wild scenes and the evil glances. Trying to ignore the attention directed at her, she felt Jean Baptiste being jerked away, and as she raised her head, a bearded face with a silly smile peered into hers.

"It's my turn!" he blurted, so close that she felt his hot, rum-tainted breath. "A kiss, my beauty!"

Quickly, she moved back, looking frantically around for Jean Baptiste. "You won't find him now; your friend has left you," said the grinning monster as others gathered around them, laughing at her distress.

"Jean Baptiste," she called, but there was no reply. She called again and struck at the stranger. She was being shoved roughly along the path when she heard a dull thud, the sound of a fist striking hard upon a human jaw. The heavy hand on her neck dropped, and looking back, she saw the inert body sprawling below her husband's hovering form. And the look on her husband's face! She had never seen him look like that before. Even in her fear, she looked again to admire him, his fists clenched, jaw set in determination, eyes radiating fury, and shoulders appearing broader than ever.

He stepped back with the agility of a lynx, drew her closely to him, and braced himself for the next stage of battle, this time with a semi-intoxicated mob of the bearded fellow's friends from the West. It was no place for a woman but there was no alternative.

Marie Anne knew she couldn't do much, but she raised her fists to show that she would use them if she had to.

Just as the battle was about to begin, there was the sound of hurrying feet and she and Jean Baptiste were encircled by twelve husky men. Dorian and others from the brigade, having discovered a loyalty to each other over the course of their journey, were ready to fight for their friends. Dorian, in his anger, looked like a black Normandy bull ready to charge.

The mob did not approach. The first victim recovered consciousness and moved away. The fight was over and the Lagimodières and their friends were left alone.

Now Jean Baptiste could speak. "What did they do to you, Marie Anne?" he asked. "Tell me! Are you all right?"

"Yes, I'm all right. But it was terrible. He was trying to kiss me — and take me away."

Leaning against her husband, she began to sob. "But thank God for our friends — Dorian and the other boys. They're good people, the ones who came with us, Ba'tiste."

"It happened damn fast," he said, still panting from the struggle with the man who tried to take him away, and looking intently at his wife to assure himself that she was unharmed. "He grabbed me, a big fellow, and for a couple of minutes he had the best of me. But I broke loose and I don't think he'll come back."

"If this is the West, I sort of wish I . . ." She didn't finish the sentence but Jean Baptiste understood. If this was a sample of life in the Northwest, she had seen enough and was almost ready to admit that it was a man's domain. Perhaps she had made a mistake.

It seemed like a proper time to make some reassessments. "Should I go home, Ba'tiste? Would there be any way? If there was a brigade leaving to return to Lachine, I suppose I could go with it."

Having seen his wife act on impulse on more than a few occasions, he suspected this mood would pass. Drawing her away, he explained in his slow manner of speaking that returning alone with a strange crew could be even more dangerous than continuing westward with him. This was no time to turn back, he told her, and moreover, he wouldn't let her go without him. He'd have to abandon the trip too if she were determined to go home. And finding a brigade with room for a passenger who would not be expected to paddle could keep them waiting at Fort William for weeks.

It would have been easy for him to become impatient with her at this point. He had warned her that she would be a disturbing influence in that land where no white woman had ever appeared. But Jean Baptiste was big enough to forget the past and try to deal sensibly with the present and future. He was talking more like a father than a husband, and if it would bring some comfort to her, he could practically promise that she would not see white men displaying more bad behavior than here at Fort William. It might be notorious for dangers, but nowhere else in the West would she see such an aggregation of amorous males as at this unbridled meeting place. It was here that cargoes of trade goods from the Montreal canoes were exchanged for cargoes of furs carried by the North canoes from the far Northwest.

Holding her closely, he said: "Fort William will be behind us. We'd better go on together!"

Having found strength from his brief and clumsy assurances, she nodded with the shadow of a smile behind her tears. "Yes, Ba'tiste. We'd better. There's the baby to think about too."

By next day the wild men were almost sober and seemed to accept the presence of a white woman they could not have for their gratification. And the more responsible Company men, having heard about her courageous performance during the recent lake storm, wanted to meet her and extend their good wishes. The gentlemanly William McGillivray, the most influential individual in the entire fur trade, bowed gracefully and promised that for the rest of her stay at the Fort, he would try to ensure her security and comfort. He chatted about Trois Rivières and Maskinonge, both of which he had seen, and made her feel at ease.

Crews were regrouping and Jean Baptiste was moving freight to a North canoe for the Pembina brigade. Without being far from his side at any time, Marie Anne wrote a tear-stained letter to her mother, repeating that she would be continuing to the Red River and hoping that, with the help of God, things would improve. It was her last chance to place a letter with a crew setting out for the East.

With new resolve and fresh courage, she took her place at the center of a North canoe when it was loaded and ready for the trip westward. This time there would be only six paddlers and a steersman in each boat, and thirty bales of freight. It would mean as much work per man at the portages, but two men would be able to carry a canoe. One disappointment was that none of the former paddlers in the Lagimodière canoe — except Jean Baptiste — would be going on to Pembina, but she might have expected as much.

When they were moving again, the route was essentially in a northwest direction by Kaministikwia River, then southwest to Rainy River and Lake of the Woods. From the moment of departure, the landscape was distinctly different from anything encountered on the previous journey. In the eyes of the observant girl, it was like an endless fairyland of rocks, trees, and water, put together by the mighty hand of a great and artistic deity. It was marvelous, too, that the steersman, without becoming lost in the network of waterways, always knew which way to turn. The travellers were now in the land of never-ending change, and there was good paddling and bad; there were many portages and still the need for caution.

Before leaving Fort William, Marie Anne heard about the churning rapids on the Winnipeg River where many good voyageurs had been sucked to their deaths over the years. But with lingering scars from the misadventure on Lake Superior, Jean Baptiste could counsel against needless risks with white water, even though canoes would have to be unloaded and reloaded with monotonous frequency.

The Winnipeg River was, indeed, the most frightening stream anybody in the party had ever encountered, but after several weeks and without further mishap the travellers came to look out upon Lake Winnipeg. Crossing the south end, Jean Baptiste's longing to see his beloved Red River was gratified. Marie Anne, watching her husband as closely as she was studying the landscape, was now convinced that she had been right in coming, no matter what pitfalls lay ahead. As she loved him, she would learn to love what he loved. She would become more tolerant of the strange people and inevitable adventures in the months ahead; his life would become her life. Marriage, she reasoned, had to be like that. She wondered how Louis Legrande was getting along and how different her life would have been if she had accepted his offer of marriage. Poor Louis! He was a nice fellow and life with him would have been very comfortable, but also drab and monotonous. Life is better this way, she mused, even if it frightens a person half to death at times.

"There's the river!" Jean Baptiste shouted.

"What river?" she asked teasingly.

"The Red, of course," he answered contemptuously without sensing her attempt to be humorous. She wanted to share his enthusiasm, but it was a moment or two before she recovered from the surprise and disappointment of her first impression. It was a slow-moving river with water the color of vegetable soup. Could this be the Red River of which he had talked so much? But he was excited and didn't notice her hesitation.

"One more portage—an easy one—and a couple of days of paddling, then Pembina. We'll make our home there."

She swallowed disillusionment. Was nothing to be as she expected? She thought the Red would have the proportions of the St. Lawrence. And where were the mighty herds of buffalo? Only two of the big animals came to view beside the water. One of the paddlers reached for his gun but he didn't shoot; being so close to the end of the journey, nobody wanted to stop to indulge in the messy work of dressing a carcass. They'd continue to eat pemmican until they reached Pembina.

A halt was called at the mouth of the Assiniboine where they met a few hunters enjoying some off-season relaxation. Jean Baptiste knew them from previous years and there was now a pleasant reunion. There were drinks for all and a meal of fresh buffalo meat, the first ever for Marie Anne. Jean Baptiste was happy to hear about the fortunes of his former friends and also to learn that the Montreal company was planning to build a fort right there at the forks where they were camping.[1] It seemed an ideal place. Others must have thought so too because there were the remains of a building long abandoned, La Verendrye's Fort Rouge, constructed in 1738. The very mention of La Verendrye brought memories of his birthplace Trois Rivières, and of Marie Anne's pretty blue dress. She had packed the dress with her belongings but was beginning to wonder when, if ever, she would have occasion to wear it again.

Two more days of paddling and the voyageurs, travelling in rain-soaked clothes and with dampened spirits, reached Pembina River. Suddenly, the rain ceased and a beautiful rainbow appeared in the eastern sky. Marie Anne wished her mother could have seen it, but in her mind she heard her mother's voice: "The rainbow is God's promise to you."

Even as she reflected upon the omen, the solid walls of the two well-built forts on opposite sides of the Pembina River—posts belonging to the Hudson's Bay Company and the North West Company, respectively — came into view. Company men in brightly colored shirts, Indians without shirts, and others difficult to classify came rushing to the riverbank to greet the voyageurs and witness the spectacle of a young white woman, said to be coming to actually live among them. Fantastic, yes, but there she was, the first white woman the local Indians had ever seen, the first to become part of the new land, the first to come determined to live in the West as a wife and mother.

But when she saw the mixed crowd on the riverside, she thought of the Fort William mob and shuddered. Instinctively, she seized a handful of slack leather in Jean Baptiste's shirt and tightened her grip. Jean Baptiste acknowledged her gesture, saying, "You'll be all right here, but hang on."

6

New life
at Pembina

Understanding Jean Baptiste's feeling for Pembina, Marie Anne wanted to be enthusiastic and speak admiringly about it. First impressions made that impossible and she spoke honestly.

"It's shabby, isn't it," she said with obvious disappointment. "Even the trees are small compared with ours at Maskinonge. The forts look strong but those dirty little shacks . . . do people live in them?"

Engrossed by shouts from old friends wearing greasy leather garments, he seemed not to hear. As he leaped from the canoe, the first one to grab and shake his hand was the rough and ready Alexander Henry the Younger, North West Company wintering partner, who missed attendance at the Fort William meetings.

"By Judas, Lagimodière, I'm glad to see you back here," he said as he brought his free hand down with hammer-blow force on Jean Baptiste's shoulder. "But tell me, where in hell did you pick up the pretty woman, a white one?"

Slightly embarrassed, Jean Baptiste helped Marie Anne from the canoe and drew her closely, saying rather apologetically—as if it were a crime in buffalo country — "I want you to meet my wife."

The trader's eyes betrayed his amazement. After an awkward pause he spoke again: "You brought a wedded wife?" Then, looking into her face, he took Marie Anne's hand, saying: "Well, you're as welcome as spring flowers, young woman, but you'll not be staying here very long. I'd give you a month and you'll be wanting a ride back to civilization."

She wanted to tell him to reserve judgment, but before she could get a word out the bluff trader, who ruled Pembina with two-fisted justice, was motioning toward the fort that was his home, shouting: "Come along, both of you; there's rum and a lot to talk about. By the way, you can pitch your tent inside the stockade wall where there's less chance of getting a knife in your guts."

Jean Baptiste, back in the country he had grown to love, amid friends with whom he had trapped and shared blankets, was immediately happy—almost talkative. "Smells good," he said, taking a deep breath of air heavy with smoke and the sour odor of decaying buffalo meat.

His return was good news, but the bigger news was Marie Anne, white, young, and beautiful. "What in tarnation are things coming to?" a crusty old trapper asked his friend as they gossiped over a pot of boiled buffalo tongues.

The other replied: "It's too bad for the girl. This country isn't much for white men and it's certainly no place for white women — never will be. This one? Sure, she's fine to look at, and every man at Pembina will be dreaming about running away with her. But, damn it, she's about as much out of place as a plug hat at a thirst dance. She won't last long here."

She knew the people were talking about her, and there was conflict within her breast: a determination to remain at Jean Baptiste's side, and an urge to escape from the strong odors, the barking dogs, and quarreling Metis children. Here, she feared, she would always be a stranger, a misfit attracting curious and lustful eyes. Indian women shuffled close enough to touch her soft white skin and departed giggling with the apparent satisfaction of having confirmed some unsuspected truth.

Alexander Henry, although convinced her stay at Red River would be short, tried to relieve the monotony by giving a dinner at his post in honor of the first white woman in all of the Northwest. It was a festive occasion with roast buffalo hump, boiled cranberries, the best French brandy, and music from Jean Baptiste's fiddle. Henry's broad-hipped and silent lady was a good cook—although not necessarily a clean one—and momentarily, Marie Anne was happy. But next day the loneliness returned. She had nobody with whom to talk for much of the time. Each day she found herself waiting for bedtime to tell Jean Baptiste of her unhappiness, only to have the deep and regular breathing of sleep reply that he did not hear. She wept in the darkness, wondering if there could be anything lovely in this godless place.

But like the rainbow after the rain, there were rays of hope. Indian women became more friendly, and gradually she found a growing fascination with Henry's fat native wife. Moreover, there was the increasing comfort of her baby's life within her. She was not alone.

For Jean Baptiste there were the two company posts offering unceasing interest. Henry, with thirty-five company servants answering to him, could report a flourishing trade; even late in the season furs were arriving by canoe, travois, and on the backs of unprotesting squaws. At the same time, Indians in "safe" groups of ten or less were being admitted inside the heavy stockade gate to exchange beaver skins for guns, shot, beads, tea, tobacco, and whiskey, well diluted with river water. To explain the large share of trade his company enjoyed, Henry had to admit to a more liberal use of the trade whiskey or "firewater." This, Marie Anne noted, was a confession of one who had earlier pronounced whiskey as the root of all evil in the Northwest.

Indians from the Cree, Sioux, and Saulteaux tribes met outside the walls, and when intertribal hatred was precipitated by liquor, quarreling and murder could result. Yet nothing was being done to restrict the use of the whiskey. To Marie Anne, it constituted one of Pembina's principal sins; the other was the common frontier relationship between sexes. It was shocking to the girl with Maskinonge ideals that traders would negotiate for Indian "wives" with no more serious thought than they might exercise in buying pemmican, and then often desert them to suit their own selfish convenience. It was a desecration of those fine emotions a wife should share with a husband, she thought.

Jean Baptiste had warned his wife that Pembina would have neither church, nor priest, but he did not prepare her for the low standard of marital responsibility. It was too easy for a white man to acquire an Indian consort by bargaining with the girl's father and making a payment of a gun, a horse, or a gallon of trade whiskey. The prevailing ideals or lack of them was clearly demonstrated the day a chief came to Jean Baptiste to buy his "white squaw." He offered the handsome price of two horses and a bag of buckshot. Jean Baptiste did his best to explain that his wife was not for sale, but the chief came again and again, each time raising his bid. Finally, when the unprecedented offer of ten horses was refused, he gave up and departed, shaking his head and reflecting upon the strange ways of the white man.

"Jean Baptiste," said his wife, "these people are committing a sin. You know that. Why does the Company allow it. Why don't they bring a priest? Why don't they?"

"Don't know," he answered, obviously not convinced. His four years in the West had proved to him how well the arrangement met existing needs. Nobody except an occasional newcomer from the St. Lawrence would object, he was sure. A native woman could be a good companion and bedwarmer—and her demands were minimum. She could skin and dress a buffalo while her man was shooting another, and she could erect a teepee while he was lighting his pipe and enjoying an evening smoke.

"Well, if they won't bring a priest," Marie Anne said as though closing the debate, "they should stop this wickedness—or at least do something to discourage it."

Drawing heavily on his pipe, Jean Baptiste said nothing. But as he knew very well, the North West Company would do nothing to discourage a custom that had proven beneficial in most cases and popular in all. Living with a woman is good for a man, he was thinking; makes him a better worker. Why shouldn't a man take an Indian woman? She was part of the West; she caused no inconvenience and gave birth to her babies without trouble to anybody around her. A white woman would demand attention and comfort—and delay the canoes for a week every time she had a baby.

Then he added that most white men and their Indian women got along well, without any strife. "Lots of the ones we know around here certainly act as if they're happy."

She looked puzzled. "If only they had the blessing of the church, they wouldn't be living in sin. What about Monsieur Henry and his Indian wife? Are they happy?"

"Yes," he replied with a grin, suggesting that there was a story to tell.

"What is it, Ba'tiste? Tell me quickly."

He hesitated, not wishing to shock her. "Well, he didn't choose her; she chose him."

It happened one night when Henry was having a party at his house. After all the guests had gone, he went to his bed and found an Indian girl—one with a good face and a pleasant plumpness—occupying it. She refused to leave. When even threats of force failed, Henry became worried and angry. What could he do? Eventually he decided to leave himself and went off to visit another fort. After a prolonged absence — long enough to test the patience of the most ardent admirer — he returned. To his surprise, the woman was still waiting for him and with no intention of leaving. There seemed nothing to do but surrender. He resolved to put up with her for awhile, but the result was a strong and loyal affection growing between them. People who knew Henry and his wife couldn't imagine them living apart now. To Jean Baptiste, this was proof that existing marital arrangements could be satisfactory; to Marie Anne, it was further evidence that Pembina should have a man of the church.[1]

She didn't like the story but gave it undivided attention. It left her wondering if all white men were able to cast such spells over Indian women and girls. Later, as she lay on the Lagimodière bed of buffalo robes and moss, meditating on their conversation, a new and more disturbing thought entered her mind. It was Jean Baptiste — in the West for four years, tolerant of the customs, attractive, young, and healthy; had he by any chance taken an Indian concubine? She wanted to know. He had never given her reason for suspicion. The question raced through her mind for hours before she fell asleep.

The answer was in Jean Baptiste's mind as he lay motionless beside her. It was not the first time he wondered how much a man should tell his wife. But he concluded again that it would serve no useful purpose to explain about Little Weasel. They had parted without ceremony when he left for the East, and he assumed that she had gone to live with her people somewhere to the west and would never cross his path again.

But Jean Baptiste was wrong. Little Weasel stayed with Indians near Pembina, and when she heard of his return, she set out to resume her place at his side. The news that he had brought another woman with him from the East only filled the girl with hatred. She heard that the newcomer was very beautiful with white skin and pleasing ways, but she was sure nobody could serve her man as well as she. For two years she hauled firewood, prepared pemmican, and shared blankets. She had a rightful claim upon him; he needed her and there was nothing for it now but to kill the white woman.

Little Weasel was not stupid. She was clever and crafty and her intentions were well hidden as she sought to gain admittance at the Lagimodière tent during Jean Baptiste's absences. Under pretense of friendliness, she would await a chance to perform her wicked purpose—poison the white woman. It was a quicker and easier method of destruction than witchcraft, for which she needed the help of a medicine man. She had no difficulty in winning Marie Anne's confidence and was busy preparing meat for the evening meal when Jean Baptiste returned from a day on the plains.

He was visibly upset while the Indian girl continued to work without show of emotion. Puzzled, he watched the young squaw's apparent devotion and realized that in case the danger of a subtle plot existed, he would have to warn his wife and tell her the truth. That night, when he and Marie Anne were alone, he related the secret.

Marie Anne's face turned sickly white. He tried to console her but she held him off. This pain was so very personal and she had to bear it alone. From the corner of the buffalo robe on the floor she gazed at the stockade logs showing dimly through the entrance of the tent. Not knowing what to do, Jean Baptiste muttered, cursing his ineptitude, longing to give comfort.

"Can't you forgive me? You know I love you." There was no reply. "M'rie, please speak to me."

Fighting faintness, she had neither the strength nor the wish for speech. Then hysteria forced her: "I hate you, Jean Baptiste! I hate this West of yours. You are cruel and wicked like this land and I can never trust you again. I was wrong! My mother told me I was making a mistake. I was wrong!" Her voice rose to a scream.

"I guess I did something wrong too," he said. "I'm sorry, damn it."

"Sorry," she cried, with the mad laughter of mockery. "You've ruined my life and broken my heart and you say you're sorry! How could you marry me with this in your heart? And be the father of my baby? What am I to do? What can I do? I ask you."

She said it over and over, now more subdued: "What am I to do?" Jean Baptiste, like a boy caught stealing apples, hung his head and twisted the corner of his leather shirt. He was ready to admit that he was wrong. Perhaps he should have told her before or just after their marriage. But he had thought it would hurt her needlessly to thus relieve his own mind. He was still not sure.

"If only I could go home," she wept, more softly now.

Or if only you'd stayed home until I returned, he was thinking. But nothing would be gained by a review of the past. It was important now to check her weeping and put her to bed. Protracted emotional disturbances might bring other troubles to an expectant mother.

He put his arms about her and kissed her with more fervor than he had done for months, and it seemed to help both of them.

"You're tired," he said as he placed a duck-feather pillow under her head. Then, lying in his arms, her sobbing gradually ceased. But she could not sleep. She had to think this problem through. It was a long distressing night, but toward morning, the wild confusion in her mind began to disappear; sensible reasoning brushed aside self-pity and injured pride. Things began to come clear. She didn't want to face two thousand miles of canoe travel to Lachine; she had no desire for more wild adventure; and clearly, whether Jean Baptiste had lived with an Indian girl or not, he wasn't a bad man. Indeed, he was a good, well-meaning man, and she was making too much of something that at least a few reasonable people did not consider sinful. Moreover, it was her own idea to come west; she had insisted against his wishes and he had been considerate for her safety and comfort on the journey. Now, in this recent sad scene, he had shown himself genuinely sorry for her distress and had come to her with love and affection when she needed them so much.

And the baby! If more were needed to fix her decision, this was it. In a few months she might be at Maskinonge — if a trip could be made without mishap — and that would be a good place for a baby. But a better place, by far, would be close to the little one's father, and her mind was made up. She was now sitting upright on the bed and wide-eyed, telling herself that she was Jean Baptiste's one and only wife, and feeling compelled to repeat to him what she'd said before they left Maskinonge: "Where you go, I go too." She must tell him, right now. Nothing so important should be kept until morning. More than that, his dreams might be troubled and his heart waiting for her reassurance.

Long before the sun's rays peeked through the seams of the tent, she tugged at his arm to awaken him. He sprang to his feet, reaching instinctively for his gun and asking in a whisper, "What is it? Where?"

"There's nothing to shoot at Ba'tiste. Come back to bed." She lifted the blanket and drew him to her, laughing at his fears. "I just want to tell you; I've thought about everything and I was wrong to make such a fuss. Look, I'm your wife and will be your wife no matter what happens."

"You wakened me just for that?" he asked, forgetting the scenes of the early evening.

Her arms tightened about him. "Yes, " she said, "that and a little more. Maskinonge is behind me. I'll never go back until we go together. I know Little Weasel is buried in your past. I belong with you, and your tent or cabin will always be my home."

For a few moments, they held each other closely. "You're not the first woman to boil my kettle but, by gad, no one will follow you," he whispered, surprised that he could put so much into one statement.

In the days that followed, Marie Anne felt a new sense of security. Her man was more completely hers. She saw him standing above the strong men of the plains like the voyageurs turned coureurs-de-bois, and with clearer vision she began to see some semblance of logic in the strange society that was Pembina. She was coming to understand those resolute fellows who accepted the dangers of the Indian country in order to enjoy its freedoms, and those fascinating, unblushing ones like Alexander Henry whose words were law. Without being able to explain it, she was recognizing an overruling force of good intentions.

It was inevitable that life in a community composed of contrasting human elements would be fraught with uncertainties and dangers. The best reminder was Little Weasel who continued to make uninvited appearances around the Lagimodière tent. She worried Jean Baptiste, but he assured himself that her actions gave no cause for alarm, until the native wife of a Canadian hunter told him the woman was planning to kill Marie Anne by one means or another. There was only one thing to do, take Marie Anne away before harm could be done.

"We'll get buffalo meat," he announced, and without further explanation the tent and sleeping supplies were packed into a small canoe. He and his wife set out northwestward on the Pembina River, travelling to country where Jean Baptiste knew herds were likely grazing at this season. With light cargo, they made good time against the current.

Jean Baptiste knew the country, knew the hills in which the river had its beginning, and the good buffalo country through which it flowed. Food would be no problem. At that season, he could shoot pigeons for a meal at any time and vary the diet with geese, ducks, buffaloes, beavers, bears, and wild berries. For three nights they camped beside the stream where the howl of coyotes sent shivers up the young wife's spine and furnished the music of isolation for Jean Baptiste. He knew the cowardly howlers would attack nothing bigger than a fawn.

On the fourth day they chose a semipermanent campsite on a knoll overlooking the river. From the entrance of their tent they could look down the stream and far over the countryside to see if buffaloes or Indians were moving. Here was beauty and solitude, and as husband and wife explored the area in search of game, they discovered an outdoor companionship, hitherto unnoticed. Marie Anne was finding a new enthusiasm for western soil and sky.

The day Jean Baptiste shot the first buffalo, his wife could hardly contain her excitement. From the moment they sighted the herd to the firing of the gun and that second of suspense waiting for the animal to fall, her heart raced madly. The shot went through the thorax of the young bull, and Marie Anne immediately received her first lesson in skinning and disemboweling a buffalo. She watched admiringly and helped when she could, even though the stench of hot entrails tested her self-control.

When the task was finished, the meat from the carcass was hung in strips from tree branches, drying for use in making the winter's supply of pemmican. This strictly western food staple had been the diet of the brigade crew from Fort William westward, and was composed of a pounded mixture of berries, dried meat, and melted fat. Now that she was preparing her own, Marie Anne looked forward to eating the food that had grown monotonous on the journey. The mixture was packed in a buffalo rumen, the second stomach compartment, to be held for the season ahead when the need might be great.

"Good," said the young man after surveying the work. "We need twice as much."

"In that case," came the reply, "I shoot the buffalo and you pick the berries."

He laughed but she was serious. She wanted to try her hand at shooting and he knew her will was not something to be bent like a green willow.

"That's fair," he agreed, "but don't miss."

"Ah! You'll show me how to do it and I won't miss."

But teaching her to shoot with skill was not going to be easy and he was sure it would take time. In this he was not entirely correct. She had watched him and remembered much about his technique. She recalled how a herd would gallop out of range almost before the smoke from the gun had cleared and understood why that first shot was so important. She practiced aiming and firing the gun, and tried crawling through the grass with the flintlock held in a position that would ensure against the loss of the gun ball. He reminded her about remaining invisible in the grass as she manoeuvred closer to the herd, and getting an unobstructed view of the selected animal. A hunter needed patience as it might require hours of time after locating the herd.

When she said she was ready for the test, man and wife set out together, walking along the river where they would have the advantage of tree cover to hide their presence. After an hour, they spotted a small herd and Marie Anne's heart skipped a few beats. She was excited. Drawing closer, they saw an old bull lying quietly, chewing his cud while females and a young bull grazed nearby. Fortune was with the hunters because they were downwind from the animals. Jean Baptiste placed a ball in her gun and handed it back to her, whispering, "Now you're on your own. Move cautiously."

The role of observer was new to him but he accepted and hid behind some trees to watch her progress as she made her way closer, moving on her belly.

Poor girl, he thought. She'll become tired; she'll get thorns in her hands; her muscles will ache. Then, for the first time, he remembered her condition. What an insane undertaking for an expectant mother! He was afraid but knew there was nothing to be gained by trying to stop it now. She has more grit than most men, he told himself. And what if she only wounded the animal? He knew very well that a wounded buffalo could be a killer.

Where is she now? he asked himself. He had to look carefully to see her inching her way through the sheltering grass with at least a measure of the skill of a hungry Sioux. At a point thirty or forty paces from a young cow, she stopped and took aim. "Be sure of your aim now," he said almost loud enough for her to hear, holding his own gun ready for use in the event of an emergency.

The thunder of Marie Anne's gun shattered the silence. The cow stumbled a few wild paces in the girl's direction and then went down. The rest of the herd, tails high in the air, stampeded away toward the distant hills.

"Marie!" he shouted, dashing from his hiding place, "Perfect!" He threw his arms around her, saying, "I shouldn't have let you do it."

"But it was fun, Ba'tiste. Now you help me skin and get ready to make pemmican."

The winter's supply of pemmican assured and cold weather settling in, Jean Baptiste concentrated on trapping, and his wife accompanied to help when she could. Like a good team, they worked in quiet co-operation. Geese flying south told of winter's approach, and Marie Anne was becoming worried about Jean Baptiste's plans for the months ahead. Surely he wouldn't be thinking of staying here for the winter, even if the trapping was rewarding.

"Where are we going to be in the winter?" she asked at length. "You know I can't have the baby here." He should have known but he looked surprised. She wondered if all men were so annoyingly obtuse. But he was not unreasonable and asked her where she would like to be for the winter. They agreed that they should return to Pembina where they could hope to find accommodation in Henry's house, or at least inside the stockade. They had to start back before the river froze, but Jean Baptiste chose to stay one more week for the prospect of additional furs.

Everybody at the settlement was interested in the Lagimodière return. Canadians, Metis, and Indians were friendly and Marie Anne's presence continued to be a matter of wonder. Their return was especially pleasing to Alexander Henry because of Jean Baptiste's previously demonstrated competence as a handy man. Moreover, his wife's charm would make life within the fort more pleasant. Henry offered the shelter of his house for the winter, stipulating only that: "You'll bring your own pemmican, of course. And you can help me keep order."

The Lagimodières agreed. Jean Baptiste promised to provide more than the necessary amount of meat and pemmican. And he became one of the local policemen. This happy living arrangement disposed of the young man's chief worries, first in protecting his wife from Little Weasel's revenge, and second, in finding adequate winter quarters for an expectant mother and her baby when it arrived.

Food and fuel would be abundant at Pembina. In addition to pemmican, there would be deer, beaver, swan, duck, fish, potatoes, and even some vegetables. Little Weasel might hover about watching for a chance to carry out some evil purpose, but the fort gates would be closed to her.

Pregnancy was not at all uncommon at Pembina, yet the aura of novelty clung to Marie Anne's condition. Canadian hunters speculated about how she would get along in childbirth. And Indians, who considered having a baby as nothing more than a minor inconvenience, wanted to be among the first to see a white specimen, and brought gifts of tiny moccasins and pieces of leather clothing. Marie Anne was increasingly grateful for the friendship of Alexander Henry's Indian wife, who knew everything about babies and promised to be present to help when the time arrived, and stay with the new mother as long as necessary.

As Marie Anne sat finishing one last small garment, she was enjoying the thought that she, as the first white woman in the West, was about to become the mother of the first white baby born in the country. In this, however, she was only partly correct, but the full story was not revealed until almost a year later when Alexander Henry recorded the details in his journal entry of December 29, 1807.[2]

As Henry related the story, a Scottish girl, disguised as a male in order to follow her faithless lover to Rupert's Land, lived in his household for about two years, or until she could keep her secret no longer. On this particular day, while working as one of Henry's servants at Pembina, this person appeared before him complaining of illness and asking permission to lie on his bed. An hour or two later, when Henry entered the room to enquire how the sick "boy" was feeling, he discovered that the "boy" had just given birth to a baby.

The revelation, coming almost a year after the birth of Marie Anne's first baby, made Marie Anne the second white woman in the Northwest rather than the first, but left her with the distinction of being the first white mother in the country. And the Lagimodière baby, born when winter's wind and snow swirled about Pembina on January 6, 1807 was, indeed, the first of its race and color in what was to become western Canada.

Alexander Henry's plump native lady, as good as her word, was present to help Marie Anne in her hour of need. With nothing more than a mumble, she pushed Jean Baptiste out of the house and took command.

"Dear Mother of God, be merciful to me in this trial and to my little one, I pray."

The girl was in good hands. The Indian woman, speaking with the help of her hands, told her how to kneel on the moss spread on the dirt floor and grip a willow crossbar lashed to two posts driven into the ground. To the older woman this was just routine, and in less time than it would take to skin a buffalo, it was all over. The baby was dried with warm moss, dusted expertly with wood ashes, and placed under the blankets with its mother.

The news spread quickly: "The Lagimodières have a baby girl," and before curious viewers had time to arrive, Marie Anne baptized the babe, asking the blessing of God, and in His presence, naming her Reine, meaning Queen.[3]

Jean Baptiste was excited and impatient; he wanted to show his small daughter to the whole population. As soon as his wife would allow it, he led the inquisitive whites and Indians, one by one, past the crib to gaze upon the wonder of a white baby. Not even an albino buffalo would have aroused more interest. The admiring Indians brought gifts of beaded clothes for the child, a rattle made from a dried buffalo bladder with a pebble inside, and best of all, a moss-lined cradlebag in which the baby could be carried on her mother's back, papoose fashion.

It was all very nice and the young mother was happy. How she longed to tell her friends at Maskinonge—especially her mother and the priest. She knew she could not get a letter out until the brigades went in the spring. By that time Reine would be four months old and still older when the letter reached Maskinonge.

In the meantime there would be a question about spring plans and travel. Jean Baptiste would want to be moving as soon as the rivers were free of ice, and she had vowed to follow him. But how safe would it be for the baby if summer travels were to take the family canoe to the far reaches of the Saskatchewan? How safe would it be to stay, with Little Weasel still nearby, wearing a smile to hide her hatred? "What will my little Reine and I do if Père Ba'tiste decides to travel?" she asked herself. Brown baby eyes looked sweetly into her mother's face and seemed to say, go too. But the question would not be that easy to answer.

7

Adventure on the Saskatchewan

The lengthening days of spring brought floods, crows, and new life. Wild flowers sprouted from every knoll and movement was everywhere—buffalo herds migrating, ducks and geese winging northward, and Indians packing teepees and leaving for parts unknown. Jean Baptiste experienced the annual recurrence of his restlessness to be moving on, and seemed willing to leave Marie Anne to speculate alone about the future of the West and celebrate their first anniversary without him.

Her interest in the future of the fur country had long been evident. She had already questioned Alexander Henry about it. "What's going to happen here?" she asked the heavy-handed trader as he watched piles of furs being pressed into bales for convenient transportation to Fort William.

Although some people said he would slit a throat for an extra beaver skin, he was flattered that a thoughtful question would be directed at him, and replied, "D'you mean change? The devil will quit hell before there'll be much change here. This is fur country, every damned foot of it, and anybody who thinks he can change it is a fool. I know, I'm crazy enough to plant a garden and bring in a hen to give me an egg now and then, but I'm telling you, woman, the Almighty made this a hard country for hard men and nobody'll ever farm it—if that's what you mean."

She did not argue with the trader. In the light of his emphatic views, it would have been pointless, but back with Jean Baptiste, she repeated the question, adding, "Do you think our Reine will see farms along these rivers—like at home?"

"Farms? What d' you mean?" The very idea was strange to him.

Moreover, his mind was on other things. The same springtime impulse that was stirring the natives was making Jean Baptiste anxious to be going, and he was hoping that his wife and baby would stay at Pembina where they would have the protection of the fort while he paddled up the Saskatchewan. By latest report, Little Weasel was leaving too and his family would be safe. In addition, the friends with whom he would travel wanted no encumbrances like white women. "Leave them here, Ba'tiste," was the advice of his friend Belgrade. "You'd make trouble for all of us if you took them. Damn it, man, there'd be two fresh graves beside the river if they went."

Jean Baptiste was easily convinced, but when he related the proposal to his wife, her resistance stiffened again. "Why shouldn't we go?" she demanded.

"Why? Because you can't trust the Indians back there." Pacing the floor, searching for reasons, he added, "You and baby wouldn't come back alive. I won't stay long."

For a moment she stood speechless, hands on her hips, and gaze fixed upon this strange thing called man. Her lower jaw protruded when she was angry or in serious thought. Speaking slowly, she said, "Jean Baptiste, I've heard you give such warnings before. Pembina was no place for a white woman, you said. You wanted me for a wife but didn't want me here. But I came and I'm getting along fine. Now I can carry Reine on my back, like a papoose. We'll make out and we want to go to be with you."

Upset, he was groping for words. "There'd be no home, you know. Just paddle and paddle all summer. Bad for Reine. Damn it, Marie, no white woman ever went on a trip like that."

"I know," she replied, "there'll be dangers." Then stamping her stubborn foot, she said a little louder, "But we're going. When do we start?"

With longer strides than usual, he set off to see Alexander Henry. The trader laughed, having guessed there would be trouble, but he had a proposal: "Better wait awhile and come with my party. We'll leave in June and you'll still have time to find good buffalo country for the fall hunting. Travel with my canoes and pitch your tent beside mine."

Henry's brigade would be delivering Pembina-made pemmican to North West Company posts on the Saskatchewan late in the season. It would mean a delay for Jean Baptiste's plans, but the advantages of being with a group would be ample compensation. A bigger party would be beneficial in the event of an attack by Indians, and Henry's cheerful company would add to the pleasure of the trip. The invitation was accepted promptly.

When Henry's pemmican brigade moved away from Pembina

late in June, two extra canoes carried Jean Baptiste's family and his Canadian friends, Belgrade, Paquin, and Chalifou, with their native "wives." It was understood that these freemen hunters could break away from the brigade at any time. They were interesting fellows. Belgrade, a square-faced Frenchman, was still carrying bits of last year's twigs and burrs in his long red hair; Paquin, slim, dark, bowlegged, and silent, was most like an Indian; and Chalifou, though small in stature, was singing when he wasn't talking, and his constant noise more than made up for any deficiency in size. As for the squaws, they were friendly but didn't have much to offer in the way of companionship for Marie Anne.

The Red River current sped them along and Marie Anne, squatting on the floor of the canoe with baby Reine strapped snugly on her back, had some sober thoughts about the days ahead. When she asked Jean Baptiste if he knew exactly where they were going, he shook his head, saying: "Somewhere back far." With mean satisfaction he was saying to himself, "She'll know who to blame when she grows tired of this. She shouldn't be here."

The brigade halted at the mouth of the Assiniboine where logs were being piled for a Company fort, and some of Henry's men turned their canoes to fork westward on the smaller river. The remainder of the party, including the Lagimodières and their friends, continued on the Red River and into Lake Winnipeg. They paddled far north, entering the Saskatchewan River at Grand Rapids where a two-mile portage was practically inescapable.

"Saskatchewan!" said Henry for the white woman's benefit. "The word is Cree and means 'swift running water'." Henry was in a hurry and consequently the brigade was travelling from daylight till dark, generally with Henry's canoe in the lead and the others following in disorderly array like a family of baby ducks.

The best break in the journey was at Cumberland House where, thirty-three years earlier, the Hudson's Bay Company, pursuing a policy of necessity, went inland from the Bay to build a trading post. The North West Company built there as well. Late season trading was still in progress and Marie Anne shrank from the thought of the curiosity her presence would provoke. She wanted to draw a veil over her face and move unnoticed among the people who had never set eyes upon a white woman, and white men who hadn't seen one for many years. But hiding her face was not practical so, with feminine resignation, she took out the little mirror with the name of Trois Rivières stamped on the back and fixed a curl in her hair to make the spectacle as good as possible.

In their anxiety to avoid embarrassing or dangerous situations created by Marie Anne's arrival at the fort, Jean Baptiste and his friends sent Chalifou ahead to prepare the way. The talkative little fellow would circulate word among the tribesmen that a beautiful white woman was about to appear and they should be on their best behavior.

The Indians were slow to comprehend. "If there are white women," they reasoned, "why have we not seen them before?" White women, the medicine man had told them, were not beautiful; they were ugly, and their men kept them hidden in distant parts.

Chalifou never lacked for an answer. "This white woman is beautiful but she has the power of the evil eye. Molest or provoke her and she will smite you with a single glance." The Indians understood, or thought they did. None wished to risk the destroying force of the evil eye, and when Marie Anne came among them they were as docile as kittens. Staying close to Jean Baptiste, she walked gracefully and smiled pleasantly, and the Indians were stunned as though they gazed at a spirit. In silence they withdrew to meditate. Then the head man decked in beaded garments, feathers, and coyote tails, came forward bearing gifts and choice meats from recent hunts. The gifts, including fine furs, were for Marie Anne, but there was a subtle reason. The very serious natives had a proposition and the leader made a speech, not long but loud.

"What's he saying?" Marie Anne asked Jean Baptiste, seizing his arm. "I don't understand."

"Haukemah," her husband replied with amusement. "That means 'queen'. They want you to stay and be their queen."

"Their queen?" She blushed and turned her face away. "Are they serious?" In a momentary daydream she may have seen herself leading her loyal subjects into battle, and ruling a tribe of native people with a fine feminine hand. "Would you stay too, Ba'tiste? Reine would be the princess. How would an Indian queen dress?" she smiled.

The Indians gazed in solemn silence, waiting for the answer. Jean Baptiste laughed, amused at her flight of fancy. Her dream ended abruptly, and returning to reality, she said she knew she couldn't accept. "Tell them I can't, Ba'tiste, but be sure to thank them. Now, I think Princess Reine needs some fresh moss."

With immobile faces, the Indians withdrew without comment. They were going to hold a feast anyway, and the meat was already cooking.

The celebration staged outside the fort walls surpassed anything seen at Pembina. The Indians were determined to honor the white woman whether she became their queen or not. French tunes from Jean Baptiste's fiddle increased the tempo of dancing, and food was abundant. Marie Anne entered into the spirit of the occasion which, coincidently, came at the exact end of her first year in the West, a year of strange and frightening experiences.

Cumberland House might have invited a longer stay, but the brigade with its cargo of pemmican had to be moving. And with thought to the baby, it seemed desirable to bring the little girl to some more settled way of living, temporarily at least.

Another freeman hunter, Bouvier by name, asked if he might join the Lagimodières and their friends when they travelled again. There was room in the canoe and the request was granted.

As the brigade set off at an early morning hour, Indians lined the shore for a friendly farewell glance at the first white woman to touch their lives. She refused to be their queen, but in their farewell they called her Ningah, meaning mother.

"You've got a new name," Jean Baptiste told her, without laughing. "You are now Ningah. That's a good name. I can use that name for you, too."

After four more days on the river, the brigade made its way around a rapids at a point called Nepowewin, and Alexander Henry pointed to the south bank where a succession of trading posts had operated. Another day and the canoes stopped at Prairie Post, owned by the North West Company, and located on a beautiful low beach extending a mile back from the water on the south side.[1]

The wintering partner in charge of the post, a chubby and friendly man, was "Mr. Laughing Face" to the Indians. He invited the freemen to settle nearby, assuring them of big stocks of game. Marie Anne favored stopping even though the men wished to take advantage of travel with the Henry party to see country farther west. The wish of the majority prevailed and the entire brigade pushed on. There was a brief stop at old Fort St. Louis, built by Chevalier La Corne when the Saskatchewan River fur trade was in the hands of the French, and again Marie Anne registered her wish to find a suitable place for a longer stay, mainly for Reine's benefit. She reminded the men of that attractive place at the Prairie Post where Mr. Laughing Face had invited them to settle. A compromise was proposed: Stay with Henry's brigade for another couple of days and then decide upon a campsite and probably say farewell to Alexander Henry.

The lady was agreeable, and two days of paddling brought the party to the place where the two branches of the Saskatchewan joined. Here, the river was faster, and in Marie Anne's opinion, the country was not as attractive as that through which they had passed. The freemen were considering turning back to Fort St. Louis or Prairie Post when the bowsman in Henry's canoe shouted, "Buffalo!"

A strange, low reverberation filled the air and a mighty black mass could be seen moving through the valley leading to the river and in the direction of the canoes. There were thousands of the shaggy brutes, almost enough to blot out a section of the landscape as they thundered their way southward, obviously bent on crossing. Terror paralyzed the travellers who knew that a stampeding herd crossing a river could swamp and wreck small boats.

Jean Baptiste and Paquin seized their guns and fired aimlessly in the hope of diverting the oncoming avalanche of flesh. The leaders in the herd, about to enter the water, observed the canoes and split, taking one part of the herd upstream and the other in a downstream direction to cross. This situation was decidedly worse. There were now hundreds of buffaloes swimming on both sides of the boats. Paying only the slightest attention to the canoes, the upstream animals were swimming and drifting closer and closer, creating tidal waves to add to the distress of the men at the paddles.

The river seemed full of bison, bobbing like corks in a tub, determined to gain the opposite shore, regardless of human obstructions. Some animals, unable to control their direction in the strong current, passed between canoes. One cow drifted so close to the Lagimodière canoe that Belgrade used his paddle to push her away. Had they made contact, the canoe would almost certainly have been upset. Not since the storm on Lake Superior had Marie Anne had such reason for alarm, and now, there was the added concern for Reine. Holding her baby with one arm and clinging to Jean Baptiste's leg with the other, she closed her eyes.

It was a bad moment but it passed quickly as the herd reached the south bank. The thunder of hoofbeats faded and while all agreed that they'd had a close call, Chalifou said what Marie Anne was probably thinking: "You never know when trouble will jump at you in this country."

Relieved now and smiling, she leaned heavily on Jean Baptiste and said, "Remember the medicine man, Red Duck? How many times was my life to be in danger?"

"Twelve times," was the answer. "How many times you got left?" Before she could respond he added, "Guess you've had enough of this country."

She said nothing, biting her lower lip and staring at the water rushing over rocks.

The men were now ready to return to the riverside location that was Marie Anne's choice, and after a midstream exchange of meat and supplies, followed by a farewell to Henry and his men, the two canoes carrying the freemen turned for the downstream journey. They made a fast return, thanks mainly to the current, and on a pleasant river bench extending far back to higher ground, not far from Prairie Post, the men erected the tents, driving the pegs more deeply than usual. Next day found them fitting stones into an outdoor fireplace, giving an air of permanency to the site.

At night they sat about the campfire, telling stories and enjoying the freedom from care. Bouvier, most recent addition to the group, was well supplied with tales of hunting adventure. He knew what it was to be caught in the middle of an Indian quarrel with no indication of friends on either side. He knew about sleeping in a leather tent during winter as well as summer. The story of an apparently dead bear coming back to life explained the loss of two fingers from his left hand.

Understandably, Bouvier didn't like bears, but his most tragic adventure with the species was yet to come. One evening a few days later, the four men from Pembina sat about the fire, smoking and awaiting Bouvier's return from a leisurely stroll by the river when a cry of human terror broke the evening silence. It was Bouvier, obviously under attack in nearby bushes.

Guns in hand, the men leaped to their feet as the blood-curdling cry came again. Marie Anne clung tightly to her baby as the men dashed forward to behold the terrible scene—an old she-grizzly with cubs close by dragging Bouvier away, her claws embedded cruelly in the flesh of his shoulder and head.

For an instant the men stood stunned, knowing it would be folly to shoot at a target indistinguishable in the dim light from the body of their friend. Marie Anne and the Indian women, anxious about their men, followed and saw Jean Baptiste rushing at the bear, striking it again and again with his gun, but doing nothing to stop the infuriated animal from carrying out its horrible purpose. In desperation, he took hasty aim and fired. The excited audience watched, sick with fear as the report rang through the river valley.

The grizzly was only wounded. Savage from pain, the animal dropped Bouvier and spun toward Jean Baptiste in a wild desire for revenge. Both Chalifou and Belgrade fired but did nothing more than momentarily divert the brute's attention. The bear was gaining on Jean Baptiste, sprinting to his canoe where there was another loaded gun. It seemed she'd take her second victim while the helpless onlookers watched. Marie Anne wanted to rush unarmed at the beast but the other women restrained her. Just inches separated the two as Jean Baptiste reached the boat, grabbed his gun, and fired into the mouth of the oncoming bear. The attacker fell dead at his feet.

White and trembling from fear, Marie Anne was the first to reach Bouvier. She knelt beside what seemed the mutilated remains. "Oh God, what can I do?" she muttered. "Can he live?" His eyes and nose were gone and he bled profusely from shoulder and head wounds. The men bent over the bloody mess and shook their heads. In this remote place there was no hope for the man's recovery.

"We must make him live." Marie Anne took charge. "You men get water. Get a robe and some moss."

Nobody raised at Maskinonge could be a stranger to accidents. Applying her hands to the wounds, she tried to arrest the bleeding. Cleanliness was important and the man must be made comfortable. As she gave instructions, the pitiful form was placed on a buffalo robe and moved to a carefully prepared bed in the Lagimodière tent.

When she had washed the torn flesh, she called for some pieces of cloth with which to wrap and bandage. But among these leather clad people there was no cloth, except ... she thought of her priceless blue dress, so dear to her and carried so lovingly over the portages on the long journey to the West. She had not worn it since leaving Maskinonge, but often she thought about a day when she would wear it again. She paused only for a minute and then called to Jean Baptiste to unpack her bag of clothes. She held the wrinkled but lovely blue dress aloft for one last look and then determinedly tore a generous strip from the bottom. "Tear some more," she ordered. "We'll need it all."

As the bleeding stopped and his breathing continued, indicating that he might survive, one of the men suggested that Bouvier would be better at the Prairie Post or St. Louis, but the self-appointed nurse had other ideas. "He mustn't be moved. We'll keep him here."

Day and night she sat by his bed, trying to bring him comfort and watching for signs of returning consciousness. "Poor Bouvier," the Pembina men kept saying. "He's slow in dying but nobody torn like that could live very long." They wondered where they would bury the body.

"Don't talk like that. You don't know. If it's God's will, he'll live. You men get more moss for his bed." The men were learning to do as they were told.

Days later, the mangled fellow regained consciousness and only Marie Anne was not surprised. She fed him prairie chicken soup and watched his strength return slowly. He could neither speak, smile, nor see, but he pressed her hand and she understood his gratitude. His eyes were gone forever, but his speech returned, and slowly his body grew stronger. Finally, he was considered fit enough to be taken to Cumberland House with a party of Crees going that way.[2]

Bouvier's departure left Marie Anne with a new worry. Belgrade, Chalifou, and Paquin, with their women, went on an autumn expedition, eastward, and with Jean Baptiste gone for much of every day, the young woman was lonely and sometimes nervous. "If only Bouvier were here!" she caught herself saying as she tended her child, a gun constantly within easy reach. "This country is crafty and cruel. I wonder if it can be tamed. I wonder what tomorrow will bring."

8

Rescue
and reward

It was one of those September mornings when bright autumn leaves exaggerated the sun's early light. Marie Anne watched her man fill a buckskin pouch with powder and balls for the day's hunt. With Reine in her arms and a prayer on her lips she shoved a package of pemmican into his pocket and instructed: "Try to be back early so you'll have the evening for Reine and me." Shivering noticeably in the damp morning air, she watched him move noiselessly along the path leading to higher ground and disappear among the willows and aspens.

At this season the Lagimodières had the riverbank site to themselves. The shapeless leather tent rested on an expanse of level benchland, beyond which to the south was park country well stocked with buffalo and other game. Nature's charm was everywhere and as far as anyone could perceive, it was a safe place to camp. Never to be discounted, however, was the chance of a hostile redman or hungry bear lurking behind a nearby clump of willows. It was a land of incalculables—often bloody and cruel—even though clear skies and singing birds conspired to make a person forget about dangers.

"Keep your gun handy," were Jean Baptiste's parting words as he left each morning to search for food. "You never know when you'll need it."

"Papa's gone hunting, little one," she told her sleepy-eyed baby as she strolled back to the tent. "He's a good papa. We just wish he didn't have to leave us alone."

Reine made baby sounds as though she understood and Marie Anne laughed with motherly admiration. "Reine, baby, whatever would I do without you?"

Instead of laughing with her mother, however, the baby whimpered as she had done too often of late, suggesting that something was not right with her. The mother's smile gave way to an expression of anxiety. She could see the child was pale—some minor baby ailment, no doubt, but how could she be sure, and what could she do to hasten recovery?

That afternoon, while Reine napped, Marie Anne sewed buffalo skins together for a bigger tent. With a dull needle and coarse strands of buffalo sinew, her slender fingers soon grew tired. She rolled the skins to one side and went for a short stroll along the river to gather wood for the evening fire. As she returned, her arms full of dry willow branches, she was startled by the sound of footsteps hurrying in her direction. She stood motionless, frightened, for it caught her completely defenseless; her gun was in the tent and Jean Baptiste would not be returning for another hour or more. Running to the tent for her gun would attract attention; by remaining perfectly still it was possible that the intruder might not notice her and would pass, but the thought of her sleeping child erased all caution. Dropping the firewood, she ran frantically through the bushes.

After going only a few yards, she found herself face to face with an Indian girl running in the opposite direction. Clearly, the girl was in trouble. Her clothes were torn, hair tangled, cheek bleeding, and terror and exhaustion written plainly on her face. Although unable to speak, her eyes pleaded for protection.

The girl's gestures indicated that she was being chased. Forgetting her own fears, Marie Anne started toward the tent, motioning the girl to follow. There was no time to lose. The pursuers would be there any minute.

The white woman's mind was working rapidly. They were all in danger. She and her baby would be even more desirable prizes than the Indian girl. Marie Anne didn't know what to do next. She wanted to help this defenseless girl but had to think of the protection of her child.

With an impulse she spread the buffalo skins she had been sewing on the floor and signalled to the girl to lie on them. The girl obeyed and Marie rolled the skins against the tent wall where they looked as innocent as any other pile of buffalo hides.

She heaved a sigh, looked at the still-sleeping Reine, and stepped outside just as a small party of braves appeared. Bent on overtaking the Indian beauty, they passed by, giving her scarcely a glance, and Marie Anne returned to her tent, weak but relieved.

It was too soon to relax; the braves halted and turned back. The white woman's heart raced madly. She could not put up an effective defense against these men who appeared bereft of conscience. But to show fear would be an error. She would remain calm. "God help me," she whispered, bracing herself for a show of composure. She seated herself with Reine behind her and the loaded gun across her lap.

The Indians came on fearlessly, without hiding their savage desires. She glanced at the baby, checked the buffalo skins to make sure there was no tell-tale movement, fingered the firing mechanism of the gun and wondered if she would have the strength to pull the trigger.

Boldly, the Indians entered, looked ghoulishly about, ignoring the white woman, and departed. They appeared to be interested in nothing else but the prize they had been pursuing.

And the thought that there might be armed white men nearby would be a deterrent.

Relieved, Marie Anne set the gun to one side and picked up her sleeping child, cradling the warm body in her arms and showering the sleepy face with kisses. She feared it was not yet safe to release the Indian girl from the intense heat and restraint. The men might return again. With thoughtful caution she lifted a corner of the buffalo hide to make sure the girl was still breathing. What she saw was a broad smile of gratitude for the security discovered so unexpectedly, uncomfortable though it might be in a roll of skins. The girl could not say it in white man's words, but her appreciation was unmistakable. She was ready to remain in her greasy, smelly prison until her rescuer considered it safe to release her.

Jean Baptiste soon returned from the day's hunt with the hind quarters of a deer on his shoulders. He was tired and hungry and was glad to squat on the ground beside the firepit over which the meat pot hung. With the usual greeting from his wife, there was nothing more to arouse his attention until she beckoned him to the tent, saying, "Come Ba'tiste, I have a surprise for you. I think you'll be interested."

Having recovered from her fright, there was a twinkle of teasing in her eyes. He was slow to respond. What trick is she up to now? he wondered, remembering the family of orphan owls she tried to raise in the previous summer. He was hungry and in no mood for nonsense, but rather than offend her, he followed and watched her unroll their store of buffalo skins.

At once a shy and shapely Indian girl lay at his feet, and the normally unemotional man gasped in astonishment. "Marie Anne! How did she get there?"

"She must be terribly thirsty, poor child! I'll get her some water." Marie Anne liked to tease and without answering his question, strolled away toward the river, leaving her husband and the Indian girl uncomfortably together.

"We've had some excitement today," she said on returning. "I'll tell you about it and you'll be thankful that we're alive."

The girl drank deeply and her eyes showed confidence as Marie Anne related the events. Jean Baptiste's hunger and fatigue were forgotten. He was astonished and his comment, "You did damned well, Marie," bespoke his highest praise.

Jean Baptiste's limited knowledge of the Cree language was sufficient for the purpose of getting her story. Her name was Mimmie, she said, and she was sixteen summers old. A party of warriors from the west—presumably Blackfoot—had attacked her family's lodge, killed her father and mother, and would have killed her if she had not managed to escape. She had no family to go back to and no wish to return to her tribe. Indeed, she appeared to have no intention of leaving the white woman who had saved her life.

It was a startling story. And to have unwittingly added a new member to the Lagimodière family seemed a trifle disturbing to him, but if Marie Anne wanted to keep the girl and the girl wanted to stay, he would not protest.

"We can't send her off onto the prairie alone, can we Ba'tiste? It would be cruel to save her from one danger only to send her into another. She seems a nice little person—lovely eyes—and perhaps she can help me with things."

Jean Baptiste, who found it easy to be charitable toward a good-looking girl, was nodding agreement but carefully avoiding a show of enthusiasm.

In the days that followed, Mimmie showed herself eager to help. She carried wood and water and proved understanding about the baby. Her wish, quite clearly, was to repay a debt to her new friends. In homespun sign language, the two women managed to communicate. Marie Anne wished she could share more of her worry about Reine's failing health with the girl. The child was growing more listless by the day. Gone were the rosy cheeks, the big smiles, and her former interest in food. The devoted mother was sick with worry. She left the child neither day nor night and tempted her appetite with selected morsels and the juice of wild raspberries. But nothing helped. Jean Baptiste hunted nearby and returned at midday to look for Reine's improvement. Neither parent spoke of it but both wondered if they were going to lose the little girl. When the baby became worse rather than better both parents remained with her and Mimmie did the chores and hunted for meat.

"Mimmie is wonderful," Marie Anne whispered to her husband. "I think she would die for any one of us. I don't know how we'd get along without her now."

But on the morning following these remarks, Mimmie's bed was empty. The girl was apparently gone. "I'm sure she's nearby," Marie

Anne kept saying. "Probably she couldn't sleep and went for a walk. Don't you think she'll be back, Ba'tiste?"

He searched the broad river flats, calling her name, but there was no reply and no sign of her. Returning, he found his wife studying the sleeping child, her hope fading and her heart sick. Reine was no better and without the Indian girl things would be more difficult.

"She couldn't have been stolen from our tent, could she, Ba'tiste? She was so kind. It would be awful if she fell into the hands of those brutes who were pursuing her."

"Got tired of us, I guess," was his reply. "Belongs to a wild race, you know."

"I don't believe it," she said defiantly. "I think she'll come back." But there was still the fear that the girl would never be seen again and the reason for her disappearance never explained.

A couple of days passed, then four and five without a clue. When not absorbed by her pale and sickly baby, the mother speculated on her husband's theory that the girl had simply deserted them. "But no!" she said aloud. "Mimmie wouldn't do that."

The sun was setting on the fifth day after the disappearance when Jean Baptiste came to the tent to warn that people were approaching from the west. He heard voices. Making sure his gun was loaded and ready, he walked to a clearing near the water to catch a glimpse of the intruders. "Women's voices," he called, "coming right this way."

Suddenly, Mimmie and a mature Indian woman emerged from the willow brush and walked briskly to the tent. Without a word of explanation, Mimmie went straight to the sick baby's place on the bed and smiled with relief in finding the child still alive. Then, with an air of authority, she turned and addressed the older woman, and both gazed studiously at Reine.

Standing nearby and trying to understand what the native ladies were saying to each other, the young mother sensed the reason for Mimmie's disappearance and her eyes filled with tears. The Indian girl looked exhausted, much in need of food and rest. How far had she walked and how greatly had she suffered in order to bring help? Marie Anne stood beside her man and watched Mimmie with ill-disguised affection.

There was no hasty action. The Indian women ate ravenously. Conversation didn't go beyond replies to Jean Baptiste's questions, and as the sun went down the tired Indians adjusted themselves to the buffalo hides intended for a tent and went to sleep.

Marie Anne couldn't sleep. She wanted to talk and ponder. Mimmie's account of her days of absence, as Jean Baptiste heard it, was brief but moving. She left to search for her Cree band, convinced that an ancient squaw who possessed extensive knowledge of healing could do something for Reine and must be persuaded to come without delay. After walking for two days, she found her people but had some difficulty in convincing the elderly lady to accompany her. But Mimmie's insistence eventually triumphed and they set out. In five days and nights, Mimmie had no sleep.

"The dear girl," Marie Anne was repeating. "But what will they do now, Ba'tiste? Are you sure they won't hurt Reine?"

"Of course not. The woman isn't a witch doctor." He had seen Indian remedies used before and believed the experiment was worthwhile. His remarks made his wife feel more at ease.

"Almost anything is better than helplessly watching our baby growing weaker every day," she agreed. She was eager to know what the Indian women would do in the morning, and hoped they wouldn't sleep late. At first light the two Crees were up and away. Knowing they would return with leaves and stems for brewing, Jean Baptiste had a good fire and plenty of wood ready. And the Lagimodière spirits were cheered by the mere fact that something was being done.

The two women returned with an assortment of roots and foliage. After boiling them down and cooling the rather repulsive fluid, Reine was given her first medicine. The child objected, as every baby has a right to, but the treatment was repeated at every mealtime.

Marie Anne watched hopefully, impatiently searching for signs of improvement. There was no change in the first couple of days and parental hope was fading. When Marie Anne was not watching Reine, she was studying the older Indian's face for signs of emotion, but there was no change of expression. In her impatience, Marie Anne might have ordered the treatment stopped, but Jean Baptiste was firm for continuation. During the next few days, the baby was at least no worse and then, after a few more days, there were unmistakable signs of improvement.

"She's better than she was, Ba'tiste. Look at her eyes. She doesn't cry as much. She's going to get better." The mother's bright eyes were as big as saucers. The change came suddenly and the medicine woman nodded her satisfaction. Marie Anne threw her arms around both the native women in turn. Mimmie showed she was happy; the older one displayed no indication of her thoughts. Her work was finished and with neither a word of farewell nor a hint of expected reward, she disappeared to return to her people.

Mimmie remained, ministered to the child until normal health was restored, and then shared a secret with Jean Baptiste. There was a happy gleam in her eyes. When she went seeking help for Reine, she discovered that her mother was alive. By playing dead when the enemy tribesmen attacked, the older woman had escaped without injury. Now that Reine was better, Mimmie wanted to return to live with her mother.

Jean Baptiste relayed the news to his wife and with tears of joy, Marie Anne embraced the girl.

"Jean Baptiste, tell her we'd like to have her with us always. There'll be a home for our Mimmie wherever we happen to be."

Jean Baptiste conveyed the message and as Mimmie walked away, Marie Anne said, "Call to her, Ba'tiste, tell her to bring her mother to see us and the little girl whose life she saved."

9

A new companionship

Wintering arrangements were made without an argument. Well in advance of November's warning blasts, Mr. Laughing Face, who was in charge of the Prairie Post, visited the Lagimodières at their tent and reported that Belgrade and his Cree wife were coming back to winter with him. There would be room at the fort for Jean Baptiste's family too.

Belgrade's wife Hawkfeather had once offered to teach Marie Anne to converse in Cree. This would provide an opportunity. Better still, the invitation would remove the necessity of going back to Pembina or building a log cabin beside the Saskatchewan. And two able-bodied males would offer additional security at the fort in case of attack.

The two women were not strangers, having travelled together in Alexander Henry's brigade. Hawkfeather was considered the most congenial of the Indian women in the party. She was not comely; her eyes beamed in different directions and she was about as shapely as a skinful of pemmican. But she was cheerful, brighter than her slow-witted husband, and generally as happy as a pup with a new bone. She knew some French and English—more than Marie Anne knew about Cree—and exchanging words promised to be a practical pastime while the men were hunting and trapping.

"Moostouche, moostouche, moostouche," Marie Anne repeated. "It means 'buffalo' doesn't it, Hawkfeather?"

Belgrade's wife laughed at the imperfect pronunciation, then nodded and offered her pupil another word to practice. " 'Wapi-scow' means 'white'."

It was the French woman's first serious attempt to learn Cree and she had lots of time for it. With a smile of triumph she pointed at Reine and said, "Wapiscow papoose."

It was the winter of 1807-'08, Marie Anne's second in the West. It would be remembered for its unusual cold and heavy snowfall. Huge drifts obliterated the riverbanks in places, and for months nobody left the fort without snowshoes. The imposing stockade constructed from split logs—four feet in the ground and nine feet above—was buried in snow up to the gunslots.

It was impossible, also, to escape the bitter cold, even inside the log house. The fireplace was little more than an indoor campfire confined by a circle of stones and with a hole in the roof for the smoke to escape. The fire only partially offset the winter wind that found every crack between the imperfectly chinked logs. Nothing less than Jean Baptiste's warm bulk at night kept Marie Anne comfortable. Reine alone was warm at all times, wrapped in a padded nest on her mother's back through most of the day, and in a bag insulated with duck feathers at night.

But the winter brought unexpected rewards. Marie Anne and Hawkfeather, so different in race and creed, discovered a community of understanding, even amusement. Among the white lady's personal belongings was the small mirror she bought long ago at Trois Rivières. The Indian woman found it and for the first time in her life, saw a perfect reflection of her own face. For a startled minute she studied the image, so much clearer than the distorted reflection she had seen on the surface of still water. Puzzled at first, she placed the mirror face down on the table and walked away as if she didn't trust it. But with fresh courage she returned and laughed loudly at what the mirror revealed to her. Marie Anne joined in the fun.

The fascination of the mirror never ended; each day, Hawkfeather returned to study the unbelievable revelations while her friend rearranged her black hair to change the amusing image.

A common reason for laughter will often strengthen the bonds of loyalty. The means of conversation was improving and admiration was growing. Marie Anne wanted to convert the native woman from her Indian ways. "What a shame this nice woman is not a Christian," she said to Jean Baptiste as she sat mending his moccasins. "She doesn't really know the difference between right and wrong. Nobody has ever told her about the true religion." Marie Anne had an inspiration: "It's up to me to tell her."

"Some day," she said to her friend, "missionaries will come to tell you about God and heaven—about Christianity. They'll tell you that scalping and fighting are wrong—and men and women shouldn't live together unless they are properly wed."

Hawkfeather was slow to grasp it all. But the pudgy and jovial woman was one who would think things through for herself. Perhaps fighting and scalping as the prairie Indians did were wrong, she conceded; she had reached the same conclusion long ago. But why was it necessary to have a priest tell a man and woman they were married? It was something between two people and nothing a third person could say or do was likely to make a union better or worse. She was sure her marriage to Belgrade did not offend the Great Spirit, and everything else depended on themselves.

Marie Anne looked annoyed. "The rites of the Church should never be questioned," she said sharply. "Marriage is a sacred institution. It should never be taken from the authority of the Church—not even in the fur country."

Hawkfeather's smile showed she was not convinced. And who said an Indian can't find the Great Spirit, or God, as well as the white man? She struggled for words and her utterances were a mixture of Cree, French, and English. But she was irritated when she recalled an Indian prediction that the white race would not be satisfied until it overthrew the Indians' beliefs and customs. Her smile departed. If, as Marie Anne admitted, one good God created all people—whites, reds and all—why would he not give every one of his creatures the same chance to discover and know him? She would insist that Indians have been searching for and finding the Great Spirit in their own way all through the ages.

The place to find him? In the woods, beside a stream, or on the broad prairies—wherever plants and animals and soil and water meet—anywhere in the great outdoors. Anybody who wanted to find him could do it, just as the newborn buffalo calf needing nourishment knows instinctively where to find it.

Here was resistance Marie Anne had not anticipated. She wasn't ready to grant any quarter in the area of religion, insisting that Indians could never know the religious truth until somebody told them. Now she was sure she must start at the beginning and tell Hawkfeather the Biblical story about creation. "How do you think we came to be on this earth?" she asked. "Well, I can tell you. I can tell you about God creating people."

The Indian woman showed interest but insisted upon telling her story about creation first. It started with a flood that covered everything. The Great Spirit reached down and brought up mud. He fashioned it to resemble a pancake, then breathed into it until it expanded to become the world. With more mud, he made trees. Two of them developed legs, arms, eyes, and the power of speech. Along came a snake that chewed the two trees off at their bases and they walked away as the first humans.

"Adam and Eve?" Marie Anne asked. But Hawkfeather had never heard these names.

With a sense of moral duty, the white woman told the Christian version of creation, of how God made everything in six days. The other listened intently as she would to any action story, but when Marie Anne insisted it was the only true story, the Indian lady laughed and said it wasn't any better than that of her people.

Marie Anne was on the verge of being offended. "Hawkfeather," she said, "you must not laugh at what comes from the Bible. Some day you'll understand that Christianity is the only true religion. Can you say the word 'Christianity'?"

The two men returned to find their supper was not ready. The discussion had to be terminated, but Marie Anne insisted upon having the last word: "Remember, you won't go to heaven unless you believe like Christians. But right now we need wood on the fire and a pot of snow to melt for water. Will you get the snow?"

That night Marie Anne prayed that it would not be long before Hawkfeather and other Indians would embrace the true faith and quit their pagan nonsense. That same night, Hawkfeather had a dream that she knew she was supposed to share with Marie Anne. Next morning, she could hardly wait for the men to leave.

Directing the white woman to sit on her bedroll, Hawkfeather, with more eagerness than clarity, told of the Great Spirit coming to her in her dream. He must have come a long way because his face was covered with frost and he was on snowshoes—the only sensible way to travel at that season. Nor did he come alone; buffaloes, coyotes, and prairie chickens followed him, gazing with admiration at him. There was nothing strange about this because he regards the birds and animals in exactly the same way that he regards humans.

Hawkfeather's story was taking a long time and she was saving the essential parts until the last. "You were there, too, Marie," she related with satisfaction. "We were all there. The Great Spirit liked you but he laughed when you argued with him and told about trying to make Hawkfeather give up the Great Spirit and believe in God. He laughed some more and told you he is both, Great Spirit to the Indians and God to white people. He said you don't need to change Hawkfeather."

The discussions continued all winter, without the men being drawn into them. Neither woman reversed her views but they made the outpost on the river ring with simple debate on topics never before challenged in those parts. The two women were brought closer in understanding and respect and the winter passed more quickly, giving place to the miracle of April. A thousand rivulets appeared to carry winter's snow to the still-frozen river. If spring had an official opening, it was the moment when the river ice broke. Once fractured, the great crust broke into fragments possessing a wild momentum of their own, crashing together with brutal thrusts, ricocheting, diving, splitting, and fighting their way through the tortured stream. Then came the sanctity of spring when the Father of all—whatever his children chose to call him—was renewing his promises of life and food for the entire family, regardless of religious convictions. There was as much spiritual refreshment for the one lady at the fort as for the other.

It was a rough rule in the fur country that when the ice went out on the Saskatchewan River, the trapping season ended. Now, as Marie Anne had expected, Jean Baptiste was proposing to leave the women at the fort while he and Belgrade travelled farther west. "We'll go along the south branch for a buffalo hunt. We'll go on horses, maybe. You stay here, Marie; you're going to have another baby—you'd be better off here. Laughing Face says you can stay. We'll come back for you."

Surely, in the light of advancing pregnancy, she would accept his advice this time. But she anticipated the scheme and was ready: "Now listen to me; Indian women travel on horses when they're expecting babies. Hawkfeather said so. Reine and I are going too."

Seizing two handfuls of his own long and tangled hair, as he always did when angry, he mumbled something uncomplimentary to women. Of course he loved his wife and child, but in moments like this he repeated a silent wish that all white women would stay somewhere east of Fort William where they would be safe and could not interfere with a buffalo hunter's movements. One good thing about Indian wives—they did what they were told. But Marie Anne's mind was set on going and the Lagimodières prepared to leave.

They started on foot while the black earth was still as soft as a cushion from the spring moisture. The men and Hawkfeather were loaded with tent, guns, and equipment, and Marie Anne was carrying Reine, now one year old. They followed the river, sometimes crossing prairie clearings, sometimes selecting a more difficult course through willow underbrush where bush rabbits darted in all directions.

They came on the third day to Fort St. Louis where La Corne had built his post more than half a century earlier. There was an evening of relaxation and sociability, and a deal for Indian horses. What horses! They were emaciated and uninviting. To Marie Anne, the thought of sitting on one of those bone-sharp backs was more disturbing than she intended to admit. She had never ridden anything rougher than a Pembina cart. Only Hawkfeather was at home on a horse; for the others it was an experiment.

"One good thing about this," the dull but cheerful Belgrade drawled, "We won't have to paddle." A spotted mare, friendly but uncertain in habits, was Marie Anne's choice. Jean Baptiste was left with a nervous black whose eyes displayed a suspicion of all humans.

"You ride mine first," Marie Anne instructed her husband. "I'll watch you and then I'll try." The mare offered no resistance as he attached a makeshift bridle, and Jean Baptiste climbed clumsily on her back and fell off on the opposite side. He performed better on the next attempt, and rode in a small circle to demonstrate at least that the animal had been ridden before. Jean Baptiste found his own horse uncomfortable by comparison but he figured he would get used to it. After all, the horses were being adopted for utility rather than amusement. They would prove most useful in buffalo hunting and there was reason to believe that these had carried Indian owners on such expeditions in the past.

Marie Anne mounted and felt totally unhappy. There was no place for her feet, nothing against which to lean, and nothing to seize if need arose. With a new coat of spring hair, the mare's back was smooth and slippery as well as sharp, and she felt insecure. Looking down she realized how completely she was at the mercy of her mount. Her main fear was for the baby on her back. It was terrifying to think of what would happen if she fell. She swallowed hard and said she was ready to start. With tent and blankets balanced as precariously as the riders, the horses were urged to move away at a slow and cautious pace.

"Wouldn't it be faster and easier to walk?" Marie Anne called, trying to be humorous. Her husband replied unconvincingly that she would love riding when she got used to it.

Her horse was the slowest, which suited her fine. She preferred to be at the rear of the group where her awkwardness would be less conspicuous and less likely to provoke laughter. By midmorning the horses were sweating profusely, adding to the riders' distress, and Marie Anne found a new reason for discomfort — a blistered rump and the nagging pain from friction at the spot.

Long before the day ended, every muscle in her body ached and she was ready to proclaim her hatred of horses. When nightfall was near, everybody was glad to dismount and the horses, after being hobbled, were glad to be released to graze. But for Marie Anne, there was no quick return to a state of comfort. Her body felt twisted and tortured. She peered fearfully at her legs to see if they were really as severely bowed and disfigured as they felt.

"You'll feel better in the morning," Jean Baptiste promised, but she doubted that one night in bed could melt away so much distress. And indeed, in the morning she felt worse. She would have rejoiced to hear that the horses had been stolen during the night or struck down by lightning. But there they were, ready to be mounted for another day of torture.

With Jean Baptiste's assurance that the discomfort would reach its worst on the second day, she braced herself and mounted. After another day, she did feel perceptibly easier and beamed at the thought of someday riding with enjoyment. But just at the time she was finding she could ride without pain, the men chose a place to make their home for the season. It was a pleasant spot beside a lively creek running into the South Saskatchewan. There were good supplies of wood and water and promising buffalo hunting close by.

Having horses simplified hunting, but the two women would have to be content to remain alone for most of each day. The danger they did not suspect was in being situated close to a route travelled by migrating Indians. Strange Indians could be ruthless and Jean Baptiste warned the women to be constantly alert.

It was midafternoon one day in the early summer when Marie Anne pointed through the trees to a band of painted Indians riding from the southwest. Even at a distance there was an air of foreboding about them. Quickly and silently, Hawkfeather seized Reine and, crouching as she ran, carried her through the bushes to a safe place. Marie Anne was alone when the score of painted braves rode straight toward her, and surrounded the tent. With no visible means of escape, she braced herself. The leader, grisly and bold, dismounted, and walked briskly toward her. From the waist up he as naked except for a leather neckstrap on which were hung small knots of human hair.

Marie Anne stood as if frozen in her tracks. "God spare us again," she murmured.

The Indian's astonishment was as great as the woman's fears, but he was quicker in recovery. What a prize, he may have been thinking. A white woman alone! His for the taking. His bulk blocked the tent entrance and he carried a wicked grin on his hideous face. With a heavy hand on her arm, he led her to where his braves could see and rejoice in his fortune. There were expressions of astonishment from his followers who had never before seen a white woman. Less disciplined braves might have rushed forward to tear the prize from their chief's grip. As it was, they stared and Marie Anne prayed as she had never prayed before. How could she escape a scalping death or something equally dreadful?

Suddenly, from somewhere in the ranks of the mounted Indians, a figure leaped from his horse, strode toward the woman and her captor, blocking their advance. He spoke excitedly to the chief. To all outward appearances, he was just another Indian challenging the chief's right to claim the woman. His words were sharp and loud and his fists were clenched. But then, strangely, he turned to Marie Anne and addressed her in her native tongue.

"How did you get here?" he asked. "Aren't you French?"

"Yes, French. I came with my husband. He's hunting," she answered in a trembling voice. "Can you save me? Surely God has sent you to save me and my family."

"I'll try," he said. "Have courage. I think I can."

He spoke again to the chief, whose fingers pressed more deeply into the flesh of Marie Anne's arm. After more heated conversation, the penetrating fingernails were relaxed abruptly. The chief, clearly disappointed, strode to his horse, mounted, and rode away with his warriors.

Her rescuer remained behind. Looking closely at him, Marie Anne was sure his skin beneath the warpaint was white. "How am I to thank you?" she asked. "Who are you? You're not Indian. How did you come to be here? I wish Jean Baptiste were here to thank you too."

She listened attentively to his reply in clear and perfect French. She hadn't heard its equal since leaving her position in the priest's house in Maskinonge. He was indeed a Frenchman whose boyhood years had been spent at Trois Rivières. Coming west with a fur brigade, he took an Indian wife and ultimately chose to be adopted into her tribe and live as an Indian.

"How strange!" she commented under her breath, realizing that she was free and unmolested and that her baby was safe in hiding with Hawkfeather. But she was still curious to know why a white man would become an Indian. "Are you satisfied with your life now? And happy?"

"Yes, I like Indians. I will never leave the tribe now."

"But why? How do you explain it?"

"Oh," he said with a slight smile, "I married the wrong woman at home. The white man in me died and now I am an Indian with a good Indian wife. You won't understand it, but there are lots of good Indians, and the way they think and live suits me very well."

Her curiosity demanded more but the man was anxious to overtake his fellow tribesmen. Stepping close to his horse he said, "May the Great Spirit bless you, Madame." And springing onto its back he called, "Adieu," and galloped away.[1]

She smiled, her lips still quivering. As the hoofbeats receded, she sank to the ground to collect her thoughts. Then, running to the bushes, she found Reine and Hawkfeather, both resting comfortably behind a clump of pincherry bushes. Hawkfeather was still giggling at the drama she had witnessed while sitting in concealment and safety.

The women had scarcely emerged when Jean Baptiste and Belgrade rode up on sweating horses. "What happened? Are you all right?" they called, dismounting in haste. They had become alarmed when they had seen at a distance the departure of mounted red men from the vicinity of their camp.

"We're all alive and nobody hurt," the women were saying together in Cree and French. Both excitedly described the incident, scarcely pausing for breath. The men, attentive and shocked, breathed words of thanks and gazed with anger in the direction of the departed Indians.

Jean Baptiste, as usual, said little but he could not hide his thoughts. More than ever he was convinced that for a woman with children, the dangers of the frontier were sure to be unending. A woman might escape a few times but eventually. . . . Fear for his family still nagged him. If he couldn't accept life in the East and his wife wouldn't leave him in the West, there seemed to be no solution.

He would test her with the question he had asked many times: "When are you going to be sensible and go back to Maskinonge?"

If he insisted in asking the same question, she would give him the same answer: "When we go back together, Jean Baptiste."

10

Better appreciation for native devotions

As spring surrendered to summer and more Indians heard about the presence of a white woman and baby at a camp beside the South Saskatchewan River, inquisitive visitors increased. The fortunate ones rode horses and dragged travois, but most of those who came were still on foot. Some carried guns bought with beaver skins, but just as many were still children of the Stone Age, armed with bows and arrows made from chokecherry wood and arrow points from flint.

With little regard for time, they arrived at all hours. Sometimes they came early in the morning when prairie chickens were still drumming on a nearby dancing ground. Just as often it was at a late evening hour when only hoot owls were expected to break the silence of night. Some of the visitors were unmistakably friendly; others were surly and hostile. A few old men with the scars of many battles showed a primary interest in Jean Baptiste's good tobacco. Younger ones — some wearing more streaky paint than clothing — were there out of sheer curiosity. They would be satisfied only when they were able to stand and stare at the spectacle of a white woman, now two years in Rupert's Land.

"Strange people, these Indians," Marie Anne was saying as Jean Baptiste relaxed after a day of riding. The haunting memory of her recent escape was still fresh in her mind as she added, "Some are like wild animals and would enjoy scalping you; others would die for their friends. Does anybody really understand them?"

Puffing languidly on his pipe, he drawled, "Some good, some bad, I suppose; just like Frenchmen."

"More bad ones," she said impulsively and then wondered if

Jean Baptiste, who was not given to profound thought, might be right. There was Belgrade's wife, as good and true as any white person, and Mimmie, the dear girl.

Jean Baptiste suddenly interrupted her: "I hear something." He sprang to his feet, reached for his gun, and stepped outside followed closely by Marie Anne. "Somebody on a horse," he said.

Marie Anne was the first to recognize the rider and shouted, "Mimmie! It's you, bless your heart."

The girl's moccasined feet hit the ground lightly and the two women embraced joyfully. The language difference presented only a small barrier, and in their excitement they were both talking, each using words unknown to the other.

Silently, Jean Baptiste led Mimmie's horse away and hobbled it while Marie Anne, taking Mimmie by the hand, rushed to the tent, saying, "Come and see our Reine, the little girl you saved from death."

The Indian girl's face radiated happiness as she held the child in her arms and mumbled Cree terms of admiration. Belgrade's wife arrived, and sensing the meaning of the reunion, hung a big pot of meat over the fire for the dinner that must follow.

Mimmie's actions revealed her thoughts. She handled Marie Anne's braided hair, and then placed a hand on the white woman's abdomen and addressed her question to Hawkfeather: "When will the next baby be born?"

Marie Anne replied, "Tell her, when the leaves fall."

The young squaw then made a proposal that Marie Anne should come to her village, thirty miles away, and have her baby there. The older squaws knew everything about maternity and the care of babies. The white woman would be made welcome. The mother and new baby and Reine would be given the best care the tribe could offer.

Marie Anne was touched. It warmed her heart that Mimmie would want her. "Thank her, Hawkfeather. Tell her she makes me happy. We'll have to consult Jean Baptiste."

As Marie Anne feared, her husband was opposed. His idea was to go back down river to the Fort of the Prairies in early August and be there for the baby's birth. Hawkfeather would supervise and they would remain again for the winter months. His plan offered the advantage that once at the fort, there would be no need to move again before winter.

Mimmie accepted the decision with childish disappointment, but she had another suggestion. Marie Anne and Reine were being invited to return with Mimmie for the annual Thirst Dance of her tribe. The visitors would live with Mimmie at her lodge. It would be like a summer holiday.

Jean Baptiste, thinking of his wife's condition, answered, "Too far for you to ride."

But Mimmie was not to be refused easily. Indian women never stop riding so why should it be harmful for a white woman?

Marie Anne chose to believe that Mimmie was right. "I just want to go with her, Ba'tiste. Why not? We live like Indians in Indian country and shouldn't be frightened by Indian customs." There was a pause, and accepting the absence of further protest as license, Marie Anne turned to Hawkfeather, saying, "Tell her, please, that Reine and I will go, and I know we'll be safe with her people."

It was decided that they would start early the following morning, and soon after sunrise, Jean Baptiste and Belgrade caught the hobbled horses and saw the two happy women and Reine ride away to the southwest.

The morning was clear. The world was green with vegetation and wild creatures were constantly crossing the trail. Redtail hawks made big circles overhead; foxes darted from one bluff to another; a rough grouse tumbled its way through the trees in a desperate effort to lead the travellers away from its brood; and a few buffaloes, separated from the main herd, grazed without alarm.

Conversation, of course, was awkward but not impossible. Mimmie, alert to every movement, pointed to birds and animals that might have gone unnoticed, and Marie Anne, to her surprise, found herself riding without discomfort. When the sun was directly overhead Mimmie managed to explain that they had travelled half-way. They rested awhile, ate some pemmican, and started again. After miles of ever-changing scenery, Marie Anne did begin to feel tired and wondered briefly if this expedition into strange Indian country was an act of recklessness. But she soon recovered her confidence in Mimmie's intentions and reliability.

The sun was setting as Mimmie and her friends rode wearily into the tent village. Dogs barked, smoke rose in curls from campfires, and Indians stood in small clusters watching the arrival of the newcomers. But when the presence of a white woman was noted, camp tempo was at once quickened. Young and old milled around to behold a white woman and a white papoose. Marie Anne smiled forcedly, trying to disguise her nervousness. Mimmie's patience with her own people was soon exhausted, and with the air of a commanding general she ordered them to stand back and allow her visitors to go to the chief's tent.

The crowd obeyed with no resistance, and Marie Anne knew she had nothing to fear once her presence was approved by the chief. He received them with such cordiality that for a moment the white woman wondered if there was a risk in accepting too much attention from the head man.

When they finally arrived at Mimmie's teepee, Marie Anne wanted to slump on the cool earth that was the floor. "Rest a few minutes," the Indian girl indicated. Soon she brought in her mother, a small lady with deeply set eyes and a nice face. Marie Anne had a kiss for each of the old lady's wrinkled cheeks; further conversation would have been labored and it was unnecessary. Mimmie's mother, knowing her guests would be tired, pointed to their bed. Reine was asleep before she was tucked in and Marie Anne, soon after.

As the first rays of morning penetrated the teepee, the camp buzzed with activity. It was the final day of preparations for the great summer festival, the Thirst Dance. Members of the tribe were arriving from distant places and the best hunters were bringing huge supplies of buffalo meat for the feasts which would follow the days of fasting.

The Thirst Dance Lodge was being constructed on a bench, a short distance back from the river, and Mimmie, staying close to Marie Anne, tried to explain. There, set in the ground to mark the center of the lodge, was a big poplar tree with branches imperfectly removed. About it to form an enclosure thirty or thirty-five feet in diameter was a circle of posts. Rafter poles were laid from the heavy central pillar to the outer ring of smaller posts. These could then be covered with leafy branches to form the roof.

I don't understand it, Marie Anne was thinking to herself. There is a serious religious quality about the preparations. But I'm not frightened; I just wish Jean Baptiste were here to share it all. It's beginning to seem like going to church.

The dance began at sunset. A fire was started near the center of the big lodge. Grouped around it were drummers, medicine men with weird and sometimes frightening headpieces, dancers with a minimum of clothing, and young men who wanted to prove themselves as candidates for the rank of brave. Although brave-making was not the chief reason for the dance, it was an appropriate time for young men to demonstrate in the presence of the respected warriors of the tribe that they, too, could be indifferent to pain. Making paired incisions in the skin and flesh of their breasts, the ambitious young bucks inserted skewers or leather thongs which were tied by leather ropes to the big central pole.

Most Indians watched eagerly. Marie Anne felt nauseated and looked the other way as the young men, straining against the ties, stretched the fibres of their raw flesh and continued to dance unflinchingly. Not until hours later when the flesh broke did they gain release from their self-inflicted torture. Those who persevered were forever braves.

To Marie Anne, the self-torture was meaningless and repulsive and she was glad when it ended. As for the dancing, it continued for two days and two nights with participants, in most cases, denying themselves food and sleep during that time. As time went on the religious tenor became more apparent and the white woman was impressed. Seeing people calling on the Giver-of-all-things, giving thanks, and praying for food and benefits from His hands made Marie Anne long for her own church. For two years she had had no opportunity to attend mass, and now the very sight of people engaged in prayer made her want to join in the exercises.

"These people are sincere in their expressions of dependence and faith," she said aloud to nobody in particular. "They do pray to their God, just like Hawkfeather said."

She began to wonder why she had been so slow to recognize the logic in Hawkfeather's explanation of the Great Spirit. The ruler of nature to whom these children of nature addressed their petitions was in some way the same as the great God of the Christian Church. Bowing her head and closing her eyes, she felt a new respect for the Indian religion. Clutching Reine firmly, she said what was in her heart.

"Thanks, O God or Great Spirit of all races, for what I have been led to see, that though our altars differ, prayer is the bridge over which all mankind can reach you. Hear the prayers of these simple people as you have heard mine. Give food and shelter to Mimmie and her people, health and faith to my loved ones, safety to my Jean Baptiste, strength to me in an hour of pain. And grant that I will see Maskinonge once again and pray in the church where my mother worships beside the little river."

Looking up, she found that the dancing was over and the devotions were ending. Mimmie, eagerly studying the movements of her prayerful lips, was standing over her. She was there to report that the feast was about to begin. The steaming pots were being opened but the feast could not proceed until Marie Anne and Reine —the tribal guests—were seated with the chief. With Reine securely on her back, the white lady was escorted to her place to eat her fill of buffalo tongue and the banquet specialty, roast lynx.

An elderly Cree lady placed a wreath of poplar leaves on the white child's head. Marie Anne beamed her gratitude. She and Reine were now the guests of the tribe, but Mimmie remained close to her white friends, still assuming full responsibility for their safety and comfort.

The Indians, who had demonstrated unusual stamina in the dancing, were now going to similar lengths in their eating. She had seen hungry woodsmen and voyageurs devouring huge volumes of food, but had never witnessed anything to match the enormous quantities of this occasion. The feast was a two-day event, apparently without intermission.

After the second day, Marie Anne told Mimmie she should return home. She had been gone almost a week, and if she stayed longer Jean Baptiste and her friends would worry. She tried to communicate her gratitude for the visit, speaking slowly and demonstratively. Mimmie's eyes assured her she understood.

Marie Anne was quite prepared to make the return trip alone, but Mimmie had other ideas. Soon after sunrise on the following morning, they were travelling back over the trail of the previous week. The birds sang morning greetings and the countryside was more beautiful than ever. The trail even seemed shorter than before, and Marie Anne admitted her complete enjoyment of the ride.

Everybody at the campsite was ready to welcome the travellers. "I'm glad to be home," she said as she slid off her horse, "but I had a wonderful time with good people, and I want to go again."

"It did you good," said Jean Baptiste. "They must have fed you well. And Reine is all right too."

Hawkfeather brought the little mirror, telling Marie Anne she should see for herself how the visit had refreshed her.

"Well, if I look better it's because I feel better. And I feel better because I've seen so many things and learned so much. And best of all, for the first time since I left Maskinonge, I feel that I've been to church. Hawkfeather, you were the first to tell me.

"And Jean Baptiste, you were right when you said there are lots of good Indians. The very best example is our dear Mimmie."

11

When the
leaves fall

"This baby will be a boy," Marie Anne told her man as they sat quietly beside the South Saskatchewan watching the sun go down.

"You sure?" he asked quickly, his question sounding like a wish.

"Of course I'm sure," she answered with a coy smile. "Wouldn't the first white baby born beside the river have to be a boy? Didn't you say this is a man's country? Besides, no girl would ever kick as roughly." There was a brief moment of silence; she combed her long hair with her fingers. She spoke again softly, as if out of a dream: "We'll have a boy and we'll call him Jean Baptiste."

The sun disappeared from view but they were in no hurry to retire. Jean Baptiste was not noted for sentiment, but on this evening he was inspired. "Sunset, little one!" he said as if to test her memory and display his own. "Remember what it meant to you when you were at home and I was out this way?"

But they had something more than sentiment to discuss. Sitting together in the dusk, they made their plans. It was already August and the baby was expected in September. Jean Baptiste wanted his family back at the fort by the next full moon.

"Yes, Ba'tiste, we'd better go somewhere before travelling becomes too difficult for me. I can go to Mimmie's village, you know. It's nearer than the fort and I'm sure I'd be happy there. I know I can trust Mimmie and her friends."

"Prairie Post is better," he answered without hesitation. "Winter quarters and no move till spring."

"All right then, Ba'tiste, but let's go soon. If we go slowly, I can still travel on my mare. Canoe might be better for me but I want to take my mare."

The matter was settled; they would leave in a few days on horseback. Belgrade and his wife, going ahead by canoe, would be there first.

There wasn't much preparation to worry about. As soon as Jean Baptiste obtained some extra meat supplies, they could be off.

With their few belongings packed on the horses they were on their way. "We'll have to go slowly, you know; only a few miles each day," she said with a sigh. "As you might guess, I'm not exactly comfortable."

"Yes." He understood. "We'll rest whenever you want," he added, wisely resisting the temptation to say that she herself had chosen this means of travel. She would have been more comfortable in a canoe. This way, however, she could take long rests when he, at intervals, went out for meat. Stops of even an hour or two would suit her very well.

By midafternoon of the first day, Marie Anne was tired. It was reassuring that she could travel for seven hours and complain of nothing more serious than aching muscles, but she'd had enough for one day. "I'm all right, I think, but I'm aching all over and must sit in a different position—or lie down."

Jean Baptiste set up the tent. They had done very well for the first day and he was secretly relieved to be increasing the distance between them and Mimmie's village. For reasons he did not explain, he never wanted his baby to be born in an Indian encampment.

"Three more days and we'll be at our winter home," he muttered before going to sleep. Marie Anne thought of his words through much of her sleepless night. Her muscles did not stop aching; the ground on which they lay did not fit her at all and the baby within kicked protestingly.

The uncomfortable night did not prevent another early morning start. They seemed to be making good time without hurrying. "We've covered half the full distance," Jean Baptiste announced early in the afternoon.

His wife replied, "That's fine because I've had enough for today."

Nodding his willingness to make camp at the early hour, he pointed to a nearby draw leading to the river, saying, "Looks like a good place for a tent, and handy to water."

She was quite willing to make the added effort to ride to the draw. Patting her mare on the neck, she spoke affectionately: "You're a gentle and understanding creature. It isn't your fault that I want to get off."

"But look! What do I see?" Jean Baptiste asked excitedly. Drawing his horse to a sudden stop, he shaded his eyes for a better view.

"Buffalo!" he exclaimed in a gasping whisper. Without taking his eyes off the animals, he untied the knots holding the tent and blankets on his mount, allowing them to drop to the ground. "You wait here," he instructed Marie Anne, reaching for his gun and checking his powder pouch. "We could use some fresh meat."

His heels hit the horse's flank and he was away, revelling in the excitement of the chase. This should be easy; he was downwind and would be well started before the creatures were aroused. His horse had been trained for the hunt and was responding perfectly.

But through the muffled thud of hoofbeats he heard a piercing scream. Looking back over his shoulder he was shocked to see the little mare racing furiously toward the buffaloes, his wife and child balanced precariously on her back. Marie Anne's face matched her terror-filled screams.

He tightened his reins and after the first moment of shock realized that the little mare, normally gentle, must have been trained by her former owners as a buffalo-runner.

His wife was trying desperately to check the mare's speed as she dashed along the slope of the valley. Jean Baptiste was not sure what to do. He brought his own horse to a complete stop, hoping to influence the mare to do likewise. She didn't. He tried to overtake her but the galloping action from the rear made her run faster. She had been trained against relaxing speed until the herd was overtaken and was clearly enjoying the run.

"Hang on," he called, though he knew she was doing it to the limit of her capacity. The safety of the child on her back depended upon her grip. She was trying to steady Reine with one hand while pulling with all her strength upon the reins with the other.

Her main concerns were for her child. Reine was screaming with fear; but common sense told the mother that the mare could not maintain this speed for long. The only hope was to hang on until exhaustion forced the animal to stop. She prayed and summoned her last reserves of strength.

Both husband and wife were powerless to stop the awful race. Not until they were in the midst of the fleeing herd did the mare slow down. Her dwindling speed allowed Jean Baptiste to overtake her and catch one rein to bring her to a stop.

"Are you all right?" he gasped, scarcely able to speak.

"I'm sick," she whispered as she climbed from the mare's back and fell to the ground. "But look at Reine, please, and tell me if she's all right."

The little girl continued to cry as her father cradled her in his arms, not knowing what else to do. "I think she's only frightened," he told her mother.

"Thank God," was Marie Anne's only answer as she sank back on the grass.

Rolling up his shirt, Jean Baptiste made a pillow for his wife's head. "Rest," he said. "I'll get the tent and bring it here." There was a faint smile on her face as her husband hobbled the mare and mounted his own horse to gallop away. "I'll hurry," he called, trying to determine where the tent and bedding had been dropped.

At best, Marie Anne could not be moved for several days, he was sure, and he'd have to pitch the tent right where she lay on the prairie, even though it was miles from water. She'd be suffering from thirst even now. His problems, he knew, were just beginning. If only Hawkfeather and Belgrade were there to help. By good fortune he soon found the tent and bedding bundles, and using a small buffalo skin he improvised a container for water and filled it at the river.

Burdened with the bundles, the water, and a tired horse, the return to Marie Anne was slower than he expected, and his impatience and his worries mounted. "God take care of her," he repeated again and again. "Let nothing serious happen."

From a distance he saw that she had not moved. When he slid from his horse while it was still in motion, she opened her eyes and said with a faint smile, "I've rested, Ba'tiste; I think I'm stronger. But I need water." He produced the skin bag and she praised his ingenuity. "Oh, that's good," she said after drinking her fill.

She slumped back and closed her eyes. Seeing her wince with pain, Jean Baptiste hurried to prepare her bed and helped her into it. Then he erected the tent over her. He tried to tempt her appetite with dried meat but she ate nothing. The pain was increasing and so was her fear.

"I'm in trouble, Ba'tiste," she said. "You'll have to help me."

"You'll have to tell me what to do."

Darkness fell and while Reine slept, Marie Anne and Jean Baptiste brought their second child into the world.

"It's a boy!" exulted the father. "A boy with blue eyes!"

The mother smiled and whispered, "Little Jean Baptiste, little Jean."

It was wonderful to have a son. Little Jean Baptiste, although somewhat premature, was healthy and vigorous, physically perfect, with no trace of handicap from the circumstances of his premature birth. But his poor father! He was beset with more domestic problems and responsibilities than at any time in his life. With the care of two babies and a convalescing wife, he had trouble in hunting enough to maintain the family food supplies. But luck was with him and he discovered small game — grouse, ducks, and rabbits — as he travelled back and forth from the spring at the river. His aim was true and nobody went hungry.

Marie Anne's strength returned quickly and before long she was ready to discuss their next move. "Always moving," she said with a hint of regret. "Someday, I hope we'll settle down and never move again. By the way, Ba'tiste, how do you think we're going to get to the fort? You can't expect me to carry two babies on my mare. It's too far to walk and we have no canoe."

"I can make a travois," he said quietly, not knowing how the idea would be received. His wife had seen Indians moving equipment and furs by this means and knew that such a vehicle would be rough and uncomfortable. The best to be said for it was that it would make the most efficient use of the horses and probably get the family to its destination. Jean Baptiste said he would train her horse to drag it. There would be no risk of another runaway for he would lead the mare.

Finding two long drag-poles he lashed them together at their narrow ends. The other ends were spread to carry a seat made by lashing smaller pieces crosswise. When it was time to try it on the little mare he carefully placed the pointed end of the contraption over the animal's withers, expecting almost any reaction. But the mare must have hauled a travois before because she was ready without hesitation to do it again.

At daybreak they prepared to leave. Marie Anne and the two children took their places on the travois seat while Jean Baptiste mounted his own horse. With a familiar burden, the little mare walked along obediently where she was led. The ground was rough and Jean Baptiste's best efforts to choose smooth surfaces failed to prevent almost constant bumps and jolts for the travois riders. Only Reine enjoyed the bumpy ride.

That evening they stopped and erected the tent beside a creek. Marie Anne was delighted to be camping beside fresh water again. "And it'll be even better to be back at the Prairie Post. I must tell you," she said to her husband, "for awhile I thought I'd never see the fort again. How thankful I'll be to be settled there tomorrow."

Their arrival at the post was a pleasant reunion. "Come in! Come in!" bellowed the amiable Mr. Laughing Face. "I wondered when I'd see you. Heard you were on your way."

"Thanks; it's good to be back," they responded as their host lifted Reine to his shoulders and little Jean made a baby squeal as if demanding recognition.

"What's this? Another Lagimodière to be sure," said the trader looking at the small baby. "A very new one, I'd say. He must have been born on the way."

"Yes," replied Marie Anne. "We hoped he'd wait to be born here but he wouldn't. We had some worries but he's all right. . . . I think he's hungry."

"Before you feed him, let me tell you, young lady, that you are now in charge of this house, and the old fort will be a better place from having you here. I'd rather have four Lagimodières than three. Even if there were six, you'd still be welcome."

Leaving her to feed the babies and settle them for the night, the two men discussed living arrangements for the winter ahead. They agreed upon terms similar to those of the previous winter. Jean Baptiste was responsible for supplying meat for the post and he would pay for tea and sugar with furs.

"By the way," the trader said, "don't be surprised if the Indians want to see that baby boy. They'll want to stage a feast in his honor."

Marie Anne settled easily into the domestic routine at the post. She was proud of her son and glad to place him on display before friendly Indians; some of them had seen Reine during the previous winter, but to them a boy rated higher than a girl and they gazed in fascination. Then, as the trader guessed, they held a powwow.

Indians gathered around the fort erecting their teepees in a big circle. They lit fires and prepared to cook large chunks of buffalo meat. News of the celebration to honor the white man's son sounded for many miles, while natives hoped for donations of whiskey from the post. At dusk, the drums began to sound and the Indians danced and feasted in alternating relays. When darkness fell, the leaders sent a message to the fort that the baby boy should be brought to them.

Marie Anne was nervous but her fears evaporated when the trader advised her to comply, saying, "These Indians have no whiskey and most of them are responsible fellows."

And so, on that moonless night, in the light of a blazing campfire, Marie Anne and Jean Baptiste took their places within the Indian circle, the baby boy in his mother's arms and Reine in her father's. The drums grew louder and the dancers bent lower, intent upon the ritual. Marie Anne's fears returned as they pranced and shrieked, and she resolved that her little one would not under any circumstances be taken from her arms.

Without warning the dancing stopped and a medicine man, wearing a headpiece hung with eagle heads, stepped forward and made a speech that echoed far along the valley. Gitchee Manitou, the Great Spirit, was implored to make the white boy a great hunter and friend of all Indians. Then, with unquestioned earnestness, a presentation was made to the baby — first a bow and then an arrow with its obsidian point imbedded in the fresh heart of a buffalo. The meaning was clear; the Indians were wishing that the arrows or bullets of the white man's son would always find their marks.[1]

The Indians had the best of intentions, but behind Marie Anne's smiles was a growing weariness. When she and Jean Baptiste retired that night, she unburdened herself: "Surely we can now be left in peace. We've had enough adventure and excitement to last for years. We've been miraculously spared. If we were in danger again, could we still hope to escape?"

"Don't know, Marie, but your old medicine man hasn't been wrong yet. Remember Red Duck?"

12

A lady
may change
her mind

Jean Baptiste hunted and Mr. Laughing Face prepared for winter by banking his house with sods. Marie Anne squatted at the river's edge, bathing her babies in sunshine from a clear autumn sky. It was the quiet season around the trading post. It was October. Yellow leaves were falling from the poplars and red ones from the willows, leaving the landscape looking naked. Buffaloes crossed the river to the south, and high overhead, great flocks of birds pointed their way to winter retreats. The rabbits had not changed color but the little bay mare was growing a coat of longer hair. It was Indian summer, the crowning delight of the year.

As the younger child sprawled and Reine played in sand or crisp leaves, it was easy for mother to feel the relaxation of all nature. After a summer punctuated by various escapes from danger, this modicum of peace and security seemed too good to last.

With her eyes fixed upon the farther shore, she was reasoning philosophically about how, at times, she hated this country, and at other times, she was afraid she was growing to love it. In these quiet surroundings, it was easy to conclude that the country was not as cruel as many people said it was. She had heard much about murder and scalping but after a year in the country, she couldn't name anybody who had been a victim of either.

With the sound of somebody approaching, however, her train of thoughts was broken and she gathered her babies and started briskly toward the stockade gate. Any unexplained footsteps should be regarded with alarm, but her fear vanished when she heard Jean Baptiste's whistle and then saw his figure emerging from the bushes with two geese hanging from his shoulders.

"You're home early. I like it when you come home early. You can take the children while I get supper," she said.

"Sure, but I see a canoe approaching from the east. Let's wait."

Her eyes beamed interest. "White men or Indians?"

"White men."

"Do you suppose it could be Belgrade and Hawkfeather? They must have changed their plans and paddled on to Cumberland. I hope they're coming back. She's such good company."

"Can't tell yet," he replied. "You'll know in a few minutes."

Jean Baptiste was more interested than he was willing to admit, and hurried away to deposit the geese in a meat hole on the shaded side of the fort. Then, joined by the trader, everybody walked to the river's edge to watch the canoe come to shore.

"Listen!" Marie Anne halted and cupped a hand to her ear. "Somebody in the canoe is singing. I know that voice. It's Chalifou's — noisy old Chalifou! He sings like a lonely crow."

Jean Baptiste's face brightened and he waved a welcome as the canoe came toward the shore. Sure enough, there were the old friends, Paquin, Chalifou, and their native ladies back from Pembina along with Belgrade and Hawkfeather who had joined the party at Cumberland House. The noisy one stopped singing long enough to shout, "Ho, Jean Baptiste, you got any grog for some thirsty Frenchmen?"

Jean Baptiste laughed and pointed out the best place to beach the canoe.

Almost before the boat touched land, Hawkfeather jumped out and threw her fleshy arms around Marie Anne. The union was a warm one, and while the other women attended to the canoe, Jean Baptiste had a bone-crushing handshake for each of his old friends.

"You stopping here for the winter?" he enquired, and his wife listened anxiously for the reply, hoping to have Hawkfeather with her.

"No!" It was Chalifou answering as usual and waving an arm to the west. "We'll stay tonight and then paddle on—up where beavers never saw handsome Frenchmen before."

That was disappointing but as Chalifou talked on, Marie Anne was getting ready to display her new baby. The native women gazed in admiration and chuckled as the young mother tried to relate the terrifying circumstances of the boy's birth. Hawkfeather, who knew the baby was expected, produced a pair of wee moccasins made with her own thick but expert fingers.

"Little Weasel's still at Pembina," Chalifou was saying. Belgrade and Paquin were smirking slightly. Jean Baptiste was clearly embarrassed. "But you'll be relieved to know, Baptiste, that she's now the wife of a trader from Montreal. As long as he's there, she won't be worrying you."

"Tell us about poor Bouvier," Marie Anne interjected, partly to change the subject.

"Bouvier? He's at Pembina," Chalifou replied. "His friends wanted him to go east to live but he refused. His face is hideous from scars and he can't see, but says he can still enjoy the sounds and smells of Red River. Says he'd rather be all dead in the West than half alive in the East."

"Poor Bouvier! Such a brave fellow! But how can a blind man manage at Pembina?"

"He has lots of friends who make sure he has enough to eat and always a place to sleep," Chalifou answered. "I believe he's happy — spends his time reciting prayers and telling stories. He tells over and over again how Marie Anne Lagimodière saved his life—calls her 'The Angel of the Saskatchewan'. Don't worry about him."

"Any white women at Pembina now?" Jean Baptiste enquired.

"None since your wife left. But there are some disturbingly good-looking Metis girls around to take men's thoughts away from the fur trade," Chalifou answered with a coy glance at his wife. "By the way," he continued, "do you remember Marguerite Trottier?"

The face of the Metis girl came instantly to Marie Anne's mind —an intelligent girl and attractive. She would have been conspicuous even in Trois Rivières or Montreal.

"Of course I remember her," Marie Anne answered, "and her husband Jutras too. They left Pembina when we did but separated from our party to paddle up the Assiniboine. I was sorry to see such a promising companion leave us. I didn't care for Jutras. I thought Marguerite's father would have been better to let the girl marry the young Cree chief who wanted her."

Chalifou shrugged. "Who can tell? But I know what you mean about Jutras. Marguerite's mother was Cree, of course, and her father being French wanted a white man for her and gave her to Jutras when she was young. I suppose if she'd married the chief she wouldn't be a mutilated wreck today."

"Mutilated?" Marie Anne shuddered at the word. "Mutilated how?"

"It was terrible. Happened early last spring on the Qu'Appelle River. She and her baby and husband were paddling with a party bringing down a load of furs. Dan MacKenzie and McDonald of Garth were along, on their way to Fort William. The Sioux attack was sudden and fiendish. War cries shattered the valley silence and there was a shower of arrows from both sides of the river. Before anybody had time to find shelter, four of the voyageur fellows were shot."

Marie Anne, listening anxiously, was already sick from anger and disgust. Here was proof that nobody could be sure of escaping atrocities in this cruel country.

Chalifou continued. "The other members of the party scattered. Jutras found shelter for himself but Marguerite was unprotected. Later, when help arrived from the fort on the river, they found Marguerite lying in a canoe, scalped and mutilated—apparently dead. But one of the men heard her whisper and understood she was asking for her child. They found the baby in the bushes, scalped and dead."

"Then she's dead, too?" Marie Anne asked in distress. "Marguerite's dead?"

"No, strangely enough. By some miracle, she didn't die. They bathed her wounds and pulled a fresh buffalo bladder over her poor scalped head. Scouts sat on guard all night with loaded guns across their knees. In the morning they placed her in the bottom of a canoe and started for the post at the mouth of the Souris River. It was her spirit as much as anything that kept her alive—damn sure of that. Before we left Pembina, she had been moved to the new fort where the Assiniboine meets the Red."

For most of the evening, as the men sat smoking their pipes and Hawkfeather played with the little mirror and brought laughter to her friends, Marie Anne brooded on the atrocities that overtook Marguerite and her baby.

She tried to return to the conversation going on behind her. The trader had furnished a quart of rum for the evening and merriment prevailed. Each man was inspired to tell his most exciting hunting story, and even the normally quiet Jean Baptiste became talkative.

But later in the evening, Marie Anne saw her husband's mood change and his face become set and sullen. She suspected that Jean Baptiste would probably want to go farther west with his friends and trap where there was less competition. She knew he was an adventurer as much as a trapper.

"Tomorrow we leave early," Paquin was saying. "We have no time to lose if we are to choose a good spot farther west and build a log tent before winter sets in."

"Farther west," Marie Anne repeated whimsically, "always farther west! When you men get to heaven and hear of a place farther west, you'll be rolling your tents and going."

"Yes, farther west!" Jean Baptiste burst out indistinctly but defiantly. "And I'm going to. Leave you and the children here and I go west. I'm going to be free again."

Marie Anne was momentarily surprised and hurt as he directed his half-closed eyes her way with evident resentment. But before she recovered, Paquin informed the speaker that there wasn't room for him in the canoe. Then, with a hand on Jean Baptiste's shoulder he added, "Besides, by morning you'll have changed your mind."

There was laughter while Marie Anne bit her tongue and refrained from answering. She would wait until morning when the effects of the rum had worn off.

The trader's house was crowded that night, with men, women, and babies sleeping on the floor. In the morning, Jean Baptiste bade farewell to his friends, showing no trace of his earlier wish to travel with them. "We'll see you in the spring," he said. As the men took their places in the canoe, Marie Anne pressed something into Hawkfeather's hand; it was the little mirror.

"Bring it back in the spring," she whispered as the other gasped with surprise and pleasure. Hardly daring to believe it, Hawkfeather asked, "Me take?" It was the most wonderful thing to enter her life and she threw her heavy arms around the white woman's neck, almost upsetting the canoe.

As the boat glided into the current and hands were raised at parting, Marie Anne felt a chill of strange presentiment. Motionless, she watched her friends disappear around the point of land, scarcely aware that Jean Baptiste stood with her. He reached for her hand and his powerful clasp caused her forebodings to vanish.

"Sorry about what I said last night. I won't leave you."

"I know, Ba'tiste," she answered forgivingly. "I'm glad I didn't respond last night."

In the days that followed, she had recurring moments of distress, thoughts of Marguerite and the parting with Hawkfeather. With more sympathy than usual, Jean Baptiste agreed that she was alone too much.

Her uneasiness did not abate and just weeks after waving to her departing friends, a group of friendly Indians brought the tragic news. The report was confused but the conclusion was clear. Their friends and another Frenchman named Caplette with his Indian wife had built winter quarters away to the west, on the north branch of the Saskatchewan. One day when the men were absent, a war party pillaged the camp, murdering and scalping the wives of Belgrade, Chalifou, and Caplette. Only Paquin's wife escaped.[1]

Marie Anne was stunned and revolted as never before. Turning to Jean Baptiste she shouted, "I can't stand it! It's all so brutal. This dreadful country! I wish I'd never seen it." She sank on her buffalo robe bed and buried her face in her arms.

He tried to comfort her, telling her that when the men came down in the spring they'd get the correct story and perhaps find that the women had not actually been murdered. But nothing could make Marie Anne forget—nothing until that winter day when a man on snowshoes came to the fort from Cumberland House. After resting and discussing business matters with Mr. Laughing Face, he reached into a shirt pocket and produced a stained and crumpled letter, saying, "Madame Lagimodière, it's for you."

With one hand on her forehead she reached for the letter and recognized at once her mother's handwriting. It was her first letter from home and she held it momentarily to her breast. Her throat tightening with emotion, she knew she had to be alone.

"Excuse me," she remarked, throwing a blanket over her shoulders and going outside into the winter sunshine. In no hurry to open the letter, she turned it over and over, dwelling on the thought that her mother had held it months earlier. Still overcome by the wonder of having received it, she broke the seal. She paused again to speculate. What incidents of luck had combined to bring mail to a woman whose only address was a tent somewhere northwest of Pembina? What had happened to the letters she had sent to her mother?

Then, seized with practical curiosity, she dried her eyes and began reading the sheet her mother had so painstakingly written.

"I hope you still live, my dear," she began. "We have heard from you only once, telling us you have a baby girl. May God smile on your little Reine and bring you all safely past the dangers that must be many in that uncivilized land."

There followed a full report on Maskinonge happenings. The syrup harvest had been good; the family priest sent his blessings; and Marie Anne's former admirer, Louis Legrande, was still unmarried. He had escorted Marie Anne's younger sister to the spring party at the Manor House and everybody along the river was speculating. There were some deaths, marriages, and numerous births. Friends and neighbors sent their good wishes. Finally, her mother begged for another letter soon, adding, "Come back, my child; this is where you belong."

Marie Anne read the letter again, more slowly, before returning to the house inside the walls. Although her eyes were red and swollen, she was smiling and composed as she squatted on the buffalo robe beside Jean Baptiste.

The men were in conversation. Mr. Laughing Face and the messenger from Cumberland House were doing most of the talking. They had grown barley on a plot of ground at Cumberland, he was saying, much to the surprise of the trader.

"I don't care what you grew last summer," the trader was saying. It's a cussedly hard country, this West, and you've got to be a fighter if you're going to stay. Think of the risks you take every year — you might freeze or be killed by animals; an Indian might take the top off your head; you could starve or just die from loneliness."

"Yes," Marie Anne agreed, gazing into space, "every one of us might as well realize that before this time next year we could be victims of the same sort of brutality that took poor Hawkfeather. Yet you men choose this country."

Conscious of the emotional strain under which she had lived in recent weeks, Jean Baptiste squirmed uncomfortably and said, "Maybe next year I'll take you and the babies home."

"You'd take us home? To stay? Do you mean it, Ba'tiste?" She stared at him in surprise. For a moment she was silent and then said: "But I don't know if I want to go—at least, not to stay!"

She was as much surprised at her own words as at his. But that was how she felt and she spoke again: "They grew barley at Cumberland this year? Isn't that what I heard you say? Wouldn't you like to see this country a hundred years from now?"

The amiable trader smiled. "It won't be much different. A few more hunters and trappers, perhaps; and still enough buffalo to feed the Indians and the white men who will venture this far. Of course the Indians, in the meantime, might decide to wipe out the whites. They could do it if they wanted to — wipe 'em out to the last man all the way from Red River to the Pacific."

Jean Baptiste's interest was awakened. "If they did kill all of us, do you think any other whites would ever venture out here again?"

The trader didn't think so. "A few of us like it here, but nobody outside the fur trade would think this country worth a fight."

"I think you're wrong," Marie Anne interjected emphatically. It was her intuition that started the discussion and she was not satisfied with the trader's view. "I think there'll be farmers here some day, maybe lots of them."

The three men laughed and the trader replied, "This isn't Montreal or Trois Rivières, you know. It's too cold; the season's too short; there isn't enough rain. No; it's buffalo and beaver country or nothing, but that suits me."

"Isn't it possible that you people in the fur business might be prejudiced?" Marie Anne was adding boldly. "Look at what Alex Henry grew at Pembina—potatoes and beets and carrots. And last time he went west on this river he took turnip seed with him. I sort of imagine this buffalo grass being plowed and made into farms, especially along the rivers. And if we're lucky, we might live long enough to see it."

The men, skeptical and obviously set in their ways, didn't laugh this time. They just snickered their scorn for what seemed like impractical feminine dreaming.

Jean Baptiste spoke. "No chance of that. The old fur companies wouldn't let farmers come into this country. They'd be foolish if they did. It would spoil hunting and trapping forever."

"Well, why wouldn't it be better to have farming?" the stubborn lady asked.

Jean Baptiste couldn't hide his annoyance. "What's the matter with you, woman?"

A smile came over her face. "Ba'tiste," she said very seriously, "do you know what else my mother said in that letter? Well, Louis Legrande—you remember Louis; he wanted to marry me before you came back—he told my mother he was sure I'd made a mistake and would soon be back to stay. Well, Louis was wrong just as you are wrong now. Men are often wrong."

She was peering through the half-open door, envisioning fields of barley and farms where now there was only wilderness. With carefully chosen words, she continued: "It's true, Ba'tiste; for the first time I'm sure it's true. This is my country, where my babies were born and where I want to live, right in this rough country where I've been frightened nearly to death a dozen times."

The men stared as if fearing for her sanity.

"What is it about this land that captures a person, even a woman?" she went on. "Perhaps it's like having a difficult child. You become fascinated because the child is so different—and might become great. Yes, Ba'tiste, I'm convinced this is my country, but soon I'd like to settle down. Will you build me a log house some day —maybe at Pembina?"

13

An unexpected touch of Ireland

Jean Baptiste's restlessness to be moving was as unmistakable a sign of spring as the swelling bellies of buffalo cows. His mind was more firmly set upon hunting farther west than at any time before and to his surprise, his wife said she was ready.

There would be a delay, however, because he had promised to stay at the fort for the first weeks of the hectic spring season when Indians from all directions converged to swap furs for sugar, tea, tobacco, powder, and whiskey. Marie Anne kept her children close to her leather skirts and remained inside the walls while Jean Baptiste, with loaded gun, patrolled the stockade. The heavy gate was kept closed and barred except to admit or discharge Indian customers, one at a time.

"Hi, Marie Anne," he shouted one afternoon as he peered through the gun slots in the gate. "Our Frenchmen!"

She rushed to his side, and looking beyond the campground where Indians milled lazily about their teepees, she saw Chalifou, Belgrade, Paquin, and the latter's wife pulling their canoe out of the flooding river and trudging up the path with heavy bales of furs on their backs. The gate opened promptly and old friends moved inside to exchange greetings and relax.

They reported good trapping, but more important was the information about the rumored tragedy. Marie Anne listened with bated breath and heard the good news that Hawkfeather and the others were not murdered but kidnapped — "taken away like stolen horses," Chalifou said. "They're alive somewhere, I'm sure. Don't suppose we'll ever see them again, the country's so big."

As for Marie Anne's mirror, it had disappeared like the women, a trophy of war, no doubt. A frown came over the white woman's face as she thought of some wicked man forcing himself upon the good Hawkfeather and staring into the precious mirror.

Kidnapping was bad enough, but it was good to know that the report about murder was incorrect. Marie Anne relaxed and entered into the gaiety of the brief reunion. Belgrade and Paquin were planning on going back to Pembina and Chalifou was going to stop at Cumberland House.

"Join us in the fall," Marie Anne invited. "But you'd never find us."

"Never fear," Chalifou said. "I'll find you if you camp anywhere beside the north river. I'll just paddle until I do find you. Or I'll sing and you'll hear me. By the way, how do you plan to travel when you go up river?"

The choice was again between a canoe and horses. Jean Baptiste favored the latter; they would be useful in the months to come, and this consideration outweighed the extra comfort Marie Anne and the children would have in a canoe. Jean Baptiste's black stallion and Marie Anne's mare, now known as Belle, had wintered not far away with horses belonging to some friendly Indians, and Jean Baptiste bargained for a third one to pull the loaded travois.

And so it was that on a sweet morning in June, the Lagimodières mounted their horses and moved slowly out of the fort gate, taking the trail to the west. Baby Jean, now called LaPrairie, was secure on his mother's back and Reine, energetic and active, was seated in front where her mother could hold and steady her. The mare pranced playfully for the first mile and then settled down sensibly. Marie Anne was on the best of terms with the mare and talked softly to her: "We make a heavy load for you, Belle, but we'll rest often, I promise."

It was pleasant to travel over nature's carpet of green, daubed with the colors of prairie flowers and alive with wild creatures. Up to a point, it was familiar territory. At the end of the third day, they camped on the spot of last year's summer home, and halted the next day where Mimmie's Indian village had been located—now unmarked except for the logs of the Thirst Dance lodge.

The route was close to the South Saskatchewan, flowing out of the dangerous land of the Blackfoot. Jean Baptiste was searching for the most suitable place for a crossing. If he had only himself to consider, he would swim the horses and hang on to one of them, but a safer arrangement was needed for his family. As luck would have it, an Indian paddling downstream agreed to ferry Marie Anne and the children across. The pack pony and the mare would swim behind the boat. Jean Baptiste resolved to swim his stallion at the rear in case either of the other animals proved unco-operative.

"Don't try to ride that horse across," his wife pleaded. "Lead him too and you ride with us."

But Jean Baptiste had ridden across the Red River more than once and was convinced his plan was best. He was not impressed by his wife's fears.

It would be a long swim for the horses because the June river was swollen and fast. They entered the water unwillingly, but once in, they swam boldly. The little mare was the best swimmer; the pack horse, with travois floating behind, was slow but powerful.

The black stallion was not a strong swimmer, but Jean Baptiste sensed no reason for alarm—at least not until the full force of the current began to carry him downstream. The big animal plunged desperately, showing unmistakable signs of tiring, and Jean Baptiste belatedly saw his error in trying to cross the river this way. But it was too late to turn back. Marie Anne, watching her husband being carried rapidly downstream, learned a new kind of desperation. She knew she could do nothing to help him without creating a still more dangerous situation.

Despite the Indian's commands to sit down, she stood erect in the canoe and called in her loudest voice: "Can you make it to shore without the horse?" In the tumult of rushing water, he could not hear, and his horse plunged on with diminishing effectiveness. Three-quarters of the way across the animal seemed to give up. Sliding into the water, the rider held on to the reins, hoping that the horse, relieved of its burden, might summon sufficient strength to swim to shore.

Marie Anne knew her husband was a strong swimmer, but the swollen stream was treacherous, and pulling an exhausted horse to shore while fighting for his own survival would be a superhuman feat. As the canoe touched shore and the two horses stood on firm bottom, Marie Anne could restrain herself no longer. Making sure the children were safe, she passed the lead-lines to the Indian and ran frantically to be as close as possible to her man.

"Jean Baptiste!" she shrieked. "Let that horse go. Save yourself. Let him go I say."

A moment later he abandoned the horse and swam straight toward her; only a few strokes separated horse and man when the animal plunged violently and went under. The brute resurfaced briefly farther downstream, then went under and did not reappear. As Jean Baptiste neared shore, Marie Anne waded into the water, her arms outstretched to help. When at last he lay panting on the soft grassy ground, she sat beside him sobbing with relief.

"Oh, Ba'tiste, stupid fellow, you might have drowned. Never do such a thing again—promise you never will," she pleaded, pressing his cold hand. "It was awful, not being able to help. I thought you'd drown trying to save that horse. But you're alive. Oh, thank God."

"Lost a damned good horse," he whispered. "Good everywhere except in water. Some horses are like that."

"Never mind about the horse. We can get along with two."

Bidding farewell to the Indian with the canoe, the Lagimodières camped nearby to dry their clothes and reorganize for the trail ahead. When they resumed travel, Jean Baptiste was riding the travois horse and progress was only slightly slower. Their course was northwesterly and if calculations were correct, they would reach the north branch of the Saskatchewan in three days.

Food was plentiful but there were dangers of other kinds. One morning they awoke to discover that the hobbled horses had wandered out of the range of visibility. There was nothing for it but for Jean Baptiste to make a search. He took his gun, hoping to see game along the way and was absent until late in the day.

Shortly before noon a band of mounted braves in war paint rode to the tent and surrounded it. The leader, in a headpiece mounted with buffalo horns, grunted something that Marie Anne interpreted as an enquiry concerning the white man's whereabouts. Trying to give no hint of her fright, she made signs to show that he was hunting lost horses and would be returning immediately. Cleverly, she began to cook meat for the noon meal, adding extra rations with which to bribe the unwanted guests to better humor.

The warriors were probably looking for Cree scalps, but by some native standards, white scalps were better than none. Not waiting for the meat to be completely cooked, she gave some to the leader and for good measure, brought him tobacco from Jean Baptiste's supply. The results were those for which she had hoped; the chief became friendly—perhaps too friendly as he squatted beside the tent to await the next meal.

Late in the afternoon Jean Baptiste returned with the troublesome horses, and at once the Indian leader's good humor disappeared. Clearly, he resented the white man's intrusion and was displeased when Jean Baptiste set about to move the tent. The situation appeared grim; but when more meat was served and Jean Baptiste explained that the white woman was feeling ill, the Indian consented to allow the family to move.

The tent was shifted but Jean Baptiste was still uneasy. During the night he loaded up family and belongings again and rode until dawn. This time he made camp in the seclusion of a wooded area where there was a better chance of escaping sharp Indian eyes. They rested during the day, and travelled again until they reached a big river. Surely they were far enough from belligerent Indians to be safe.

"Well, where are we, Ba'tiste, and how much farther?" Marie Anne enquired. He was not sure but judged this to be the North Saskatchewan.

Jean Baptiste went hunting, following the river, and soon encountered a white man whose tent was only a short distance upstream. The stranger was an Irishman, Patrick O. Dublin, known to the Indians as Potlatch. He confirmed that this was indeed the North Saskatchewan but warned that it was at least eight days canoe travel to the mouth of the Vermilion River.

"How far by horse?"

The man was noticeably startled. "Do you mean you're taking your family on horses? My friend, you must be crazy!"

"You can think what you like," came the reply, "but I want the horses for buffalo hunting when we stop. Hard on wife and children but we're getting there."

Jean Baptiste was beginning to see that the choice of horses for this expedition was an error, but was not ready to admit it. His family would have been better off in a canoe although there was no need to say it aloud.

Patrick O. Dublin was not an ordinary specimen by any means. He was, strange to say, a scholar and a botanist even though he lived as a recluse. He had been active in the fur trade in Peter Pond's years, but left it when he could no longer tolerate the cruelty to animals imposed by the steel traps. That evening he paddled to a point close to the Lagimodière tent and pulled his canoe ashore. When he saw Marie Anne, he stopped abruptly as though confronted by an apparition.

"Well bless my Irish soul, she's white! You didn't tell me. Niver did I expect to see the day! A white mither and two white young'uns out here!"

"We're glad to see you," Marie Anne said as a greeting. "We don't see many of our race."

"Ah, and I'm glad to be feasting my eyes on the likes of you," the stranger replied. "But why wad a refined body like you come to this rump-end of the universe? It can be na place for two such brawly children." He stared in silence and then spoke again. "I wouldn't believe it if it were not before my eyes. You see, I had a sweetheart once, and thought to marry her. She had a mouth and hair like yours. Lord yes, like yours!"

"And you changed your mind, Mr. Dublin?"

"I did not change your mind until I had to. I loved her dearly and lived for the day when she'd be boiling my potatoes. Yes, yes, but human kind is strange. I was being deceived. Yes, deceived! I thought I was the only one cuddling her. But I was wrong and I left Ireland to live in Montreal and then in this Rupert's Land."

"Will you never go back, Mr. Dublin?"

"Niver! But don't call me Dublin. That name's dead. Just call me Potlatch."

"You live alone?"

"Alone, lass, but it's not a bad life. The sons of Ireland love freedom and independence, and this riverbank has its points that not even a Galway farm could offer. You'll onderstand, I'm no' strictly alone, in the sense that I live in a community of growing things — flowers and animals I mean. I regret that I must kill to live, but I'm on good terms with most of the wild things around me and I don't destroy more'n I need."

Marie Anne was smiling. To encounter such an unusual and refreshing character was indeed a surprise. The accent was one with which she was not familiar, but it was no obstacle to the pleasure of listening to the man's forceful expressions.

"Imagine finding the likes of him out here," she said after he paddled away toward his tent. "He's probably a good and loyal fellow and it's worth coming a long way to meet him." Jean Baptiste agreed, saying he'd be a man to call if help were needed.

Potlatch came again next day. Jean Baptiste was away with his gun, but Marie Anne welcomed her neighbor who brought a fresh mullet for the evening meal. He talked about life there on the riverbank and about prairie flowers. Before long she was following him to a place where wood-violets grew. Violets were her favorite flowers and she picked a bouquet to fix in her hair for Jean Baptiste's pleasure when he returned. Then, back at the tent she found company awaiting, a party of Indians on horses, inquisitively studying the habitation. Naturally, she was nervous. Though her children were safe and a man was beside her, strange nomads were never to be taken lightly.

"Fear nothing, madam," Potlatch said as he straightened his weather-beaten body and raised a noble chin. "I know these heathens and I'll expound wi' them. Just stay close to me lass."

Thankful for the strong confidence created by this new acquaintance, she did as she was told. He opened the conversation boldly and explained to the natives that these white people were friends of the traders and of the Indians. The chief's curiosity was evident; he wanted to know more about white women. Did all white women look like this one? Why did white women not follow white men into this land years before? Would the little white girl grow up to be a beautiful woman too? And then, when the old Indian's gaze fell upon the tender face of the Lagimodière son, he grunted with fresh interest and leaped from his horse to get a better view.

Instead of crying, the child smiled winsomely at the big man and the chief was captivated. At once he wanted to own the child, wanted the smiling boy with a burning urgency. He was ready to bargain. His first bid was the horse he was riding. He handed the reins to the mother, fully expecting her to take them. She knew what he meant by the gesture.

"No, positively no," she said in a trembling voice. The Indian supposed he would simply have to raise his price. Seizing the reins from the horse on which one of his followers sat, he extended the leathers, indicating an offer of two horses.

She was frightened, and turning to Potlatch, said, "Tell him he can't have my son at any price, not even if he takes my heart out."

"There's no deal, chief," the Irishman roared, but the Indian was still unconvinced. He made another offer. He would give two horses and his own son.

Again Potlatch roared, "There's no deal, you loon!" and this time his thundering voice echoed through the river valley.

Marie Anne held her baby tightly and wept; then, gaining strength from Potlatch's courage, she shook her finger at the Indians and scolded them in words they could not understand: "Don't you say any more about my baby. Now go away!" Although her words were strange to Indian ears, she obviously made her meaning clear enough and to her surprise, the usually ornery prairie tribesmen turned their horses forthwith and rode away at a gallop.

"Well, I niver expected to see a white woman wi' your face and your spunk, madam. You give me a new faith in womankind. And damn it, I might as well say it as think it: I only wish I had met up with one like you."

They were the finest compliments she had heard since coming to the West, and she blushed with warm appreciation.

"I'm sorry, too," Potlatch added, with the air of a general, "that you are not of the Irish breed. The followers of St. Patrick would be proud to claim you. Ireland, you know, has a few accounts to settle with the Sassenach neighbors, and you possess the mither-stuff from which victorious chieftains spring."

Marie Anne was overwhelmed at the wonder of meeting such a man so far from civilization. Nobody would expect to encounter such fine speech in the fur country.

Jean Baptiste returned with the tongue and hump of a buffalo cow, and after listening to two reports about the Indian visitors—one in French and one in Irish—he announced: "Tomorrow morning I'll catch the horses and we'll be travelling."

Marie Anne tried to disguise a sigh; these days at the river were restful and refreshing and Potlatch was a profitable discovery. Now she had to face the return of trying to mother a family on a horse's back. But before she was ready to speak, Potlatch had something to say to Jean Baptiste.

"Look here, young fellow; I like you well enough but you're a confounded ass if you continue to travel that way. Just because you have a missus who's as game as a foxhound is no reason for expecting her to ruin herself. Be reasonable, mon! With two weans on her back and anither i' the nest, it's not decent. You'd better take care of yon lass because you'd niver come by anither like her. If I'd known the Almighty made her kind, I'd have been looking for one instead of coming here to live like a bleedy hermit.

"Now don't be troubling yourself to argue wi' me, Mr. Lagimodière," the Irishman went on as Jean Baptiste attempted to speak. "I'm in no mood for controversy, now or any time. I'll just relate my proposal and you can prepare to accept it. I've got a canoe. I fully onderstand ye cannot chase buffaloes with a boat when you go on west. Nivertheless, that canoe will serve your family needs better than a whole herd of cayuses. You'll take my canoe and I'll take your two horses."

Potlatch was not through expounding yet. "If you have any contrary views, Mr. Lagimodière, you may as well keep them to yoursel'. I don't know how I'll manage your horses but that will be my concern."

Jean Baptiste tried again to voice an objection to the plan but didn't get far. Potlatch was still talking. "I'm not asking for your opinion, Mr. Lagimodière. It's for the gude of your family. You've made a trade. It's very simple. Onderstand?"

Jean Baptiste nodded his capitulation and Marie Anne, still trying to smother her mirth, said, "Mr. Dublin—I mean Potlatch—you're awfully good. We'll never forget. I hope you'll enjoy the horses. Take care of my little mare. She's a sweet thing."

Potlatch admitted he might have trouble caring for both horses, but promised that if he could not accommodate both, it would be the little mare he would keep. And as for the canoe: "It's just a stone's throw from here and it's in good repair. Now, you come wi' me to find the ponies."

Everybody went to find the hobbled horses. They were not far away and the mare whinnied her reply to Marie Anne's call.

"I'm sorry I'll have no oats for them, just as I have no oatmeal or potatoes for myself," Potlatch said. "But I'll try to be a good friend to them just the same."

The hobbles were removed and Potlatch led the animals toward his tent, calling back that he would be around in the morning to help pack the canoe. "And if there's anything else you need, I'll be honored if you'll tell me. Good e'en my friends."

Next morning, with the expert assistance of the quaint son of old Ireland, the canoe was loaded and Marie Anne, with a broad smile on her face and children on her knees, took her place on the bottom of the boat.

Potlatch wished his departing friends well. To Jean Baptiste he said, "May your gun niver jam on you," and facing Marie Anne, his remark, with sentiment: " 'Tis a crown for your gallant head more'n a canoe for your bottom that you deserve."

The western sky appeared brighter than ever before and she spoke cheerfully. "It'll be better this way, Ba'tiste. I don't suppose a man could understand how difficult it is to support three babies on a horse."

"Three?"

"Yes, three, Ba'tiste, even though you've seen only two."

They were paddling upstream on the broad North Saskatchewan. To Marie Anne there was something both splendid and terrifying about it. They were seeing new country and being drawn into the spirit of adventure on a bigger scale. On the other hand, every day took them farther from Maskinonge and deeper into country where the waters of Indian society were more turbulent.

14

Westward,
still farther westward

They moved upstream day after day and Marie Anne blessed Potlatch's Irish heart for the exchange that gave her a secure seat on the bottom of a boat instead of the precarious place on the back of a horse. The children, too, were safer, but for Jean Baptiste, struggling constantly with a paddle, it meant harder work. As he pondered the nature of the deal—two horses for one canoe—he believed he got the worst of it. "Damn that Potlatch," he said. "He had an appearance of honesty but you can't rely on faces."

But Marie Anne, after settling the children on blankets, took up a paddle and began matching strokes with those of her man in the stern. It was heavy enough and tedious but to her surprise, the rhythm and grace of good paddling could become fascinating.

Trading posts came to view along the river but Jean Baptiste showed no wish to stop until he identified the North West Company fort opposite the mouth of the Vermilion River. There they went ashore and received a warm welcome from friends of Pembina years, Henry St. Martin, Joe Laflam, and their native wives. Marie Anne laughed at the expressions of surprise when they saw her: "What? You still here in the Northwest?"

"Of course I'm still here," she said with slight impatience. "Where did you think I'd be?"

"Gone back to the East—or dead," the blunt St. Martin replied. "Nobody at Pembina thought you'd stay. And two years ago when you left with the little girl on your back, the betting was that neither of you would last a year out this way."

"Ah, but there were circumstances you didn't understand. A wife should be at her husband's side, wherever he may go. Being close to him will increase her safety."

"Perhaps; but however you explain it, you're a brave young woman," the man replied.

She corrected him. "No, not me; it's Jean Baptiste who's brave." But her answer was lost as the two native women brought their Metis babies for the white woman's inspection and admiration. And while Marie Anne was being charmed by the dark eyes and creamy skins of these babies of mixed parentage, the Indian women were gazing in wide-eyed wonder and envy at the blue eyes and white skin of the baby Jean Baptiste. Investigating fingers touched the baby cheeks and the native women were satisfied that the little fellow was real.

Marie Anne's presence at Vermilion River was reason enough for celebration. Excuses for gaiety were rare, and even the Cree Indians spread their robes and pitched their teepees for an extended stay. The best meats were placed in the iron pots and rations of rum were handed out. Marie Anne was worried and enquired from her husband if they should move on.

"No," he replied. "You can't leave now. There won't be any trouble."

The Crees were at that moment forming a circle and drawing the company trader and Jean Baptiste into it. The tribesmen squatted on their blankets and stared inwardly. Seeing the white men relax, Marie Anne ceased to worry and watched with interest to see what would happen next. At an inconspicuous signal, the Indians began a ceremonial chant and the head man, marked by extra feathers, lit a longstem stone pipe, took a few puffs, and passed it around the circle. Each man drew from the mystic stem. It was the Peace Pipe ceremony, a declaration of peaceful intent. Marie Anne recognized it from descriptions she had heard and was impressed.

"Indians must forgive readily," she said to Jean Baptiste when they were together at the end of the day. "Either that or they forget quickly."

"Why?" he asked.

"Because they were getting along fine before the white people came. Isn't it true that the whites did the Indians more harm than good, Ba'tiste?"

"What do you mean?" he asked without much interest.

"Whiskey and smallpox, that's what I mean. And new troubles over Indian women. These people must know that white men will take their lands as they want them, like they did along the St. Lawrence. I can't help but wonder why their leaders haven't decided that this has gone far enough and ordered massacre or something."

"Don't forget," he answered sleepily, "Indians wouldn't have guns today if it wasn't for the white traders."

"I suppose that's so," she answered, still not ready to quit the subject. "But when they had nothing better than bows and arrows, weren't they just as well off? I wonder, Ba'tiste, if having guns is really a good thing for them."

He had neither the time nor the will for such debates. She had too much time, he reasoned. Perhaps when the next baby came she would quit this needless talk. Hoping to silence her, he offered a concluding thought: "Don't worry; Indians know the white men won't ever bother taking this western land. It wouldn't be worthwhile."

She was not to be silenced so easily. Speaking with revived enthusiasm, she said, "Did you see the turnips and potatoes growing beside this post? Did you see them?" He didn't answer and she continued: "Look Ba'tiste, maybe this hasn't occurred to the Indians, but just imagine how many turnips there would be if all of this country was planted to them. Look how many there are in one short row! We've come hundreds of miles since we left Pembina and, who knows, it may be turnip land all the way. Doesn't it make you wonder, Ba'tiste?"

But he was asleep. Everybody is interested in furs and buffaloes, she mused, and nobody is interested in turnips. If I see Mr. Potlatch again, she told herself, I'll talk to him about turnips. He won't laugh.

When Jean Baptiste said it was time to move again, his wife asked, "Much farther?"

He was tired of hearing that question and answered curtly: "Halfway to hell. We'll go till we find good trapping."

They left a message with the trader for Chalifou in case he came that way: "We'll be in a tent at the mouth of some stream running into this river; might be far west."

As usual, they travelled through long summer days and slept on the riverbank through short summer nights. The children seemed to accept the new life pattern readily, sleeping on blankets on the floor of the canoe for part of each day. Time passed without incident but not without some monotony.

"Why is it that life here is all extremes?" she asked thoughtfully. "It's either monotonous or too exciting for comfort. For days we sit in the canoe and nothing happens; then the Indians ask me to be their queen or they want my scalp for a souvenir." She laughed and asked Jean Baptiste, "Aren't you dying to know what's around the next bend?"

"We'll see when we get there," was all he said. He was not a philosopher. He had no intention of trying to be another Potlatch. He was intent upon beavers, noting every little stream running into the river and wondering about its beaver population.

"I'll tell you what I would like to know about the next bend in the river," she said with edge to her voice. "I'd like to know if you will find what will satisfy you. Don't forget this baby will be born before long and I would like to be sure we don't find ourselves in a spot like we did the last time. If you're going to paddle on and on like this, it would be better for me to float back with the current to Mr. Laughing Face's Fort of the Prairies."

"And stop at Potlatch's?" he asked sarcastically.

"Don't say things like that, Ba'tiste," she answered with anger in her voice.

Although he made no reply, she guessed he would stop at the next likely stream. And he did. The family tent was pitched where the small river entered from the north. Exploration proved it to be the mouth of the Red Water River, just a day's paddling below the North West Company's Fort Augustus.[1]

After a few days, Jean Baptiste suggested moving the family tent to the riverbank beside the big fort. There Marie Anne could depend upon help from the native women when the third Lagimodière baby was born. It was a happy proposal and soon after the move was made—about mid-August—the baby arrived, a girl to be called Josette. She was the first white child born in the area destined to become the Province of Alberta. Like her brother and sister she soon became the object of great curiosity and admiration among the native people.[2]

In the absence of mishap humans are inclined to take new risks. After several weeks of relative peacefulness, Marie Anne adopted the habit of settling her children for an afternoon sleep and then walking the short distance to the river to obtain a pail of water. It proved to be a mistake. Returning on one of these occasions, she caught a glimpse of an Indian woman with a small bundle in her arms, hurrying from the Lagimodière tent toward the Indian encampment. Dropping the pail of water, Marie Anne ran frantically to her tent. As she feared, her son was missing. In a fury of rage she followed the woman.

"Give me my child!" she demanded. The suspect glowered and pretended that she did not understand. Although the Indian was twice as big as she was, the young mother held her in a firm grip with one hand and jerked open the blanket with the other. There was baby Jean, undisturbed and smiling broadly, as usual. The native people who gathered stood startled and motionless while Marie Anne breathed fury at the thief, threatening anybody who might consider stooping to such stealth in the future. She learned another valuable lesson and never again left her children unattended.

Fort Augustus proved a pleasant place to stop for awhile. But beaver skins were good in September and early that month the family left the post, regretfully, and moved back to the campsite at the mouth of the Red Water River. The riverside dazzled with autumn beauty. Before long, the place had become home for these resourceful people.

After a few days, Chalifou arrived, coming this time with a canoe carrying a wife and two children.

"The last time we saw you, you were travelling alone," commented Marie Anne.

Not even his heavy tan could hide the blush on Chalifou's face. Awkwardly, he explained that he had grown tired of travelling alone, and while at the Cumberland House celebrations had met this Metis widow with two small children. He concluded that fate had brought them together. "She thought well of it," he explained, "and here we are. The more I see of her, the better I like her."

"By the way," he added in a different tone, plainly pleased to change the subject, "I have a present for you from Vermilion River." He produced a leather bag which he placed at Marie Anne's feet. "The trader at the post insisted that I carry it," he said.

"Turnips!" she shouted with delight. While the others laughed, she continued: "They'll be good with buffalo meat. We need some vegetables in our meals. I'm sure the children need something like this."

"Is it true that you're going to teach the Indians to grow them?" Chalifou asked with a chuckle. Everybody laughed.

Chalifou's wife could speak both French and English, and although she wasn't willing to taste the turnips, she was bright and Marie Anne was interested. Chalifou pitched the family tent beside the Lagimodière's and while the women became better acquainted, the two men discussed plans for the fur season.

Late in September the two families had an unexpected visit from the former ruler of Pembina, Alexander Henry, who was on his way to Rocky Mountain House. As usual, he was in a hurry, but he remained long enough to admire the young family and tell the Lagimodières that they would be made welcome at Fort Augustus if they chose to winter there. Marie Anne considered Fort of the Prairies to be her adopted winter home, but she thanked Henry for his offer, thinking that Augustus would give much better shelter than a tent on the riverbank.

But the beaver hunting and trapping promised to be even better than expected and the two men wanted to remain. Jean Baptiste hesitated to suggest it, but after rehearsing it carefully, he offered his wife a deal: "If you and the children will stay here for the winter, you can decide where we go in the spring. I promise." Much to his surprise, she agreed, but with one condition—the men must build a log tent with a stone fireplace.

It took time and hard work, but before the river froze over in November, the new structure for the families was completed, with poles and grass and soil for the roof. It was crowded and had neither windows nor floor, but everybody in it was busy with babies or beavers—and everybody was cheerful. For Marie Anne, after two years in the Northwest, this was the first home bigger than a tent that she could call her own.

15

Storm
and calm

A blanket of snow fell early, as if mother nature was in a hurry to send her living things to bed for their winter sleep. The forest setting beside the Red Water River needed nothing more than the first snow and the log cabin to complete the idyllic scene.

"It's a nice little house and it won't blow down like a tent," Marie Anne noted when it was made ready for occupation. She was right and it was an excellent demonstration that boys like Jean Baptiste and Chalifou, raised in the wooded valley of the St. Lawrence, never lost their acquired skills with an ax. But their axmanship was better than their calculations. When four adults and five children found sleeping space on the floor of the one-room structure, breathing impolitely in other faces was unavoidable, and anybody obliged to make a midnight trip outside knew it could not be done without stumbling over at least one human body.

Such crowding was not conducive to peaceful relationships through a long winter, but it was too late to start building another house. The two mothers, normally friendly, became irritable and quarreled. The men agreed that some change in living arrangements would have to be made. When it became clear that trapping and hunting at the Red Water location was not going to be as good as expected, Chalifou announced his intention to move with his family to another area.

Marie Anne watched Chalifou and his family depart just before Christmas and admitted mixed feelings. Now there would be less household congestion and fewer quarreling children. Clearly, the cabin would be more livable, but Jean Baptiste, hunting and trapping by himself, would now be facing the risks and dangers of winter weather alone. She worried about him. Each morning as he set out, flintlock in hand, she urged him to be back by sundown and demanded his promise to turn toward home at the first sign of a blizzard.

The storm of which she'd had a haunting fear broke unexpectedly on a day in January, and she watched it gathering force like a round stone loosened on a hillside. Within minutes, snow was blowing in blinding gusts, blotting out every landmark that might have guided a traveller. Darkness fell early and Jean Baptiste was not back. Sick with fear, Marie Anne struggled to feed her children and prepare them for bed.

"Where is papa?" Reine asked. "Isn't he coming home?"

"Of course he's coming home," mother replied, trying to reassure herself.

Baby Jean whimpered from the increasing cold entering at log joints and cracks in the chinking. The worried mother held each little hand and knew that her stone fireplace would be less than adequate this night. Piling all the blankets on one bed, she lay down with the baby in one arm and the two older children held close to her with the other. She sang to them, and as they became warmer, they went to sleep.

But Marie Anne did not sleep. The scream of the wind and the thought of Jean Baptiste caught in its cruel clutches filled her with horror. Now and then the gale sounded like a human cry. She would rush to peer through a crack in the door and listen until convinced that the sound was nothing more than wind in the treetops.

Daylight ended her sleepless night and Jean Baptiste was still missing. "If only there was something I could do!" she said to herself. "If Chalifou's wife were still here to stay with the children, I'd go out to search. Jean Baptiste might be lying in the snow not far from home. I must venture a short distance."

Her resolve, as all her decisions, was firm. Leaving the baby asleep and Reine and Jean moderately warm and fully occupied with the building blocks their father had cut from poplar wood, she buttoned into her warmest coat, threw a blanket over her head and stepped out into the driving snow. Keeping in mind the awful danger to herself and the children if she ventured too far and lost her way, she knew she dared not go beyond the range of visibility from the cabin. Her restricted search was in vain and she was about to return to the children when, in spite of her resolution to exercise caution, she was horrified to discover that she was lost. Standing knee-deep in a drift of snow, she tried to see through the blinding blizzard, but her cabin had vanished. Her own footsteps were obliterated almost as soon as she made them, and she could see nothing that would offer even a clue to the direction of home. Wisely, she remained in one place, hoping that visibility might improve, even momentarily. Instinctively, she dropped to her knees and prayed for guidance for the sake of her little ones.

Arising from her prayers, she seemed to find fresh courage and new hope. She began studying the wind. She recalled walking against the wind when leaving the cabin and reasoned that she should now be going with it. She struggled on and soon came to the riverbank. Following the river could bring her to her cabin, provided, of course, that she followed it in the proper direction. Responding to her intuition, she turned left and plunged on through the drifts until she was confronted by her cabin. Josette was crying and Reine said she was hungry. With tears of relief, Marie Anne gathered all three of them in her arms and sank to the buffalo robe bed, closing her eyes in silence.

She knew now the futility of trying to find Jean Baptiste. There was nothing more to do but wait in hope. The storm did not relent and night came again without sign of husband and father. She spent another sleepless night, stubbornly denying the tale of death and disaster borne on the gale.

Toward morning, the storm abated and soon after dawn Jean Baptiste stumbled in, his face almost beyond recognition from exposure and frostbite. He collapsed into his wife's arms and was put to bed. She massaged his legs and sore feet to restore circulation while murmuring, "Ba'tiste, you did come through. I was frightened you'd freeze. But everything will be all right now. How we need you! You must be hungry. I'll get you some food." But her words were wasted because Jean Baptiste had fallen asleep.

When he awakened hours later, she had hot buffalo meat broth for him, and he related the gruelling experience from which less resourceful and less hardy men would have perished. When the storm erupted, he made a shelter from willow sticks set up teepee-fashion on the leeward side of a big spruce tree and waited for the storm to end. His only food was the raw and frozen flesh of a fox shot for its skin.

There was gratitude in Marie Anne's heart but a frown on her face. She knew from experience with frostbite that Jean Baptiste's ordeal had not ended; he would not be able to resume hunting for days, maybe weeks. But whatever the future held, she knew she would have to find a solution to the immediate problem of finding food for the family. Supplies were already so low that after feeding her family, she denied herself more than a nibble, saying she had lost her appetite. Knowing very well that if fresh supplies were to be obtained, it would be for her to find them, she plied Jean Baptiste with questions about winter hunting until she felt ready to undertake the task alone.

"We need meat, Ba'tiste," she said casually. "I'm going hunting with your gun. There's plenty of wood for the fire and you can watch the children and feed them from what is left. Reine will help you. I'll be back before dark and if I'm lucky, I'll bring something for our supper."

He sat up as if in shock. "Marie," he gasped, "you can't do that!" But realizing their position, he relented. "I guess you have to. But be awfully careful and follow the river so you won't get lost. Don't go far." Still weak, he fell back, muttering, "Be damned careful."

It was heavy walking in the deep snow, there being no crust to carry her. She tramped until midday without seeing any game. Then a grouse appeared and she fired at it but the shot was wide. Tired and discouraged, she turned toward home. Within sight of the cabin, she caught the faint outline of a rabbit, and like an old hand, she shot it and proudly carried it home. It wasn't much for a family of five but she was too tired to think more about it. After the rabbit and bannock supper, she dropped on the bed and was quickly asleep.

Next day the young mother set out again, trying to ignore her aching muscles. But the day started better and before long she shot another rabbit. She wished a young buffalo would come along but knew the herds at this season were feeding on more southerly ranges. She would have to settle for less.

"But what's this?" she mumbled with surprise. "Fresh tracks in the snow—too big for a coyote and too small for a buffalo." The tracks led against the wind which should allow her to get closer to the animal. She followed as quickly as deep snow would permit, well aware that she might be on the trail of some ferocious creature. But the family need for meat was uppermost in her thoughts and she plodded on, keeping her gun ever ready.

The tracks led into the bush, out onto the river and then back to high ground. Stalking was tiring and she fell periodically in the soft snow. Worst of all, there was no assurance that she could overtake the animal. Indians sometimes followed tracks for a day or more.

Suddenly, she heard the crack of a breaking twig. She stood motionless and to her astonishment, saw a handsome buck deer meander from the bluff of trees ahead, straight toward her. Her impulse was to shoot at once, but caution told her that a deer in motion would present a more difficult target and she could not afford to miss.

Suddenly a big, gaunt wolf bounded to the edge of the bluff, stopped, considered the futility of chasing an able deer in the open, and immediately looked disinterested. When the wolf halted, so did the buck, turning his antlered head toward its pursuer. Neither payed any attention to the motionless human form studiously watching the drama.

Marie Anne raised her gun, and aiming with meticulous care, she pulled the trigger. The big buck dropped in the snow. And taking warning, the startled wolf seemed to somersault in the air and disappear into the woods. Marie Anne could hardly believe her eyes.

But the meat was still far from the cabin and she wanted to be back with her family before dark. With her small knife she set to work to bleed, skin, and dress the deer, remembering how Jean Baptiste did it when she assisted him. She was clumsy but determined and she completed the job.

Two major problems remained to be solved—how to carry the first part of the venison home, and how to protect the remainder from meat-eating animals. She divided the carcass and laid aside what she hoped to carry home that day. A nearby spruce with basket-like branches solved her second problem, and she hoisted the remaining pieces high enough in the tree to lodge beyond the reach of prowlers.

The sun was drawing close to the horizon when she began the long and difficult walk with meat, flintlock, and the small rabbit. The last of her journey was in semidarkness but there was triumph on her face when she stood inside the cabin and announced, "I shot a buck!" The family ate well that night and her story of the adventure brought Jean Baptiste to laugh loudly and approvingly.

The next day, Marie Anne left the cabin early, pulling the small sled Jean Baptiste made for hauling firewood. When she commenced the return with a load of deer meat, the runners cut deeply into the soft snow and the effort was almost too much for her. Eventually she took to the frozen surface of the river where there were fewer drifts. Sometimes when she stopped to rest, there was the wicked temptation to give up, but with the perseverance that was characteristic of her kind, and with fatigue matched only by her immense satisfaction, she was finally at home.

Treating herself to a day of rest first, she repeated the trip and brought in what remained of the carcass. Jean Baptiste speculated that they had enough food to last until he was strong enough to hunt again.

Lengthening hours of daylight and the first spring thaw brought the Lagimodières to talk about plans. This time, according to the deal made in the autumn, Marie Anne would decide where the family would go. "First we'll go to Fort Augustus and get rid of those smelly furs," she ruled. "Then we'll go downstream and see our friends. As for this last winter's trapping, we might as well have gone back to winter with Mr. Laughing Face. It was a mistake to stay here, wasn't it Ba'tiste?"

"You never know about trapping until you try," he replied,

never pleased to be reminded of a mistake. Although his feet were improving, he was still handicapped and irritable. When the river was free of ice, the family set out for the fort, canoe weighted down with furs and growing children. Paddling against the current was always heavy work, but Jean Baptiste was now better with his hands than his feet and enjoyed using his muscles again. It was an advantage to be one of the first trappers at the fort in the spring, and the Lagimodières were able to trade for flour, sugar, gunpowder, and brightly colored cloth for children's summer clothing. Chalifou and his family were present, and with a few beaver skins worth of well diluted rum, Jean Baptiste relaxed for an evening with his old friends. All but Marie Anne were feeling merry; she wanted to be moving. She had not revealed a secret hope that after three years on the Saskatchewan, Jean Baptiste would agree to paddle toward Pembina that summer.

When she told him he was annoyed by her intrusion, but he yielded: "All right, we'll go. But why the rush? How far do you want to go?" She gave no direct answer but said it would be nice to see their friends along the river highway. And so, the downstream journey began. Since the winter at Pembina, most of their paddling had been against the weight of moving water. Now they would travel with greater ease.

They stopped briefly at the mouth of the Vermilion River where the head trader greeted Marie Anne as "the great promoter of turnips." Smiling, she thanked him for the bag of roots he had sent the previous autumn and added bashfully, "Would you have a few turnip seeds to spare? I do want to see them tried in another part of the country."

"Sure. All kinds of them," he answered, explaining that the seed had been sent with supplies from Montreal and he had no intention of planting more than a row or two. Men didn't really need vegetables, he noted, and he would be glad to give all the remaining seeds to this woman with the fanatical enthusiasm for turnips.

She was pleased. She knew what she wanted to do with the seeds. She would leave some with anybody who displayed an interest in cultivating and planting a plot of ground. She wanted to talk with Potlatch.

Days later, as the canoe bore the family farther downstream, she said shyly, "I'd like to stop to see my little mare."

"To see old Potlatch, you mean," Jean Baptiste grunted.

"Yes, partly, Ba'tiste."

"All right. But you've been in such a hurry, you won't be stopping long."

Potlatch had built himself a log hut and on the flattened side of one log was the residential name, "Glenanne," carefully carved with a knife. Jean Baptiste didn't notice but his wife saw it at once and blushed.

An overgrowth of whiskers hid his emotions as he appeared at the cabin door but Potlatch's deep Irish voice rang clear and captivating as ever. "Just one new Lagimodière?" he roared. "Confound it, I thought ye'd have twins this time. But come inside. I didn't think ye'd go by. You look more like an Irish queen than ever, lass. Bairning seems to agree with you."

"What a nice new house, Mr. Potlatch." She studied the interior and said, "A man with such a house should have a wife."

"Aye, you're a bright body by why must the female mind dwell eternally on matrimony? Dash it, can't a man have a good home without paying for it with his independence? Nobody wanted to be my wife when I bided in a tent, but since I've built this wee place, I've been obliged, I regret to inform you, to eject two she-devils who thought to move in."

Jean Baptiste was inspecting the log work and taking no part in the conversation. He had nothing against Potlatch, except that he talked too much.

"Tell me about the little mare, Mr. Potlatch," Marie Anne said. "I've missed her."

"Now, there's a story, madam. I missed her too, missed her for a bluidy fortnight and thought she was dead."

"You mean she strayed away?"

"I mean no such thing. Both horses were stolen. Some red devils would rather steal a horse than a hizzie's heart. But come now, all of ye, an' I'll show ye the mear and tell you all I know concerning her adventure. Whether or not she suffered brutality at the hands of the lifters I canna' say, but I assure you her travels were not without a bit of romance."

They walked to a grassy flat close to the river where Potlatch had constructed a corral and rough shelter from poplar poles. Beside the structure was a big coil of hay which the devoted Potlatch had recovered the previous summer by pulling long grass by hand and piling it carefully. Inside the corral was the mare.

When Marie Anne assessed the scene, she knew that no horse in Rupert's Land had received better care. "Oh, you dear, dear Belle," she breathed, rubbing the mare's nose and running fingers through the long winter hair, still holding fast. "But is something wrong with her? I know! She's going to have a baby."

At the same moment, Jean Baptiste recognized the mare's condition and asked, "How did that happen?"

"Ah, yes," Potlatch replied. "She's heavy wi' foal and I'll tell you all I know. It was soon after you left, nearly a year past, that the two horses were stolen."

"Are you sure they were stolen?" Jean Baptiste asked.

"Yes, I know it. Their hobbles were cut and left lying on the prairie where they were grazing. I searched for miles and found no trace. I concluded we'd niver see the two beasties again. But ten days later—or was it a couple of weeks?—I went out of my tent on a morning and what should greet me but the familiar whinny of this grand mear. I fancied her before but I loved her thereafter."

"But who brought her back?" asked Marie Anne, drawing closer.

"Don't let your impatience rule you, miss. I'll tell you how I reconstruct her adventure. After the thieves ran the horses a good many miles, the devils released them wi' their own horses and expected them to stay. But our little mear didn't fancy the new associations and when she found opportunity, she began the return trip, alone."

"You mean she came back all by herself? Good for Belle! How far do you suppose she travelled to get here?"

"How far she came we'll niver know, but it is most probable she came fifty or sixty miles. I'm no' suggesting, mind you, that her thoughts were exclusively on returning to me. She didn't get herself foaled by coming straight home. After associating with an Irishman, she believes she should have something to show for a long trip. And by the soul of St. Patrick, she's showing you something."

"Oh, I wish we could stay to see Belle's baby," Marie Anne said, obviously as interested as if her best friend were having a child. "It's so exciting!"

"Madam, the foal will be your property if you should ever want it. I'll keep it for you—if the horse thieves don't get it, that is."

"You're so good, Mr. Potlatch. How long will it be before the baby comes?"

"That I canna' say but I'll be looking for a horse wean within a fortnight."

Marie Anne's eagerness to get back to the Fort of the Prairies vanished. Gladly she would have camped and waited to see the foal. But Jean Baptiste, with no sentiment for it, wanted to be going.

While the canoe was being loaded Marie Anne placed a small package in the Irishman's hand. "They're seeds," she said quietly as if they were contraband. I'd like you to plant them and when we meet again, tell me what you think of what grows."

"Seeds!" said the surprised Potlatch. "What kind of seeds?"

"Turnips," she answered. "Just wait till you see them grow."

"Indeed, I know all about turnips. Lots of times I near wrecked my bleedy back lifting them from Ireland's soil. But do you think they'll grow here?"

"They will grow. I know they will," she replied eagerly. "And when it's proven, there'll be talk about planting this country to people too."

"You don't really expect your old man to forsake hunting and take to planting?"

"No, Mr. Potlatch, Jean Baptiste will never be a planter. He won't even listen when I talk about turnips. If he was interested in planting, we'd be living quietly at Maskinonge today. But the people who come when my babies are men and women—they're the ones who will plow and build solid homes along the river."

"You're the first person to so express hersel' in my presence. It's nigh heresy, you know, to think of such a thing out here where men worship furs, but woman, you've said something that's been running through my mind. If the buffaloes and fur-bearers were to leave and niver return, I believe I could grow enough food right here to keep myself and a family. But the traders don't want to believe it. They'd like to hold this land for furs in perpetuity. But they can't do it. It may be a frosty country and rainfall may be scant, but there is soil. Lord, lady, what soil! I've dug holes to examine it and the best of Ireland's loam is mean by comparison."

This was the encouragement that Marie Anne needed, and coming from Potlatch, she hung to every word. "Then you'll plant the seeds, Mr. Potlatch?"

"Indeed I'll do that—and anything else ye may bid."

"I hope we'll see you again, soon," she said with sincerity in her voice. "But things are so uncertain in this land. If we don't meet, will you please let me know, somehow, about the mare's baby and the turnips? Yes, and about yourself."

"I'm not so brash as to be sending you messages about mysel', but I will report on the foal and the turnips. And mind, the foal is for you or your weans."

A few more days brought the Lagimodières to Fort of the Prairies and the never failing welcome from Mr. Laughing Face. And, glory be, there was a letter waiting for Marie Anne, addressed by a hand that told its own story—that of the blind Bouvier.

"Blessings on his great French heart!" she exclaimed as she opened it. The writing was indistinct and much of it totally illegible, but she struggled to understand all the news it contained. Among other things, a rumor about—the word looked like "settlers."

"Do you suppose settlers would be coming to live at Red River, Ba'tiste?" she enquired. Without waiting for his answer, she reminded him of his words: "Remember? You promised I could decide where we'd go this year."

He guessed what she was about to say. To her surprise, there was pleasure in his expression when he heard her pronouncement: "Ba'tiste, we'll go back to Pembina."

16

Coming home
to Red River

By the time the Lagimodière canoe neared the south end of Lake Winnipeg and the mouth of the Red River, Marie Anne might have admitted to being tired of the journey. There was the constant exposure to sun, wind, and rain; the monotony of eating fish at every meal; and the annoying regularity of long and tedious trips every time she was expecting a baby. But she had chosen the expedition this season and she did not complain.

The sight of Red River brought a vision of relaxation at Pembina and an early release from housekeeping duties in a canoe. A broad smile of relief came over her face, but when she mentioned the river's natural beauty, Jean Baptiste laughed loudly and left her to guess the reason for his amusement.

"I know why you're laughing," she said. "You're thinking about the first time I saw that river, five years ago; I thought it was ugly and said so. I know it seems funny, but a person's judgment can change with circumstances. This time, Ba'tiste, I have the feeling of coming home and I like the idea."

"What is Red River?" Reine interrupted. "Is it red?"

"You'll see it in a few minutes," she was told. "You saw it before but you were small."

"The river doesn't change," Jean Baptiste said, working harder against the current. "We might make it to the mouth of the other river before the end of the day. We'll stop there to see the new fort built since we left. It belongs to the Montreal men—Gibraltar, they call it."

Pleased with the prospect of a visit there, he became more talkative and told his wife all he had heard about the new post and the robust fellows like John McDonald of Garth and John Wills who planned and built it.[1] As it happened, Wills was present when Jean Baptiste pushed the family canoe ashore at the confluence of the Assiniboine and Red rivers.

"So you're the Lagimodières!" Wills shouted in greeting the family. "I've heard a lot about you people but didn't expect to meet you. But here you are, all five of you, to be sure." Looking at Marie Anne with undisguised admiration, he said, "We heard the Indians ran away with you, ma'am. Now that I've seen you, I can't say I'd blame them for wanting to keep you." She blushed, smiled, and graciously acknowledged an introduction to Benjamin Frobisher, Jr. and Alexander Macdonell who both appeared with enough buckles, lace, and good clothes to distinguish them, also, as Company officers. Her unique position in the West was enough to interest any of them, and that she was bright and beautiful too was sufficiently inspiring to send gentlemen searching for their best clothes.

Jean Baptiste remarked on the excellence of the fort's location in relation to the best sources of pemmican, and complimented the superb workmanship in its construction. "We think it's a good post," Wills replied. "But we weren't the first to choose the site. A St. Lawrence River man named La Verendrye built here almost seventy-five years ago; but there was nothing left of that fort when we came."

"La Verendrye, of course, from Trois Rivières, near our home." Influenced, no doubt, by the good French brandy supplied by the Company men, Jean Baptiste spoke first this time. Marie Anne was left to simply smile her approval for the recognition of the most famous voyageur from their home district.

"May your courage and beauty never grow less," Macdonell proposed, and the men touched glasses and gazed at Marie Anne as they drank. She nodded gracefully but wondered why she, as the guest of honor and the one to whom the toast was directed, was not even offered a sip of that brandy.

Fish and baked potatoes were served for dinner and Marie Anne resolved again that if they ever settled down she would grow potatoes as well as turnips. Surely there could be nothing more delicious than potatoes; she hadn't tasted them for three years. Benjamin Frobisher sat beside her and she decided to appeal for his help.

"Do you think I could get some potatoes for planting later on?" she asked shyly. The question seemed to fit nicely into the Frobisher thoughts of that moment. He knew Jean Baptiste's reputation as a hunter and thought it would be helpful to have him for a neighbor, and nice to have the young woman nearby at all times.

"Why don't you and your family settle down near here?" he

asked with a winning smile. "It's attractive country and the soil along the river is probably as good as any. If you do, I'll see that you get plenty of potatoes for planting."

Overhearing the exchange, John Wills had something to add: "Potatoes? That girl can have potatoes and anything else she wants, short of the fort itself."

Jean Baptiste was noticeably uneasy and grew impatient to be moving. Early next morning the Lagimodières paddled away, anticipating two days of travel before reaching Pembina. A few new cabins were seen beside the river, but the countryside was unchanged and Pembina had enough familiar faces to make the homecoming welcome a heart-warming experience. Jean Baptiste had no trouble in borrowing a cabin, and with it came gifts of pemmican that would meet all immediate food needs.

Paquin and his wife were there, Bouvier, Marguerite Trottier, and others. The genial Alexander Henry the Younger, prominent wintering partner in the North West Company, was no longer there; and Little Weasel was absent. Nobody knew where the Indian girl and her new husband had gone, but Marie Anne was no longer worried. She was sure she could now cope with any situation likely to arise.

She found Bouvier living in a small cabin solicitously tended by an Indian lady whose appearance would never have attracted a man with vision. Studying the woman, Marie Anne was shocked by the lack of cleanliness. The blind man seemed to read her mind and spoke out.

"She's good to me, my little Mandan; she cooks good food and keeps me warm in bed. I think she loves me in her own way and I'm lucky to have her. She belongs with me now and I wouldn't know how to get along without her."

He whittled away at wood and small chips lay everywhere on the floor. Although his face was scarred and twisted, it bore the expressions of a man at peace. And when his guest was about to ask what the carving would be, he anticipated the question and said, "It's a bear I'm making this time, but I suppose it's too soon for you to see the shape. Mandan will show you some of the things I've made."

The native lady came shuffling through the chips carrying an armful of carvings for Marie Anne to see. "Why, Bouvier, these are exquisite. You made them and you can't even see!"

There were figures of bears, beavers, foxes, and one human head, a delicate beauty, reminiscent of something she couldn't quite capture—a spirit, it seemed, rather than a thing.

"It's you, Madame Lagimodière—you, the angel of mercy and patience who saved my life. You are responsible for the talent these humble carvings display. It's true I haven't eyesight, but I see with my touch and my understanding. The head is yours, perhaps more like you than other people can know."

In the days and months that followed Marie Anne was often with the blind man who was invariably cheerful and ready to converse on any topic she suggested. He was wise and thoroughly informed about local happenings, making him an ideal companion and the only person besides Potlatch with whom she could discuss some of the matters closest to her heart.

"Did you hear there may be a farm settlement beside this Red River?" he asked her.

"I didn't exactly hear about it, Bouvier, but I think you wrote me something of the sort. And then I dreamed the strangest dream about settlers."

"Well, I dreamed too," he said, "the sort of dream that always comes true. The talk is that a Scottish earl wants to bring people to settle. I believe the first of them are on their way and something tells me we'll see them right here.[2] I know people say it's a crazy plan; they say the same earl failed when he tried the scheme in the East. But this might be different. That earl is a Scotsman and if I know his race, he'll try again and again till he succeeds. We'll see settlers on Red River."

Jean Baptiste walked in as Bouvier finished his speech, muttering, "What damned nonsense is this you're talking?" As usual, talk of settlers made him angry. "Settlers in this country would starve, bloody well starve!" Attracted by his words, other residents joined in the discussion. The majority were ready to sneer at the idea of using the soil for farming. Almost without exception they contended that people who couldn't hunt and live off the land would never survive for long in the West.

But one contrary opinion was unchanged. Marie Anne's mind dwelt on turnips and potatoes. If they plant turnips they won't starve, she was saying to herself. I'll plant them myself next year and when they grow I'll be able to show them to people who come here to settle. Whatever happens, I must plant in the spring. She was anxious for Jean Baptiste to remain at Pembina for the winter so that she could have planting space the following spring.

And before spring, there would be a new child in the family.

"What will we call this one, Ba'tiste?"

"Call who?"

"The new baby, of course. What do you think of Benjamin?" she asked.

"All right, I suppose, but it's more English than French. Is it Frobisher you're thinking about?"

"Perhaps it is. I'm not sure. He was a nice man. But I just like the name."

"No use deciding now. The baby might be a girl."

But it was a boy and he entered the world boisterously, just before the end of the year 1811, and giving birth to him almost exhausted his mother. Many times she rejoiced that she was at Pembina rather than at some isolated hunter's cabin on the North Saskatchewan River. In any case, he was given the name Benjamin, and like his mother, was drawn to the soil to become a successful farmer. It was with Benjamin that his widowed mother went ultimately to make her home.

The arguments about settlers continued at Pembina. Paquin's viewpoint was typical: "I can't understand the Hudson's Bay Company giving approval to a settlement scheme. Mark my words, if settlers do come, the pedlars from Montreal will make it damned unpleasant for them. Things are bad enough now between the two big companies but they'll get worse. You might see an attempt to build a colony but it won't last." Only Hugh Heney, who was in charge of the Hudson's Bay Company post at Pembina, and Bouvier, stood ready to defend the idea of settlement. Marie Anne remained with unshaken convictions about the importance of testing the Northwest for farming, but because of Jean Baptiste's strong opposition to the principle, she remained moderately silent.

Only on one occasion, when provoked by emotional pressures, did she speak boldly. It was as if she had been conserving her energy for that moment and her voice had the ring of missionary zeal. Everybody around her listened and marvelled.

"Don't be so sure that a colony can't succeed. In this strange land, you can expect the unexpected. You men should know that. You were among those who said a white woman couldn't survive here, but you should now be convinced that you were wrong. What's the matter with you that you can't think of anything except shooting and trapping? I say that turnips and potatoes and barley and maybe wheat could become more important than furs. Our children will live to see it. If Jean Baptiste will stay in one place long enough this next summer, I'll plant more turnips and potatoes than any of you have ever seen. And if my family can't eat them all, there'll be others who will be glad to get them."

The men did not like being lectured by a woman, but they concluded at once that her tongue was sharper than theirs. They were not convinced because they did not want to be convinced, and they chose to drift away rather than face her in argument.

There were no converts but there were decisions demanding immediate attention. The most urgent concerned summer plans. What compromise could be found between Jean Baptiste's perennial desire to travel, the welfare of the four small children, and her own longing for a place with enough land for a garden? Had he only himself to think about, he would go back to the North Saskatchewan River and penetrate new country, but he wasn't thinking only of himself. He had already settled it in his mind that his children needed some moderately permanent home, and before spring he must find it.

"Where do you want to plant your turnips?" he asked, surprising his wife.

In a flash, her arms were about him, her eyes smiling into his. "You mean we can stay beside the Red River?"

Yes, that was what he meant and after some discussion, he asked, "How would you like me to build a log house on the north of the Pembina River, not far from here?" For reasons best known to herself, that location would now have been her second choice, but she was ready to accept it and said so. Before a day had passed, however, Jean Baptiste came into the temporary home and announced, "I'll build a place for you on the Assiniboine, near Mr. Wills' fort, where you'll be close to your source of potatoes for planting."

That would be even better, she agreed, but why the sudden change of plans? He didn't want to explain, but Little Weasel had come back to Pembina.

17

The first
settlers arrive

Rumors of trouble filled the Red River Valley. There was talk of war with the United States, increasing violence between the two big companies engaged in the fur trade, and open conflict between Sioux Indians and Red River Metis who met regularly on the same buffalo hunting range. And people with French names who whispered gleefully about Napoleon's succession of victories in Europe—until his ill-fated advance on Moscow—wondered soberly when he would send his armies to recover British North America.

For a woman with four small children—the oldest only five years of age—and a husband given to frequent absences from home, the 1812 outlook was frightening. When Jean Baptiste proposed a family cabin on the Assiniboine instead of the Pembina River, it was natural that she would think of John Wills' offer of shelter at the solidly built Fort Gibraltar if it were needed. Moreover, Hugh Heney, the Hudson's Bay Company trader at Pembina, speculated that the settlers—if they ever arrived—would be located somewhere in the vicinity of the junction of the Red and Assiniboine. She agreed at once to locate on the Assiniboine, naming just one stipulation: that the exact site on the river would be of her choosing.

As big flocks of migrating geese flew north, the six members of the Lagimodière family were moving by canoe in the same direction. It was only a short downstream journey to the mouth of the Assiniboine and the big fort where John Wills had a drink of rum for Jean Baptiste and a renewed promise of seed potatoes for his wife. He encouraged the proposal to build a cabin on his river, not far from the fort, and offered to accompany them in the search for a nice site, high enough to be above the flood levels.

The search did not take long and Marie Anne pointed with approval at a riverside clearing offering an attractive site for a cabin with open space beside it for a potato and turnip garden. There, on the east side of a point later known as St. Charles, Jean Baptiste erected the aging buffalo skin tent. Then, stripped to the waist, he strode away with his ax to tackle the first logs suitable for building. The chips were soon flying and before sunset he had cut, dragged, and notched the first row of logs for the house his wife hoped they would occupy for more than a mere season or two.

With baby Benjamin suspended from a strong branch in his leather carrying bag, and five-year-old Reine watching the other two children, Marie Anne was free to start her digging. But this was not ordinary digging and she had every reason to be discouraged. As time would prove, the soil was immensely fertile, but it was tough to cut with a spade, heavy and sticky. It took all her weight to force the implement into the earth, and all her strength to lift and turn a loosened clod. It was heavy and painful toil, but the dream of potatoes and turnips—perhaps wheat for flour—spurred her on. Jean Baptiste snickered with a hunter's contempt and withheld the sympathy he might otherwise have offered when he saw her blistered hands. The cultivated plot was not as big as planned, but it would be big enough for the test and demonstration which was to be more important than even she had anticipated. After more spade work and more blisters, the precious turnip seed was planted in two straight rows, and the few potatoes delivered by Mr. Wills were carefully cut in pieces and spaced to fill the remaining part of the garden.

Daily, she inspected her garden, searching for growth and, daily, her impatience increased when nothing showed. She wondered if she should dig up the pieces of potatoes she had planted and eat them to prevent total loss. Jean Baptiste advised her to do it. But after a few more days, she called from her garden to come and see. To her joy and his indifference, she was able to point to both turnips and potatoes breaking through the heavy soil, exclaiming loudly, "They're growing! We're going to have a crop and a change of diet from pemmican. When you see Mr. Wills, tell him to come and see."

At about the same time, the single-room log house with a sod floor and roof, one rawhide window, and a stone fireplace with mud chimney, was ready for use. Jean Baptiste was proud of his handiwork and said it was as good a house as any between Gibraltar and Pembina. Surrounded by her children, her garden, native vegetation, and the new house with enough wall bunks to accommodate everybody, Marie Anne felt more settled and content than at any time since coming to the West.

John Wills, enjoying Marie Anne's enthusiasm for her planting project, brought in a garden hoe and presented it to her. For the balance of the summer, when she was not attending to the needs of her children, she was hoeing and speculating about the probable date when the crop would be ready for her table. The potatoes would mature before the turnips, and when she could restrain her curiosity no longer, she dug one potato plant and recovered enough tubers for one big meal. John Wills was invited to dinner on that great occasion when the Assiniboine soil yielded its first domestic vegetables and proposed a toast to the lady who might be making agricultural history.

The Lagimodière children, who had never tasted potatoes, were ecstatic about them, and even Jean Baptiste conceded that Marie Anne's experiment was worthwhile. Before that day ended she was back in her garden, digging sod in order to extend the planting area for next year.

It was only days thereafter that the best reason for testing the riverside soil became clear. While Jean Baptiste was enjoying some idle hours at Fort Gibraltar, two mounted riders were seen approaching from the north. The horsemen rode boldly to the fort gate where John Wills and Alexander Macdonell stood ready with a welcome if the travellers proved friendly. The first to dismount was Miles Macdonell. He was carrying two proclamations, one from the Hudson's Bay Company confirming the grant of land to be known as Assiniboia to Lord Selkirk, and the other from the earl, appointing Macdonell to the position of governor of Assiniboia. He reached for the hand of the other Macdonell, who happened to be his cousin, and then introduced his riding companion, Dr. Edwards.[1]

Jean Baptiste was one of those who stood silently by as the new governor explained that the main body of his working crew, coming to make preparations for Lord Selkirk's settlers, was at that moment paddling up the Red and would arrive within a few hours. They were grateful to Hugh Heney of the Hudson's Bay Company post at Pembina who had sent horses to bring the governor and doctor from a point below St. Andrew's Rapids.

John Wills introduced the two travellers to various local people whose curiosity brought them to the gate. Among them was Jean Baptiste Lagimodière, described as the "best hunter in the country." Freemen like Jean Baptiste, and Company men, could be pardoned for wanting to gawk at the man who had the nerve or foolhardiness to lead sodbusters into the fur country.

But it was too soon for animosities and the meeting was all friendliness and cordiality. Men of both companies sat on the grass and talked freely until late in the afternoon. The canoes carrying Miles Macdonell's workmen soon came into view and drew to the east side of the Red, opposite Fort Gibraltar where Hugh Heney and William Hillier had set up their tents to receive the newcomers.

Miles Macdonell and Dr. Edwards crossed the river to join their fellow travellers and direct unloading. Canadian and Metis trappers with not much else to do at that season crossed as well. They were surprised to see among the cargo a pair of young cattle, a bull, and a heifer that stepped obediently from a big canoe and walked quietly to higher ground. Jean Baptiste, among the spectators, watched the animals as though he had never seen their kind before.

Here was another anomaly the local people would not understand—bringing domestic cattle requiring feed and care to a country already overrun with wild herds of a related species. Their flesh would not taste any better than buffalo meat.

The two young cattle, Jean Baptiste was astonished to hear, had been discovered at Oxford House, between Hudson's Bay and Lake Winnipeg, likely brought from Scotland as calves. Hoping the cattle would serve the settlers, the Selkirk men requisitioned them, christened them Adam and Eve and hoped they would be fruitful and multiply in the settlement.

After Jean Baptiste paddled back to his cabin that night, he had much to tell Marie Anne: "The settlers have arrived with two cattle, and Miles Macdonell is going to choose a place for them to farm somewhere between here and the mouth of Red River."

Marie Anne caught the excitement of the moment and wished their cabin was closer to the scene of activity. "Things will be so exciting from now on," she said.

Jean Baptiste replied, "Yes, too exciting."

"What did you hear today?" Marie Anne asked eagerly each night when her man returned home.

On the fourth night he reported: "Tomorrow Miles Macdonell is going to fire a cannon at noon and read something he thinks is important."

"What do you think he'll read?"

"I don't know. Something about the land and making himself the boss, maybe."

"I'm going to be there," she said sternly. "You won't approve but I'm going."

"Why do you want to go?" he asked gruffly. "No women there. I can tell you about it."

She considered it her duty to keep in touch with developments along the river. The next morning the entire Lagimodière family paddled to the east side of the Red. Macdonell's plan was to fire the cannon and then read the proclamation that authorized the transfer of the land of Assiniboia to Lord Selkirk. Following that he would read Selkirk's order that made him, Captain Miles Macdonell, the governor.of Assiniboia.

Momentarily, Macdonell's interest seemed to be in the presence of a white woman and children more than the public proclamations. But Marie Anne remained close to Jean Baptiste and Macdonell's attention returned to the orders of the day. His manner was rough and autocratic, but with the help of the cannon's roar, he proved convincing. After reading what only a few of his listeners understood, he considered himself fully and formally installed in office. To celebrate the event, the North West Company officers present, Canadians, Indians, and all were invited to his tent for refreshments befitting such an occasion.

Strange to say, Miles Macdonell's rum had lasted better than his food supplies and during his days opposite Fort Gibraltar, his men were obliged to live on catfish caught in the river. That was all right for a few days, but what would they eat during the winter ahead? The governor was understandably worried, and seized the opportunity to talk to Jean Baptiste about securing his assistance.

"In a month or two," he said, "we'll have a second group of people—men, women, and children—the real settlers. How can we ensure food supplies for them through the winter? I've been advised to take all these people to Pembina so we'll be closer to buffalo herds. You'll understand that my men can build cabins and cut firewood, but they wouldn't know anything about hunting buffaloes. People tell me that you're the best hunter in the country. Would you consent to hunt for us this fall and winter? You'd need some assistants, of course, but we're prepared to pay you."

Jean Baptiste was interested, but did not like the idea of long absences from his family. He knew he should consult Marie Anne. "I'll let you know tomorrow," he told Macdonell.

Naturally, Marie Anne was unhappy about the prospect of living for long spells without her husband, but she recognized that his services would be invaluable to the settlers and that the task was one he would want to accept. She would not block the plan.

"You'd better go," she said. "You must leave us with a big supply of firewood and pemmican and promise to come back as often as you can be spared."

Miles Macdonell wanted Jean Baptiste to start his hunting operations as soon as he could get away. Macdonell planned to remain for some days at the forks to select a site for a colony fort which he intended to call Fort Douglas, honoring Lord Selkirk's family. His choice of location was a point of land formed by an eastward bend in the Red River about a mile north of the Assiniboine. There, at what he would call Point Douglas, his helpers dug up some soil to plant a bushel and a half of winter wheat he had brought from Scotland. Having completed the preliminary arrangements at Point Douglas, Macdonell started for Pembina. At the same time, Jean Baptiste was riding south, and by the middle of September, he and several of his friends were making their way westward from Pembina to the grazing ground known to be a favorite with the buffalo herds.

About the time of the first snowfall, a fleet of nine canoes brought the first of the real settlers—seventy men, women, and children—to stop briefly at Point Douglas.[2] After months of travel to York Factory on Hudson's Bay, and then further by canoe, these people were tired, homesick, and frightened and urgently in need of reassurance. Having heard of their arrival, Marie Anne knew her duty; placing her own little ones and a bucket of turnips in her canoe, she paddled to the forks and along the west bank of the Red to extend a simple welcome, especially to the women. No longer was she the only white woman in the country, and no longer were her children the only ones of their kind.

The travel-weary women, mainly from Scotland and Ireland, rejoiced to see Marie Anne and her children, and surrounded her to relate their worries and fears and ply her with questions. They told about the sixty-one dreary days on the big sailing ship, about quarreling between the Scottish and Irish people, and about the grueling trip from York Factory without seeing a friendly face. Now, there was the unexpected pleasure of meeting a white woman who came to see and cheer them and bring the first fresh vegetables they had seen in months! Here, best of all, was proof that a white woman could live in the country.

"Ah, Mrs. Lagimodière," said Mrs. McLean, who had given birth to a baby daughter on the sailing ship, "if I hadn't met you, I'd have been ready to start back to Scotland. And are you telling me that those healthy children were all born out here? How wonderful!"

Marie Anne smiled with satisfaction. She had a further message: "My man is hunting meat for you right now and he's the best hunter in the country. If you should be short of food this winter, I'll have some frozen potatoes and turnips to spare and you can have Mr. Macdonell send a sleigh for them."

Marie Anne had a new feeling of joy as she canoed her way back to the cabin that evening; she had seen white women at Red River and had done something important for them.

The ensuing winter was indeed difficult at Pembina. The buffalo herds, ever unpredictable, remained farther to the west and food supplies were short. Jean Baptiste was doing everything possible, but the spectre of hunger grew clearer until February 2, 1813, when the colonists were reduced to a reserve consisting of fifty-nine pounds of meat borrowed from the men of the North West Company.

"What are we to do?" men and women were heard to ask. "That trifling amount of buffalo meat will be gone by the end of the day. We're on the brink of starvation."

But before nightfall that day, the crisis vanished. Four sleighs loaded with buffalo meat came from Jean Baptiste and his hunters, and a sleigh was being dispatched to the Assiniboine to get the frozen turnips and potatoes Marie Anne had promised.

The potatoes lost palatability from being frozen, but the turnips suffered only slightly, and to people who had no other food except buffalo meat and fish, the lady's produce not only helped to prevent starvation but actually tasted like something prepared for a feast. She was the one who brought cheer when it was needed urgently, and she was now the one whose determination to grow turnips and potatoes created a new confidence. To no one's surprise, one of the babies born at Pembina that winter came to Point Douglas in the spring with the good name of Marie Anne McFetter.

Jean Baptiste, as good as his word, was back home on the Assiniboine a couple of times during the winter and then back to stay when the settlers moved down to Point Douglas. He was frequently at the point and saw Peter Fidler come down from Brandon House to survey the land for the new farmers, laying out long, narrow riverlot farms of about one hundred acres each. It was the best arrangement, beyond question, allowing the residents to live close to their water highway and contributing to sociability and effective defense in the event of attack.

At midsummer (July 18, 1813), when prospects for the colony's success appeared brighter, Miles Macdonell started on the long journey to York Factory to meet another contingent of settlers. These were men, women, and children from the Parish of Kildonan in the Scottish Highlands. But their sailing plans were disrupted after ship's fever broke out and seven people died during the crossing. The captain chose to put in at Fort Prince of Wales, a long way up the coast from York Factory. With the unexpected delay, the surviving immigrants decided that they should not attempt the seven- or eight-hundred-mile canoe trip to Red River until spring. Their only alternative was to make log and driftwood shelters upstream on the Churchill River. Miles Macdonell returned to Red River without even seeing the people from Kildonan.

But this was not the only problem. Drought spoiled most of the crops planted at Point Douglas and the oats were frozen. Only the potatoes and turnips were successful. Worst of all was the rumor that men of the North West Company were trying to incite the Indians at Rainy Lake against the settlement. "These whites," the Company men were alleged to have told the natives, "are not the ones who come to trap and trade. These who come to farm will take your land and destroy your way of living."

Jean Baptiste, whose sympathies were still with the fur traders, said, "We'll see shooting here before this time next year."

"I hope you're wrong," his wife replied without taking her eyes off their fifth baby Pauline. "I hope the settlers and our family can live quietly. Why can't we be left in peace to do more planting? I think that planting food crops is the most honorable of all occupations. Can't you agree with that, Ba'tiste?"

18

Caught
in the conflict

The great hall at Fort Gibraltar rang with music and dancing on that first night of the new year, 1815. Settlers and others living nearby were present to enjoy North West Company hospitality. There was something incongruous about it and questions were being asked in whispers: "Has the Montreal company had a change of heart? Is this a promise of friendship from the people who have violently opposed settlement?"

But whatever the reason, settlers, freemen, and native people were present and having fun. Black bread, cold meat, and rum were there for the taking, and the Company's own piper was in fine fettle, making music for the highland dances, while Jean Baptiste was there to fiddle for the jigs.

North Wester Duncan Cameron was the apparent essence of good humor. He smiled benignly at the women and directed good-natured greetings at the men. "Who said he was an offensive man?" a settler's wife asked indignantly. "He's a nice man and so well dressed with expensive lace. He's handsome in that red coat. Wouldn't it be thrilling to dance with him!"

Cameron was trying to please everybody, except in choosing his own dancing partners when he was pleasing himself. For the French minuet, he asked Marie Anne and together they commanded the eyes of everybody on the floor. As their dance concluded, Cameron bowed, saying, "I trust the fairest woman at Red River will favor me with a dance at the next party here at the fort."

"Do you plan to have another party, Mr. Cameron?"

"I do, and rather soon. Will you attend?"

"You surprise me," she answered. "I thought you and your

Company were opposed to settlers and now you seem to be working for their pleasure. A change of policy?"

"No, it's not that. It's just that, well, we think we should get to know the settlers and give them some advice. We may be able to spare them from danger and loss."

The words puzzled her as she watched Cameron withdraw. What advice would his Company have for the settlers? And what new dangers except those created by the North West Company itself?

She knew there was an undertow of suspicion and fear throughout the valley. True, there was a show of friendliness when the first Selkirk men arrived. But ever since that day in the previous January when Miles Macdonell had issued an order forbidding the movement of pemmican from Selkirk's territory without permission, bitterness between the North Westers and leaders in the settlement had mounted steadily. Naturally, the men of the Montreal Company resented the idea of a settlement. They knew that crop-minded people who wanted to keep cows and sheep had ruined the fur trade along the Mississippi and the same could happen here. The North Westers had always been denied the right to ship goods by Hudson's Bay and now, to have the rival Company backing a colony of farmers on the banks of their river lifeline was just too much. To make matters worse, Macdonell seemed to be going out of his way to annoy the Montreal traders, and they had come to believe that their very survival now depended upon complete destruction of the Selkirk colony. But if that result could be achieved without violence, so much the better.

There was another winter party at the fort and then one in the spring, each of which was preceded by sinister displays of wild riding and shooting by native people on settlement trails. The Metis, of course, were friendly to the North West Company. If anything had been needed to place the halfbreeds more securely on the North Westers' side, it was Miles Macdonell's order that there must be no more running of buffaloes by mounted hunters. The Metis hunted almost exclusively on horseback and Macdonell was fearful that their methods would drive the herds beyond the reach of his people who did not have horses.

Fear was mounting and every time a gun sounded, the Point Douglas folk jumped. But now, at the last of the Fort Gibraltar parties, servants of the Company talked gravely to settlers and their wives, warning that life at Red River was no longer safe—never would be. Indians could fall upon settlers at any time and failing that, the Metis would certainly lose their patience and strike to kill.

The settlement, the Company men pointed out, was all a mistake anyway. Nearly three years had passed and starvation stared the settlers in the face almost constantly. Crops were disappointing and it was doubtful if Selkirk actually had a legal claim to the land.

Then Duncan Cameron, with a fine display of sympathy, made his cunning proposal, offering free transportation for all settlers who would agree to go to Upper Canada where Cameron's Company would furnish food for a year and help in finding free land. There, he promised, the settlers would be away from Red River trouble and could build for their future.

After overhearing a North West Company man making a definite offer to a settler, Marie Anne could see more clearly the purpose of the parties at the fort. Her emotions changed from alarm to anger. She could see now the plot to destroy the settlement.

"Supposing there is trouble here on the river," she mentioned to her husband next day as he and his friend Paquin sat smoking beside the cabin. "Which side will you be on? Paquin is all right because he's only worked for one side, but you've been with the pedlars and you've also worked for the Hudson's Bay Company and the settlers."

Jean Baptiste drew his short-stemmed pipe from his mouth and chuckled, "Guess I'll stay on good terms with both as long as I can. But I don't like the way things are going."

She pressed him further. "If there's a showdown, who would you want to win?"

"I don't know," he replied. "I sort of like those settler fellows, but that Miles Macdonell! He's trying to make us all mad. He has no right to give us orders."

Paquin spoke up: "Yes, he'd order everybody to stop shipping pemmican out of this country. It's not his pemmican."

"Of course, but I can see his purpose when he did that," Marie Anne added. "He wants to be sure he won't be caught without enough food for the settlers. He's responsible for them, you know."

"I know that," said Jean Baptiste, "but other people have to eat, too. How are men on the brigades going to live? The men with the Saskatchewan canoes depend on this pemmican and Macdonell had no right to seize five hundred bags of North West pemmican coming from posts on the Assiniboine."

Paquin was nodding, then added, "John Wills was right. Macdonell is going too damned far. He has no authority to steal pemmican. I wonder about Selkirk, too. Everybody says he hates the fur trade. I wonder if he has a real claim to this land. He could be bluffing."

Marie Anne didn't think he was. The settlers who arrived in June—the Kildonans who wintered beside the Churchill River and walked to York Factory in the snow—spoke well of the earl of Selkirk, she said. "You old hunters just don't want to think anybody can farm here. You'll get your surprise yet."

Paquin winced. "I'll bet a twist of tobacco that if the Montreal men will wait awhile, these settlers will destroy themselves. It may not be long. They call themselves farmers and they don't know how they'll feed themselves. If it weren't for Jean Baptiste and his crowd, every last one would have starved in the last couple of winters. They can't farm here. They put seed in the ground and get nothing back. They let dogs and coyotes take the sheep they brought. They shoot one bull because he was cross and let the other stray away and fall through a hole in the ice. The pedlars' Company won't be bothered by them very long."

"All right," Marie Anne replied, "but who will win if there's a fight for the river?"

Jean Baptiste was the first to answer: "The North Westers, of course."

Paquin agreed. "Sure they'd win. They'd have the Metis on their side. They're tough. They shoot straight and their guns are always cocked."

It wasn't a good time to be leaving the Red River community, but Jean Baptiste had reason to see Peter Fidler at Brandon House and announced his intention to be going. It was the month of May and Marie Anne's potatoes and turnips had been planted. The river-banks were beautiful with new leaves and flowers and Marie Anne thought she and the children might accompany him, just for the outing. She walked to Point Douglas to report that she would be away for two or three weeks and would call again when she returned.

"Those people around the settlement look like frightened children," she told her husband that evening. "I wonder if we should stay in case we're needed." But Jean Baptiste thought nothing would happen for awhile, and if his wife wanted to go, she might as well forget about the settlers.

The Assiniboine water was high and mosquitoes were abundant and brutal, but otherwise the canoe offered a pleasant change. "This river is so different from the Saskatchewan," Marie Anne observed. "Just one bend after another. We seem to be going in circles most of the time." She was correct. Jean Baptiste explained that it was about a hundred miles to Brandon House if a person walked, but close to three hundred miles when one had to follow the curves of this loopy river.

"Three hundred miles? That's far longer than I expected the trip to be. But we're not in a hurry and we have a home when we're ready to go back. Ba'tiste, I'm enjoying this."

Peter Fidler was a blunt fellow with thick brown hair, broad shoulders, and big feet. And Brandon House, built on the Assiniboine just above the mouth of the Souris River in 1793, had seen stirring times and Indian attacks. Jean Baptiste had been there before but to Marie Anne, it was a new experience. It might have been called Peter Fidler's House because of the unquestioned authority with which the inimitable trader ruled. He greeted the Lagimodières and showed them where to erect their tent.

"Who would have believed it?" he bellowed. "A white woman at my house, and by the highest heaven, such a one as any man would slit a throat to claim." But the manner in which he gazed at her made her feel uncomfortable, even frightened. Peter Fidler was not one to hide his feelings. Marie Anne knew nothing about his private life or the many half-and-half children who bore his name, but she made up her mind to stay close to Jean Baptiste.

Fidler wanted Jean Baptiste to go on to the post on the Qu'Appelle, but their conversation was suddenly interrupted by the sight of a man on horseback coming from the east. Both horse and rider were obviously tired. When the man, a Metis, dismounted, Fidler asked, "How far did you come?"

"Red River."

"What's happening there these days?"

The stranger replied in frenzied terms: "Much happened. No more settlement. Some of people go east, some go north. All gone. Houses all burned. Settlers never come back."

Fidler received the news sternly. He had tried to help the settlers, but at heart he was a trader of furs. Jean Baptiste was silent although he had mixed feelings. Only Marie Anne was clearly shocked.

Excitedly, accusingly, she said, "That's the work of Duncan Cameron. I believe he's capable of murder. From now on, I'm completely on the side of the settlers, and I hope they come back and farm in spite of Cameron and his gang."

The Lagimodières and Peter Fidler listened while the visitor related the rest of the disturbing facts. There had been a series of Metis demonstrations, obviously inspired by the North West Company, and the colony people were stricken with fear. When the terrorized settlers were offered free transportation to Upper Canada the men, women, and children from over a dozen families—134 souls in all—took places in Company canoes and bade a final farewell to Red River. Duncan Cameron had been trying to effect the arrest of Miles Macdonell. Finally, with a warrant from Archibald Norman MacLeod of the North West Company, who held a Canada Jurisdiction Act appointment as a justice of the peace, Macdonell was charged with theft of pemmican.

Things were going from bad to worse. A more determined Metis attack on Point Douglas was threatened. Young Cuthbert Grant and Peter Pangman, with hybrid vigor and native boldness, were ready to act at the North West Company's bidding. Miles Macdonell decided to surrender in the hope of saving the colony, and with an assurance of no further destruction during the summer, he gave himself up to be sent as a prisoner to Montreal for trial.

But as the traveller from Red River admitted, Macdonell's surrender did not end the assault. The bois-brulés made forays at once to shoot the settlers' horses, plunder, and threaten murder. Almost all residents who had not accepted transportation to the East gathered a few belongings and set out by canoe northward. Only John MacLeod and a couple of courageous young fellows remained behind, as though they had a chance of guarding the crops and homes against savage attacks.

"We must return to our house," Marie Anne said to her husband, and before he had time to reply, she turned to Peter Fidler saying, "Please excuse us, we have to be on our way."

The Lagimodières returned to find their cabin unmolested, but at Point Douglas the destruction seemed almost complete. A death-like stillness hung over the settlement. Where homes had stood, there were now only ashes. Even those guilty of the burning and looting were absent. Evidently they, like the Company officers, concluded that the colony was completely knocked out.

But they were wrong. The uncompromising John MacLeod remained to defy Alexander Macdonell, Cuthbert Grant, and all their scheming followers. Although standing against scores of armed and mounted insurgents, this man with iron determination was still the one in charge of Point Douglas when Marie Anne found him in the blacksmith shop, one of the few buildings to escape burning. It was his fortress and he welcomed her, knowing she would be a good ally. He knew her loyalty to the settlers.[1]

"It's been a hell o' a time, Mistress Lagimodière," he said, relating the events. "Miles Macdonell may have been a fool at times, but he was nae coward. He'd have fought it out with Grant's villains, but there were women and children to consider. He yielded tae the urging o' settlers who were more frightened than prudent, and surrendered in the hope of ending the trouble. But Grant served notice to the settlers tae get out and there was nae end to anything until the place appeared abandoned and houses burned."

"But how did you escape, Mr. MacLeod?"

"Ah weel, I just decided I'd take a stand against the sinners and if I was murdered it would be no huge loss. As it was, my luck lasted and I was able tae show those wicked fellows that a MacLeod can be baith stubborn and mean."

"How in the world did you manage to keep them back?"

"Weel, when I decided to stay behind tae mock the devils, I had time tae lug that three-pounder cannon from the fort tae my wee place. I had plenty o' gunpowder and cut up a chain for use as shot."

"Did you use it?"

"Indeed I did. I wouldn't want to saw all that chain for nae purpose. Tae show them I knew how tae use my wee cannon, I drove a link right through the horse Big Simeon was riding."

"I know Simeon. They say he committed his first murder when he was seventeen."

"He didna' like what I did and I could hear him shout a promise he'd take my life for it. But I figured they'd take it anyway if they could, and it seemed a proper time to end timidity. Sae I called tae them and said, 'Now ye bronzed bastards, if ye feel like firing my hoose too, just come a wee bit closer and get your gizzards filled wi' chunks o' chain.' They did come closer and I filled the air wi' smoke and din and bits o' iron and we'll never know how many were hurt. They seemed tae be convinced because they gathered up all their men who fell from their horses and withdrew. They didna' bother me again. But the two lads who were with me have since gone south to Pembina."

"That's wonderful," she said. "Now, do you think the settlers will come back?"

"Weel, the ones who went east in Company canoes will no' return, but we'll see the others again and I'm sure the earl o' Selkirk is not finished with his enemies yet."

"Then we'd better see to it that the potatoes and turnips in the gardens have a chance to grow so there'll be food for next winter. I'll keep the weeds down."

"You'll keep the weeds down? In all the gardens? Well, bless my soul! I do believe you would, Mistress Lagimodière. Do you know, if I had you and that hunter husband of yours wi' me in my wee fort, I believe we could have annihilated that whole gang. As it is, they'll be back for my blood."

In the days that followed, Marie Anne came by canoe to weed gardens. Her children—all five of them— accompanied their mother and amused themselves while she pulled the long weeds and used the hoe on the short ones. Sometimes Jean Baptiste came too, but he had hunting to pursue. More often, John MacLeod assisted. Unfailingly, it was the woman, working as though lives depended upon it.

She and John MacLeod were at work in the gardens when hoofbeats were heard on the trail from the north. Alert to possible dangers, MacLeod started toward his log shelter, beckoning Marie Anne to gather her children and follow. He knew that once inside his wee fort, he could swing the muzzle of his three-pounder and furnish protection for them all.

But MacLeod had too far to go to reach his building, and the two mounted men spurred their horses into a hard gallop to cut him off from his arsenal. They timed their charge well, giving him no chance to reach his doorway.

MacLeod stopped and faced them. They drew close to him and dismounted. While the lean one held both horses, the big, hairy-faced one held his gun at close range and said, "We've got you this time, MacLeod. You'll not bother us again. We'll shoot you now or you'll swing from a tree beside our campfire tonight. Whichever way we do it, it'll be the end for another damned intruder."

It was Big Simeon, the ruthless Metis who had sworn to kill MacLeod. With him was Charlie Joe, another who had suffered indignity from MacLeod's cannon. "What'll it be, MacLeod? Shooting now or hanging tonight? 'Tisn't everyone who gets a choice from me. Say it fast or, by God, I'll say it for you."

MacLeod straightened himself and with apparent composure, looked the wicked Simeon in the eye, saying, "Why must such an important decision be made sae quickly? It would be a grave mistake for a man in my position tae die before telling ye a few things ye should know. I can't tell you anything after I'm dead, ye know Simeon. Noo, the first thing I have tae tell you is that ye can probably kill MacLeod today but if ye do, you'll live to wish ye hadn't. You're fighting a battle ye canna win. Do you get the point, ye dull bastard?"

MacLeod had two purposes in trying to engage and confuse the big fellow in conversation. He knew that Marie Anne had hurried her children to the river where she left the family canoe, and it was important to give her all possible time to get away from these men who seemed void of conscience. As well, delay holds hope for anyone facing disaster.

"That's a hard decision ye asked me to make, Simeon," MacLeod continued. "But you're a sporting man and I'll make ye a proposition; you drop your gun and you and I can determine who is the best man with his fists. You're twice as big and you'd enjoy killing me that way."

"Don't be a fool, MacLeod. I've no time for that. You stand right there in front of my gun while Charlie Joe fires your building, and when you've seen your fort in flames, then I'll decide if we do you with a bullet or a rope. Fire that house, Joe, and be fast on it. I'm in a hurry to see how MacLeod's eyes look when he's dead."

At that instant, Marie Anne, who had left her children at the river and armed herself with Jean Baptiste's buffalo gun, approached unnoticed and stood motionless. "I'm in this too," she shouted, "and you who like killing and burning so well might as well know this gun is loaded."

As the slow-witted Simeon turned to look upon the woman, MacLeod sprang to grab the barrel of Simeon's gun. Simultaneously, Marie Anne pointed her gun at Charlie Joe and instructed him not to move. He was unarmed and seemed quite willing to obey.

It looked like unequal combat. Simeon was bigger, stronger, and more brutal than his adversary. He was already winning the struggle for the flintlock, but as he was about to wrest it away, MacLeod reached the flint and knocked it off the gun, rendering the weapon useless except as a club. The enraged Simeon jerked the gun away and swung with all his might at the Scotsman's head. MacLeod ducked and the gun slipped from its owner's hands and landed a dozen yards away. Now the two were on more equal footing.

They stood facing each other. "I'll keep this one away," Marie Anne reassured MacLeod. "If he moves, I'll shoot. Don't let Simeon get hold of you. Don't let him close enough to bite." She never took her aim away from Charlie Joe, but she was aware of every blow being struck. Simeon's punches were heavy but they often went wild. He wanted to get MacLeod by the throat. But if MacLeod was not big, he was at least agile and slippery. He was no stranger to fighting, having learned the rudiments of self-defense on the hillsides of Scotland.

Simeon landed a sledgehammer blow on MacLeod's shoulder, but it wasn't a vulnerable spot. The smaller man managed to strike Simeon's pugnacious face, and blood flowed from his nose. Simeon reached new heights of fury, lunging ineffectively at MacLeod with both fists.

"Don't you move a muscle," Marie Anne repeated to Charlie Joe. "My finger's on the trigger. And Mr. MacLeod, don't let that brute seize you."

While his head and shoulders hurt, MacLeod had gained some confidence that he could outsmart and perhaps outfight the bigger man. But it was too soon for optimism; the giant's next blow struck the side of his head and he fell to the ground. Simeon leaped in the air to fall with all his weight upon his foe, but MacLeod rolled sideways and Big Simeon landed in the dust with a heavy thud.

Both men were on their feet in seconds. Marie Anne could hear Simeon's teeth grinding savagely. He rushed at MacLeod and both men went down again, rolling in the dirt while Simeon pounded MacLeod with telling blows. Marie Anne's heart was beating madly as she prayed that MacLeod would find new strength. She worried about her five children left at the riverbank, but she dared not relax her watch on Charlie Joe. Sweat stood out on her brow as the two fighters rolled, got up, and went down again.

MacLeod's cheek had been laid open by Simeon's teeth, but he was lasting well and had escaped every trick Big Simeon had tried so far. But after a stinging blow to his bloody nose, Simeon shook himself free, got to his feet, and backed away, withdrawing something from his pocket.

Marie Anne screamed, "He's got a knife!"

Simeon rushed forward with the knife held high to strike. If he couldn't outguess the giant quickly, MacLeod would be cut to pieces. Marie Anne thought it might be better if MacLeod would turn and flee; MacLeod, too, may have considered running, but that would have settled nothing and Marie Anne would have been left with two attackers.

Whatever was to be done, had to be done quickly. MacLeod crouched and seized a handful of dry dust, and as Simeon came within striking distance, he hurled it in the giant's eyes. His aim was perfect. Simeon was momentarily blinded. He lowered his knife and struggled to remove the grit from his eyes. MacLeod, in the meantime, stepped closer and landed a carefully aimed blow at the big man's jaw. Simeon fell to the ground as though the bones in his legs had dissolved.

Marie Anne cheered and shouted, "Don't let him get up."

Bleeding and panting, MacLeod stood over the man like David over Goliath, ready to strike again if he threatened to get up. But Simeon showed no sign of getting up or fighting again. He was breathing but was thoroughly knocked out. Even after he opened his sore eyes he remained silent. By this time, MacLeod had his flintlock, and he and Marie Anne were now in unquestioned command. She wanted to rush to the river to see that her children were safe but did not dare do it yet. She had to believe that Reine was big enough to watch the smaller ones.

"What are we going to do with these men?" she asked. "We don't want them here."

MacLeod was exhausted but hadn't lost all interest in mirth. "There was talk about a quiet hanging beside a campfire tonight," he said dryly, trying to stop the trickle of blood from the wound in his cheek. "That's exactly what folks who set out to kill and burn houses deserve. But, no, we'll not hang them. I'd prefer to let them live to remember the day when a woman's courage and a Scotsman's luck beat the bloody scoundrels at their own despicable game.

"What about it, Simeon? Will ye leave this settlement alone and never come near it again if we postpone the hanging?"

Simeon did not answer. He was still slouched in semiconsciousness and in no condition to make weighty decisions about the future. Nor was he capable of sitting safely on his horse, but neither Marie Anne nor John MacLeod wanted him as a boarder. "Hey you,

Charlie Joe," MacLeod called. "Bring yon horse this way. We'll have tae tie the big galoot on his horse to get him going, but by the Blood of Bruce, we're not letting him stay here, even if he has nae more fight in him than in a blackfaced wether."

The limp body was hoisted to the horse's back. There was enough leather rope to tie his feet together under the horse's belly. Then, giving the horse a slap on its rump, MacLeod had a parting word for Charlie Joe: "You and your subdued friend would do well to travel as far as possible before sunset in case we change our minds about the hanging. And tell the big lout when he recovers that if I ever see either of you near this place again I'll presume you're inviting me to shoot tae help rid Red River of its rats. And by the way, I'll keep that gun your dull friend was going to shoot me with. I might need it."

MacLeod heaved a sigh of relief when Charlie Joe mounted his own horse and led away the other with its ungainly burden.

Marie Anne returned to her children and found them hungry and frightened, but otherwise well. "We're going home," she said to MacLeod, "unless that cut on your face needs attention."

The cut and the bruises, he assured her, were as nothing at all. "But what's a man tae say to a woman who has saved his bloody life? If this settlement survives, by God woman, a lot of the credit will belong to you."

She blushed, advised him to wash that wound carefully, and go to bed early. He watched as she paddled away toward the Assiniboine, and said to himself, "Never did I see the like. Red River should not forget." Then thinking of something else, he ran along the shore and shouted, "Will you be coming to hoe turnips tomorrow? I'll be here tae help you."

19

Living without Jean Baptiste

Hoeing resumed a couple of days after the memorable struggle, and both Marie Anne and her Highland friend took extra precautions. When not close to MacLeod's fortified cabin, they kept their muzzle-loaders beside them and eyed every trail leading to Point Douglas. Simeon might well return with a score of his angry friends. But he didn't, and for days nothing broke the silence of the valley except MacLeod's booming voice.

"Lord A'mighty, woman, I can't forget what you did. I ken damned weel that I'd not be alive to hoe a garden if you hadn't kept Charlie Joe at the blasting end of your gun."

"I only hope we're not wasting our time here," she answered. "It depends on the settlers. Do you think they'll come back?"

He was about to reply when his alert ears caught the sound of voices on the river.

"Hish," he said, reaching for his gun. "A canoe—from the north! Gather your weans and go along tae my shop. I'll follow as soon as I see who's here."

The canoe drew to the shore and a middle-aged man with sharp features stepped out and strode boldly up the riverbank in the direction of the private fort. MacLeod recognized him as Colin Robertson, formerly with the North West Company and now in the service of the Hudson's Bay Company and Lord Selkirk. MacLeod went to meet him.

Robertson had come over the long water route from Montreal, en route to the Athabasca region. But having passed the eastbound canoe brigade carrying the settlers who had left Red River, he felt constrained to make an inspection of the settlement or what remained of it. Shocked at what he saw there, he changed plans instantly.

"I'm going to find the settlers and bring them back," he told MacLeod and Marie Anne. "I'll see to it that they're back in time to harvest their wheat and potatoes and build cabins before winter begins. They'll be back, even if I have to carry them," he concluded, revealing the strength of will that made him useful to the earl of Selkirk.

Robertson didn't stop long. He was angry and bustled excitedly until his crew was ready to start again. Then, as his canoe moved into the current, he shouted, "I'll see you again soon."

Robertson located the depressed refugees at Jack River, far north on Lake Winnipeg. Some were sick; all were unhappy. They didn't know what to do. They seemed fenced in by circumstances. An exclusive diet of fish and the appearance of scurvy added to their misery. Many wished they were back in Ireland or Scotland. Some regretted their refusal of free transportation to Upper Canada, and only a few entertained ideas of returning to farm at Red River.

But however divergent their views about the future, they needed a leader and Robertson was their man. On one point he was adamant: They must go back to Red River. They were soon on their way, relieved that a decision had been made. At Point Douglas they saw the remains of their houses. It was not easy to hold back the tears and even more difficult to know where to begin rebuilding. With no homes and not much food, the oncoming winter appeared bleak, and pessimism returned.

"Why waste another year?" a woman asked, almost hysterically. "I'm ready to go all the way home, or if Cameron will still take my family to Upper Canada and give us land there, I'll leave tomorrow." Others agreed. "We refused to go before but when things keep getting worse, we're fools to stay and shiver and starve and worry."

Marie Anne listened to the embittered women. Their frustrations were not difficult to understand. After eight years in the country, she knew much about scurvy—knew that a fish diet was conducive to it. Hawkfeather had shown her how to brew a spruce tea that would prevent or cure it, and she had discovered that when potatoes or turnips were a part of the regular diet, scurvy did not occur.

"It's too bad you lost your houses," she began, "but you haven't seen your crops since you came back." The women admitted that they hadn't visited their little fields, and Marie Anne firmly instructed them to follow her. "Bring pails with you; we'll dig potatoes for your supper."

The women followed her halfheartedly. The crops were not great, but they were the best to be grown in the valley soil since the coming of the first settlers. When people who had not tasted vegetables in a year ate boiled potatoes and turnips with their fish that night, the Red River soil and climate assumed a brighter glow. Here was fresh evidence of fruitfulness, and if talk about going east in North West Company canoes didn't end, at least it instantly diminished.

As Marie Anne made her way back to Point Douglas the next day, the conclusion came to her that the men of the settlement were ready to begin again if only their women would agree to settle down. MacLeod agreed with her theory, saying, "I guess so, but convincing them is your job."

Mrs. Dunbar, whose complaints were the loudest just hours earlier, was the first to be converted. Rushing from her tent to meet Marie Anne, she said, "I didn't know potatoes and turnips could be so delicious. This valley looks better today. I'm not sure I would agree to leave. Mr. Robertson says he'll send a message to Montreal for help to protect the colony, and I guess my old man can build us a house anytime he likes."

When Marie Anne met Colin Robertson later that day, he said, "I think we've seen the miracle of potatoes. Do you know, I've seen more men driving stakes into the ground where they intend to build than on any day yet."

But the danger from attack was as great as ever and nobody could fail to see it. No one could tell how soon the hired hatchetmen of the North West Company would strike again. It could be any time, perhaps even before the settlers could have the satisfaction of harvesting their wheat. As a constant reminder of the threat, there was the grinning Duncan Cameron, sitting like a well-fed monarch at Fort Gibraltar, now and then donning his red coat and taking a menacing walk in the direction of Point Douglas.

Making daily visits to the settlement Marie Anne saw cabins rising from the ground and the ugly symptoms of scurvy disappearing. Wives and mothers looked for her and her children who were always with her. They had questions for her, questions concerning clothing, gardens, babies, food, and even disagreements with husbands. She had time for everybody's problems.

"Have you heard?" she asked excitedly when she met John MacLeod on one of her morning strolls. "Robertson has had word that a new governor has been appointed for this colony and he's already on the way, travelling with another group of settlers. His name is Semple—Robert Semple—and he's an old soldier." To MacLeod it was good news. It would mean, among other things, that when the party arrived, the settlement would have added strength from added numbers and fresh leadership. There would be a new balance of power in the country.

"Semple, eh?" MacLeod repeated contemplatively. "Weel, I hope he's a fighter and not just one of the forgiving kind. I've still got some links o' chain for yon cannon and it would be unfortunate to waste them. I'm keeping one for that Simeon bastard and one for Duncan Cameron."

Colin Robertson grinned in silence, betraying both amusement and approval. He believed in firmness in dealing with an enemy and resolved to take the initiative without waiting for Semple. It may have been to impress his own people and give them confidence that he ordered his men to capture Cameron when he walked in the direction of Fort Douglas. Then, having taken Cameron prisoner, Robertson seized Fort Gibraltar, thereby gaining control of the entire west bank of the Red River. But when Cameron became repentant and promised to end the attacks on the settlement, Robertson relented and gave him back his fort.

As the month of October wore on with shorter days and colder nights, Jean Baptiste came home from one of his hunting expeditions with a bigger supply of meat and a conviction that trouble would break out again and soon. He told his wife after they retired for the night: "The bois-brulés are getting ready and Cuthbert Grant is riding with them every day. Looks like a plan for murder."

Marie Anne was troubled. She sat up in bed and spoke sternly, "We must warn Robertson. Cameron is crafty. We can't let the bullies spoil the settlement again. I'll fight too if Grant comes back."

He was sorry he'd told her. He couldn't understand why his wife would become involved in this quarrel. But she was determined and vowed that if he didn't talk to Robertson, she would consider it her duty to do it. Reluctantly, he agreed to see Robertson in the morning.

At Point Douglas, Jean Baptiste saw men piling wood for winter fuel and chinking cabins. Others were taking fish from the river to be eaten with potatoes and turnips stored in pits below their cabins. They were more cheerful than on his last visit. He didn't stop to socialize but walked straight to the fort. Robertson was in a jovial mood. "Well, Baptiste, what brings you here at this morning hour? Why in hell doesn't a man with a pretty wife and five children stay at home more?"

When Robertson's light-hearted blustering ceased, Jean Baptiste came right to the point. He was not one for needless words at any time. "Halfbreeds up Qu'Appelle way are getting guns from the North West Company. Grant says they're going to kill everybody next time. They're not fooling. Marie Anne said I must tell you. Now I go."

"Heavens, Lagimodière, don't go yet. You just came in from the west? Who did you see? Are you sure you understood?"

"Sure, I understood. I saw Grant. He's mad. He says he'll kill MacLeod first."

Robertson sat silently for an instant. "Mind you, I'm not surprised. But what's to be done? We're not ready for that gang. I must get a message to the earl of Selkirk in Montreal. He has to be told that we can't survive without soldiers. I think he'd see that we get some protection. But how is one to get a letter to him? It's a hell of a time of year to ask anybody to make that trip. One would have to go through American territory to be safe—twenty-five hundred miles it looks to me and on foot all the way."

There was silence as Robertson gazed at the ceiling. "There's one man hereabouts I'd trust with that letter," he said. "Do you know who I mean?"

Jean Baptiste answered, "No."

"You, Lagimodière! Who the hell else? If you can't get through, the devil can't."

Jean Baptiste was not expecting such a request. Sure, he could get through if anybody could. It wasn't a question of taking care of himself in the outdoors that flashed through his mind; it was the risk to his wife and children when he was away.

"What about my family?" he asked Robertson.

"Look Lagimodière, you don't need to worry. We'll look after them. We'll take them right into this fort if necessary. And, of course, you'll be paid for your time and trouble. What about it?"

"I'll talk to Marie Anne. I'll let you know quick."

Marie Anne was already at Point Douglas, calling at the Meikle home where there was a sick baby. Naturally, she didn't like the idea of Jean Baptiste making that long and dangerous trip. Her first impulse was to say no, but she agreed about the importance of getting armed protection and she answered, "Jean Baptiste, I wouldn't let you go just for the pay. But these people aren't safe. I won't stop you. The children and I will worry, but if you go our prayers will follow you. You know that."

Yes, he knew that. He was not worried about dangers and hardships to himself. Such things never bothered him. The life of danger had been his choice.

"All right, I'll tell Robertson I'll go."

Within an hour of leaving the fort, Jean Baptiste was back sitting with Robertson.

With anxiety on his face, Robertson closed the door and bolted it.

"Well, what is it Lagimodière? Will you or won't you?"

"You said you'll take care of my wife and family. Then I'll go."

Robertson reached for Jean Baptiste's hand, held it firmly and said, "By the gods, Lagimodière, you're a man I'm glad to know. Now, when will you be ready?"

"Ready?" Jean Baptiste asked with surprise. "I'm ready now."

"I suppose you are but I'll have to prepare the letter. Let's say the morning and in the meantime don't talk about this to anybody except your wife. Say you're going hunting."

"I don't talk much," Jean Baptiste replied quite needlessly.

There was solemn conversation in the family cabin that night, and Marie Anne insisted that she was proud to think he would undertake such a task. Still, she couldn't hide her concern.

"Robertson will take care of you," he repeated.

She replied, "I know that. It's not for myself or even the children that I'm worried. It's for you, Ba'tiste. Winter is coming and the dangers. . . . The children and I will manage somehow, but we need you and you must hurry back."

While Jean Baptiste and his wife were engaged in serious conversation, Colin Robertson was bent over a candle-lit table at the fort, preparing two letters to be carried by "the faithful Lagimodière" to Montreal; one was to the earl of Selkirk explaining the dangers facing the settlers and the urgent need for a military force; the other was to the Hudson's Bay Company's legal agents in Montreal, explaining the agreement with Jean Baptiste.[1]

On his last evening before departure, Jean Baptiste gathered his family and a few belongings and moved into Fort Douglas. There Marie Anne and the children would be safe—as safe as they could be anywhere—and from there Jean Baptiste would leave on the great trek. His wife had a few last-minute repairs to make on his leather clothing and Colin Robertson had a few final words of advice.

"Better stay well to the south," he cautioned. "The Fond du Lac route is longer but probably safer. If those North West knaves learn of your purpose, they'll try to waylay you and they wouldn't hesitate at murder. You'd better go straight to Pembina, then through Minnesota to the Sault and along the south shore of Lake Huron to Detroit and then to Montreal."

Jean Baptiste was listening but not very intently. "Don't worry," he said. "I'll find Montreal."

Early on the morning of October 17, when the first wisps of smoke were rising from Red River cabins, Jean Baptiste was gathering his equipment—a couple of blankets, an ax, his trusty gun, an extra pair of moccasins, and a parcel of pemmican. It was enough to be carrying but a man should not start with less.

The morning was cold but as yet there was no snow and walking would be good. "Be at Pembina midday tomorrow," he said. "Maybe get a friend to go part way with me from there." He kissed each of his children, still in their beds, held Marie Anne momentarily in his arms as tears trickled down her pink cheeks, and then, with the briskness that was typical of all his physical activity, he strode away. Marie Anne followed, walking slowly until a bend in the trail removed him from her view.

There, sheltered by Red River's leafless but kindly trees, she sank to her knees in the crisp cover of leaves and prayed: "Please travel with him and see him through, for the sake of all these people and for our little ones."

20

The awful day
of Seven Oaks

"Don't worry yourself! You and the young'ns will be safe here at the fort," Colin Robertson told Marie Anne many times after Jean Baptiste's departure. "For him it'll just be like a long hunting trip and then you'll have him back."

It was all very well for Robertson to rationalize, but it wasn't easy to banish the thought of him being so far away. More than the distance there was the nagging fear of danger on his path; at midnight hours she was haunted by thoughts of him freezing or starving or being murdered. She longed for a message but after staring through the blackness she knew it was too much to hope for.

Six days after she watched him disappearing on the trail, however, came the report for which she had prayed. At the gate of the fort stood an exceedingly fierce-looking Indian, his ugliness accentuated by the absence of part of his nose. He was Peguis, chief of the Saulteaux tribe, and had come to see "Lagimo's squaw." He was not really a stranger along Red River and, as many people knew, he was Jean Baptiste "Lagimo's" friend. Years earlier, when Jean Baptiste was new in the West, he intruded upon an Indian fight to rescue Peguis from a party of Sioux scalpers. Thereafter he was Jean Baptiste's friend, and now he was present to tell his friend's "squaw" that he had seen Jean Baptiste arrive at Pembina on foot, and saw him leave the next day with two companions from former years, Belland and Parisian. The chief did not know how far the two acquaintances would accompany him, but he could report that Jean Baptiste was in good health and had charged Peguis to see that no harm came to Marie Anne and the children.

After reporting, the chief, ever loyal to his friend, announced that he would hunt and camp close by until "Lagimo" came back. Any suggestion that his attention would be unnecessary fell upon deaf ears; in accepting the responsibility, his Indian pride mingled with determination, and Peguis would not relinquish.

Marie Anne meditated. As the setting sun made long shadows, tears filled her black eyes; Jean Baptiste was thinking about his family—she knew he was. And the old chief, whose mutilated face would frighten most people, became beautiful to her.

She wasn't frightened about her own safety, although life within the fort could court more risks than living in the riverside cabin where her neutrality in Red River's turbulent society was more likely to be accepted. Loneliness, she believed, could become serious although people in and about the fort were thoughtful and kind. John MacLeod was a daily visitor; rough and ready as he was, he tried to be helpful and she liked to see him come. He couldn't hide his admiration for this woman to whom he had a personal debt, and he liked children. Reine and Jean delighted to sit on his knees and listen to stories about Scotland and ships and shepherds.

"Yes, yes!" he said. "You'll be lonely a wee and loneliness doesn't go 'way like croup or a colic. But remember, lass, if you be needing a man's ear at any time, John MacLeod will be honored to give you his."

"Then you knew all about Jean Baptiste's trip, Mr. MacLeod."

"I did that," he replied, "and I'll be saying a Presbyterian prayer for him each day."

"You are a good man and you help me to believe that all will turn out well."

"Of course they'll turn out well unless we are so feckless as to surrender to Duncan Cameron and Alex Macdonell and their blackguards. But Robertson is not one to yield. He was a Nor' Wester himself long enough to learn a few wicked tricks. He'll shake his highland fist at them the way traders understand."

But Robertson's rule was not to last for long. The fourth of November—eighteen days after Jean Baptiste's leaving—the news spread along the river that canoes were approaching from the north bearing the new settlers and a new governor. At once the settlement vibrated with excitement. Protesting babies were cleaned up and men and women who had any choice donned their best clothes.

Suddenly, the settlement's population was more than doubled as eighty newcomers—men, women, and children—came ashore. Some were embraced by friends or relations; some were happy to be at Red River, and a few were ready to cry. But it was upon the new governor, Robert Semple, an Englishman born at Boston and an ex-army officer, that most eyes were fixed. He showed no emotion, but stepped from the canoe as though he had done it a thousand times. Colin Robertson, with the hesitation of a man trying to make an assessment, strode forward and seized Semple's hand. "I'm Robertson," he said. "I've been holding this colony together until you arrived. Now you're in charge."

"I'm grateful, Mr. Robertson. But don't be rushing to resign your responsibility. I'll need your advice and help. First, tell me how we're going to take care of these people I have with me. It's already becoming too cold for them to live in tents."

Robertson was pleased to think he was still wanted. Straightening himself, he told the governor that the settlers with cabins would take some of the newcomers for awhile, and the fort would have to take the rest until more permanent arrangements were made. Sharing Marie Anne's quarters at the fort that night would be a tired Irish mother and two children; the place would be crowded but gratitude would make the sacrifice easy.

Semple was a fresh experience for Red River. In appearance, he was more like a poet than an army officer. He knew exactly nothing about the fur trade, and although he asked for Robertson's assistance, he was not one to take kindly to more than a little advice. It wasn't long until Robertson, with scorn in his voice, was referring to him as "that muddle-headed Englishman."

It was a mild winter and that was a blessing. Meat supplies were coming from Pembina fairly regularly, and the settlers were moderately comfortable. Building operations continued. For six days of the week everybody was busy and on the sabbath, William Sutherland, the Scottish elder noted for long prayers, tried to fill the role of minister.

With no winter attack from the west and no threats from Duncan Cameron, Semple was inclined to believe that the dangers had been exaggerated. He felt that now, with the settlement population strengthened, the Nor' Westers would rather retreat than fight.

Robertson didn't agree. "When spring comes, look out," he warned. "If you think Cameron's crowd is subdued, just demand the return of the colony guns the halfbreeds took to Qu'Appelle and see how they respond."

Semple did act on the proposal and his order was ignored. In doing nothing to enforce the demand, he lost prestige. Near spring, when Semple was making a tour of Hudson's Bay Company posts farther west, the more practical Robertson seized the opportunity to test the attitude at Gibraltar. He sent one of the settlers to Cameron to enquire if the North West Company men would still transport discouraged settlers to the East. Cameron fell into the trap, promising to assist any who would quit the settlement. Robertson, being a man of action, decided to strike while Semple was away. He ordered Cameron's arrest and seized Fort Gibraltar.[1] On Cameron's desk at that moment was a letter addressed to a North Wester colleague at Fond du Lac, proposing that Indians in that area be directed to fall upon the Red River settlement.

Robertson was now convinced. Red River could expect trouble. A letter from Alexander Macdonell to Cameron was intercepted, revealing that a storm was gathering at Qu'Appelle and it would, when it broke at Red River, make the attack of the previous year seem like a joke. It would end the threat of settlement in the fur country. This was the information awaiting Semple on his return. Still Semple was not noticeably aroused.

Robertson became increasingly anxious. The help expected from the East had not arrived. There was no word about Jean Baptiste and Semple was apathetic. "Perhaps he's dead," neighbors said when Lagimodière's name was mentioned. "Nobody should have expected him to be able to fight his way through all that winter snow anyway." Marie Anne became quiet and sad. John MacLeod's calls were as regular as ever, and the Saulteaux chief came occasionally. She tried to be cheerful until the day in May when a free-trader from Fort William reported a murder down that way—"a fellow called Lagimon."

The stout spirit of Marie Anne threatened to crack. "It's Jean Baptiste! They killed him!" she cried almost hysterically. Semple tried to comfort her, repeating the assurance that the Company would take care of her and the children. But his words were lost and so were Robertson's attempts to set her at ease. Only when John MacLeod called did she brush her hair back and show an interest in talking. "What shall I do, Mr. MacLeod?" she asked.

"Do?" he replied. "Do nothing unusual, lass. We'll bide a while before we confess your old man's not coming back. Providence is mysterious, ye ken, and I'm not for burying the deed until I'm sure they're deed. In the meantime, with the stuff you've got in you, you'll have concern for the fate of this poor damned community."

"Have you had any news about the Metis?" she asked, bracing herself to talk about other things.

"Not much. But Alex Macdonell is getting saucy again. He robbed the English Company's supplies and had his men lift bales of furs at Brandon House. It's highway robbery, o' course, and it's a bad situation. The letters Robertson came by in his own rough way leave no doubt in my mind about the enemy's intentions. We could put up a good fight for a man like Robertson."

"Yes, you could," she answered. "We all know what you did when you held the blacksmith shop." She was already becoming more relaxed.

MacLeod continued. "But that governor fellow goes around as if he didn't believe the Qu'Appelle crowd had guns. He's going to get a shock and the poor settlers will be fleeing again. I hate to think on it."

By seed time when hearts should have been full of hope, fear was mounting. Robertson could control his patience no longer. He took Cameron into custody again and told Semple he had no intention of sitting there to be shot down by the attackers from Qu'Appelle. He was getting out and he would take his prisoner, Cameron, with him. "But remember my advice. You'd better dismantle Fort Gibraltar while we hold it and float the logs to this place and concentrate on the defense of Fort Douglas."

Robertson's canoe departed for Lake Winnipeg, carrying him and his prisoner Cameron.[2] And strangely enough, Semple did take the hint and had his men raft many of the Fort Gibraltar logs to the point, to reinforce Fort Douglas. Six days after Robertson left, Indians from the west brought another warning. Cuthbert Grant had two hundred mounted men ready to ride to Red River to meet an incoming brigade from the east and ensure its safe passage into the Assiniboine. Chief Peguis, whose lodges were set up on the east side of the bigger river, opposite Fort Douglas, was at the fort early in the morning to talk with Semple and "Lagimo's squaw." With his customary loyalty toward the white settlers, he was prepared to place a force of his young warriors on the point to protect the settlement. Semple, however, did not think it would be necessary. "There'll be no fighting," he said. "I'll talk to Grant."

Turning to Marie Anne, Peguis said, "Before big fight, you and papooses come to my teepees. Safer there!"

When anything of importance happened on the plains, the native people were the first to know about it. Early on that day of disaster—June 19—the chief was back at the fort to take Marie Anne and the children to live with him and his squaw, who accompanied him to offer her smile of approval.

Marie Anne was inclined to remain at the fort, but the chief's mind was set and MacLeod advised her to go. Without further discussion, she gathered children, clothes, and blankets and followed her Indian friends to the river where the canoe was pulled out on sand. But the effects of worry and sleeplessness were taking their toll, and as she stepped into the canoe, she slipped or fainted and fell with a splash into the water. The older children screamed when they saw their mother almost disappear, but the gallant chief was quick to plunge into the stream and drag her to safety. On a grassy spot close to the water she sat motionless in her wet clothes until she was ready to try again.

She soon took her place on the bottom of the canoe with her five children in front of her. The silent chief paddled directly to his teepee on the east side where his lady fussed about to find dry clothes for the white woman. Marie Anne knew at once that she was among friends she could trust.

It may never be known if Cuthbert Grant really intended to attack the settlement on that day, the blackest day in the area's history. Midway through the afternoon the watchman in the Fort Douglas tower saw a troop of mounted men, thought to number thirty or forty, approaching from the west. They were the Metis, to be sure; they had their own way of riding and no other group in the country could present such an imposing sight. Almost at once the riders veered to the northeast as if to bypass the fort by half a mile. Whether the leader was intent upon making his way to the river to offer protection to the incoming brigade, or planned to turn later to strike at the settlement may never be confirmed. In any case, the alarm spread and settlers rushed for shelter in the fort.

While Marie Anne sat in safety in the chief's teepee, Governor Semple called for twenty men to follow him on foot. He would go out to engage Cuthbert Grant in conversation and hopefully settle everything. Twenty-seven men seized guns and followed, enquiring at the same time if they should take the three-pounder cannon. Semple's reply was, "No, we won't need the cannon. I'll talk to them."

From the opposite side of the river, Marie Anne and the Indians watched. They saw Semple and his little troop making their way northward until the two lines almost met. The horsemen were now seen to be more numerous than the governor reckoned and he decided to send back for the cannon. The scene was clearer now: Cuthbert Grant was leading sixty or seventy mounted men, some of them painted like warriors. One of Grant's men—Boucher by name—came to meet Semple. Angry words followed.

"What do you want?" Boucher enquired.

"What do you want?" the governor replied.

"We want our fort," Boucher answered, referring presumably to Fort Gibraltar.

"Then go to your fort," Semple replied.

"You!" shouted Boucher, "You destroyed our fort, you damned rascal."

Semple grabbed the muzzle of Boucher's gun, and at this critical moment a shot was fired. More gunfire followed and the battle was on. Marie Anne grew uneasy and tense. Peguis, on the other hand, spoke without emotion, as if the topic was buffalo hunting, saying, "Halfbreeds know how to fight. Semple make big mistake. He needs Indians to help him. Maybe all white men get killed." Marie Anne walked alone along the river to get a better view, praying for the safety of the defenders.

Bloody and disastrous as the battle proved to be, it was all over in a matter of minutes. Peguis was right; the halfbreeds were too strong for the settlers. Lieutenant Holte, who had been at Semple's side, was the first to fall. In another instant Semple received a bullet and the Red River men were more disorganized than ever.

The slaughter was terrible and in the heat of battle, the wounded Semple was shot again and killed. When the firing ceased twenty minutes after it started, twenty men on the settlers' side were dead, with one dead and one wounded on Grant's side.

One of the few survivors on Semple's side was John Pritchard whose name was to become well known at Red River. Cuthbert Grant released him when he promised to return to the fort and advise its surrender. There would be no more shooting, Grant said, if the surrender was without needless delay and the settlers would abandon the settlement. The day passed but other sad ones followed. The settlers were frenzied. A dozen or more women had been dashed into widowhood. Of course they would surrender and leave the fort, hopefully never to return. Again many were fleeing to the north; again silence settled over Red River, but this time there was less of the burning and destruction that had marked the previous departure. The reason was clear. At Marie Anne's suggestion, the Peguis camp, including warriors, was moved across the river, a dramatic reminder to the Metis that the Indians might resist further acts of mischief. Again, too, the stubborn John MacLeod refused to leave, and with Marie Anne and the chief, there was a conference each day. Still, she found little about which to be cheerful. Her husband was presumed dead although neither she nor John MacLeod accepted it. The settlers she had grown to know and like had been forced out for a second time, and the settlement might never rise again. Without yielding to fears, she wondered what the future held for her and her children.

After occupying Fort Douglas a short time, Cuthbert Grant and his men rode away and did not return. But soon after the fateful day of slaughter, the fort was the meeting place of North West Company men from Fort William and the West. The gathering took the form of a celebration marking the certain end of the Selkirk scheme.

As Marie Anne watched the great men of the Company coming and going through the gates of the fort, her anger grew. Wicked men she believed them to be, doubtless the moving spirits behind the killings of June 19. Perhaps she should tell them of her scorn. But why would they give her a hearing? She removed the idea from her mind. But a few days later when making her way along a local footpath, she came face to face with two of the visitors. Alexander Macdonell from Qu'Appelle recognized her and without introducing his friend MacGillivray, he greeted her.

"Oh, Madam Lagimodière! How nice to encounter you. I was thinking about you. Very sorry to hear about the death of your husband."

She hung her head without replying and Macdonell continued, "But you look more irresistible than ever. If you ever need a man's assistance, day or night, you can call on me. It's possible that you and I could do much for each other. Come to the fort for a talk."

He moved closer to her and gestured to take her hand but she drew away, looked him coldly in the eyes, and addressed him: "You! You're really sorry I lost my husband. You would like to assist me! Mr. Macdonell, I hope I never need assistance so much that I would have to invite you. Innocent and gallant you would like to appear! You'd like somebody else to take the blame for the attacks on these settlers. I suppose you'd say it was Cuthbert Grant's idea to come down here armed and leave a score of dead settlers and more widows and orphans. Oh yes, you're nice people!"

"Now, now!" he said. "Don't get excited. You're just upset."

"Perhaps I am upset, but I could say more. If Jean Baptiste is dead, you and your friends probably know much about it, and I'm glad I don't have to live with your conscience. Don't you or Cameron or MacGillivray ever come near me!"

Then, collecting a bit of composure, she added, "Don't be sure your troubles with Red River farmers are over. You can't destroy the spirits and ideas of good people as easily as you think. I hope I'm still around when this settlement is big and strong and you and your miserable partners are forced to behave yourselves and watch people growing potatoes and turnips and wheat, and keeping cows. Your fur trade will not last forever."

Peguis and his squaw were unfailingly kind, but Marie Anne knew that she and her children could not remain in the chief's tent all winter. With Fort Douglas occupied by North Westers, she could not consider it as a refuge either. She was ready to accept widowhood and think about the responsibilities it would impose. Colin Robertson's promise was to furnish support in the event that Jean Baptiste met with an accident, but with the fort now in enemy hands, his well-meaning assurance held only small comfort.

John MacLeod was trying to be helpful, but there was a limit to what he could do. Mutual admiration was obvious and she was not overlooking the possibility that he would ask her to marry him, but it was too soon to think seriously about such a thing. Moreover, as a good Presbyterian, he probably wouldn't care to adopt another church.

A short distance south of the Peguis encampment, opposite the mouth of the Assiniboine, was an unused cabin. It was built by a freeman, Bellehumeur, and almost immediately abandoned. Vacancy was like an invitation to move in. The former occupant left it clean and supplied with firewood, and on John MacLeod's advice, Marie Anne and the children moved into it and called it home. As long as Peguis and John MacLeod remained near, she would feel secure and not be hungry. A more troublesome question could not be ignored: What would she do if and when circumstances separated her from those loyal friends?

Perhaps the time had come for her to consider going back to Maskinonge, but somehow the thought of leaving this land that brought such a strange assortment of joys and sorrows was not yet convincing. She would remain at Red River for the winter at least and when the canoes were moving in the spring, she would address the question again.

Christmas, 1816, was close at hand. It would be the second Christmas without Jean Baptiste, another lonely one, and nobody in the family, except the youngest members, could look forward to it.

But John MacLeod was right. "Providence is mysterious," and three days before Christmas, as the winter sun was sinking close to the southwestern horizon, a familiar figure was seen trudging wearily over the encrusted snow toward Marie Anne's cabin. He glanced curiously in all directions, obviously not sure of his surroundings, then walked cautiously to the cabin door and knocked. Jean Baptiste was back, as though back from the dead. Marie Anne shrieked for joy and embraced her man. Tears and laughter mingled as never before and Christmas, 1816, was the best the family had experienced.

21

Jean Baptiste's adventure story

It took Jean Baptiste more than a year to complete the long and hazardous journey, and it took Marie Anne another year to get the full story from her modest and uncommunicative man. It made her hate the Alexander Macdonell gang more than ever.

When he set out for Montreal on that late October morning in 1815, he believed he would be back with his family before midsummer. But little did he realize the hardships and dangers—even designs on his life—that lay ahead.

At Pembina he met two old friends, Belland and Parisian, who volunteered to accompany him for part of the journey. Belland's horse and cart would make travel less onerous. But after a few days of the luxury of cart travel the men were at Red Lake and in enough snow to end the use of wheels. On Jean Baptiste's sober advice, the two friends returned to Pembina while he and an Indian known as Monkman continued eastward on foot, breaking trail all the way. Monkman, like Jean Baptiste, was a man of few words, and the two walked for hours without speaking. But it was reassuring to have a companion in this rugged new country.

Robertson's advice had been to follow a course well to the south, giving Fort William and its unfriendly Nor' Westers a wide berth. But as the men labored on in deeper snow, the Indian suggested changing routes, following the shorter north shore of Lake Superior even though it carried a larger risk of being seen by the scrappy Highland Scotsmen at Fort William. Jean Baptiste agreed.

On reaching Rainy Lake the two stopped at the cabin of John Tanner, "the white Indian," who had been at Red River a few times. He remembered Lagimodière and invited the two men to stop and enjoy his Indian wife's cooking for a few days.

Tanner filled the evening hours with the strange story of his life. His father was an English clergyman living on a farm in Illinois when the boy, at the age of nine, was kidnapped by Saulteaux Indians from the woods where he was gathering nuts. He was carried northward to Lake Huron and Sault Ste. Marie. A Saulteaux squaw of high rank in the tribe, having lost her only son, wanted the white boy as a replacement. She became devoted to him and the loyalty and admiration were mutual. Together, they travelled to Red River, hunted on the prairies, and returned to Rainy Lake where a poor marriage replaced a fine filial relationship. Red Sky of Morning turned out to be a domineering wife, but she was a good cook and John Tanner figured that most other women would have averaged no better.

The short stay at Rainy Lake was pleasant, but John Baptiste could not forget the serious purpose of his trip and knew he must be on his way. Tanner had advice about the route and Jean Baptiste thanked him and agreed to stop by on his way back.

The country was rougher, the snow deeper, and sleeping conditions no better, but they were making good progress. Their main worry was in finding food because the rabbit population was at a low point. They saw deer occasionally but an entire carcass was too much to carry and the animals did not appear when most needed. At one point they subsisted for six consecutive days on rock moss, boiled to make it a little less like itself and a little less like hay.

Approaching the Lakehead, they knew there would be food at Fort William. But to reveal his identity and his errand at the place he had been advised to avoid would have meant certain arrest for Jean Baptiste. So it was decided that Monkman would venture to the post and ask for meat while Jean Baptiste remained in hiding. As might have been expected, the reception at the fort was unfriendly, but the Indian had the sense to give up rather than jeopardize Jean Baptiste's purpose.

In the meantime, Jean Baptiste was encountering unexpected troubles of his own. A dog picked up his scent and barked loudly, bounding toward his hiding place. Fearing that the barking would arouse suspicion at the fort, Jean Baptiste shot the animal, then rushed out to recover it, knowing that dog meat rations would be highly preferable to famine.

One thing he overlooked, however, was the possibility that the dog's owner was nearby. As he brought the dead animal back to his hiding place, a big man hauling a toboggan came into view and walked straight toward him.

"Who the hell are you?" he roared. "You'd shoot my dog! You'll pay for this with your damned neck."

Jean Baptiste recognized crisis. It wasn't just his own safety that filled him with fear. If he lost the impending battle, the important letter would never reach the earl of Selkirk. He braced himself and gathered his hard fingers into fists.

The big fellow dropped the rope of the toboggan and raised his gun to swing a killing blow. But Jean Baptiste was quick to move and the gun struck the point of his left shoulder instead of his head. It left the arm feeling paralyzed, but with his right hand Jean Baptiste managed to land a jarring blow to the side of the attacker's face. The enraged man winced and backed up to swing again. And while his adversary was bending for what was intended to be the fatal blow, Jean Baptiste sprang at him with a battering-ram punch to the chin. The blow landed fairly and the man slumped in the snow. The fight was over.

Jean Baptiste was uncertain what to do next. He couldn't leave an unconscious man in the woods where he might freeze, but to drag him to the fort and risk being caught was equally unthinkable.

Monkman returned and stared with wide-eyed amazement at the spectacle of man and dog lying in death-like stillness in the snow. "What did you do?" he gasped.

Jean Baptiste said he would explain later. The best course of action, he reasoned, was to take the dog with them, load the man on his toboggan, and drag it out to where the Nor' Westers would find it. "Then we get away, fast."

Jean Baptiste was relieved to see that the vanquished man was breathing. By the time they had pulled the toboggan to a well-beaten path leading to the fort, his consciousness was returning and the travellers, with the dead dog slung across the Indian's shoulders, set out at a brisk pace to the east. Not until later in the day did they halt to reduce their load by dressing the dog. Jean Baptiste alone knew how close his mission had come to failure. Colin Robertson was right; they should have kept well away from Fort William.

To save time, the men crossed stretches of ice along the north shore of Lake Superior. Once before, that lake had tried to swallow Jean Baptiste and now it tried again. "Jump," he shouted when he saw the ice separating, almost at his feet. He jumped to safety but Monkman was not fast enough and fell into the icy water. Had Jean Baptiste not been present to pull him out, the Indian would have drowned.

At Sault Ste. Marie, Jean Baptiste and Monkman parted company and the former went on alone. It would be faster and it might be safer. He was now travelling along the top of Lake Huron and winter's cold was moderating. At Drummond Island, he met Captain Livingston, Lord Selkirk's friend, who accompanied him as far as York, later Toronto. Winter was retreating, but becoming fatigued, he was anxious to reach his destination and was glad to accept the offer of a sleighride part way to Kingston. For the last part of the journey, however, he was back on foot, just as the great trek began.[1]

In Montreal he went to Lord Selkirk's house and knocked at the door. "Does the earl of Selkirk live here?" he asked the servant who opened the door.

"Yes," the servant replied, with no invitation to enter.

"Then I'll see him," the caller said. "I have a message for him."

The servant, scanning the shabby specimen before him, replied firmly, "Oh no! You can't see the earl. I'll take the message to him, but you can't come in. Besides, the earl and Lady Selkirk have guests."

Jean Baptiste frowned in anger. "You tell the earl I come from Red River to see him. He'll have time to see me. Now don't waste time."

Ladies and gentlemen in Montreal's finest clothes were dining at the earl's table when the servant reluctantly reported, "A messenger, Sir! Says he's from Red River and must see you."

The earl excused himself from the brightly lit table and went at once to the door. When he heard that Jean Baptiste had come with a letter from Colin Robertson, the earl bade him come in, read the letter at once, and remained to ask questions. Then, taking Jean Baptiste's hand, he said, "You've done well Lagimodière. I'm grateful to you. I'll have more questions about the state of things out there and then I want you to rest in Montreal for as long as you choose. When you're ready to return, I'll have letters for Robertson and will ask you to carry them with all haste. Now you'll have dinner and sleep in my house tonight."

Jean Baptiste warned that he would not stop long in Montreal. He was anxious to be on his way back to Marie Anne and the children. Selkirk acted quickly. He appealed to the lieutenant governor of Lower Canada for soldiers for the protection of his colony, but the North West Company influence in Montreal proved so powerful that the request was denied. The best he could get was a commission making him a justice of the peace, and permission to take an armed escort westward for his own protection.

As soon as his plans were completed, Selkirk told Jean Baptiste that he might start back and he, Selkirk, would follow with a body of disbanded Swiss soldiers—the de Meurons—he hoped to hire. "I urge you to return by the same route," he said, "except that you must avoid Fort William. You may assure Colin Robertson that I'll be coming to his support very soon. Otherwise, Lagimodière, keep your mouth shut and your gun handy. Good luck."

The earl placed additional letters in Jean Baptiste's hand. Along with the all-important letter to Colin Robertson, there was one to Duncan Graham at York asking him to furnish this man with a good gun and garden seeds for Red River. There was also one for his friend Captain Livingston at Newmarket instructing him to furnish a canoe.

It was now spring and Jean Baptiste could be happy that his return journey would be with less discomfort from cold and less hardship arising from food shortages. Moreover, with open water and a small canoe, he would make better time. Selkirk hoped to keep the knowledge of Jean Baptiste's movements from the North West Company men, but their connections were so widespread and effective that secrecy was nigh impossible. The Scots directing Company affairs were soon aware of Jean Baptiste's return and word went out to intercept him at any cost. Even wintering partners in Minnesota were alerted to watch for him and tell the Indians of a reward for his capture—twenty pounds in currency, two kegs of rum, and two carrots of tobacco. "When captured," the instructions advised, "see that he is brought a prisoner to Fort William."

With an invisible net set out for his capture and fine rewards to his captors, the man had only the slightest chance of escaping. He was taken at Fond du Lac, beaten when he resisted, and taken to Fort William to be deposited in the "butter vat prison." He was relieved of the letters he carried for Robertson and informed that Red River was again in the hands of the North West Company. His wife, he was told, was among those killed by the halfbreeds.

Fort William was in all respects a terrible experience for the prisoner. While Company officers attending the annual summer meetings celebrated nightly, he was cooped up like an animal; with disgusting frequency, officers and servants came to gaze between the bars of his cell door, as though he was a strange monstrosity.

One of those who came looked vaguely familiar. The man glanced aimlessly at first and then suddenly his expression turned to wrath. Simultaneously, the two men recognized each other as the memory of the short but vicious fight they'd had in the snow a few months before flashed through their minds.

"It's you, you devil! Now they've got ya where ya belong and 'tis me who'll have the pleasure of killing ya. Ya'll never get out a this and ya'll never shoot another dog. If I had my gun I'd finish ya right there in yar cell. Damn ya!"

Jean Baptiste remembered the man's savage nature, and as he saw him turn and walk briskly away toward the governor's quarters, he could only expect some evil purpose. He was right. The Nor' Wester, Butcher by name, reported that the prisoner in the butter vat cell was the one who shot his dog and beat him up. He wanted the privilege of killing him. The fort's officer laughed and said, "If you want to fight that Lagimodière fellow, we'll bring him into the great hall after supper tonight and we'll all enjoy the show. It'll be a fight to the finish, I suppose."

"Can I club him?" Butcher asked, and the officer laughed again, then said that if it was in the nature of a public performance, there should be no clubs.

"But he might knock me out again," Butcher replied.

"Take him on. You're half as big again as he is, and you must be in better condition than a man who's been eating prison fare in a cell for the last month. You can beat him."

A hundred or more officers, voyageurs, and trappers assembled for the first entertainment of the season. Butcher, surrounded by his colleagues in the North West Company, was the favorite to win. He jerked off his leather jacket, displaying broad shoulders and hairy chest and deposited the garment carefully on the floor close to where he would be fighting. When the guards brought in Jean Baptiste and removed his jacket, he looked at the crowd and knew he didn't have a friend in the hall.

"Go to it," said the referee. "The last man standing will be the winner." The spectators cheered and Butcher, mumbling curses, struck his opponent in the chest. Jean Baptiste, still unsure of what this was all about, struck back instinctively, jarring the Nor' Wester from head to foot. He was not at his best but struck again and again and brought blood to the bigger man's nose. Infuriated, Butcher punched wildly, landing a blow to the side of Jean Baptiste's head. He fell to the floor striking the other side of his head against a hard object hidden with care under Butcher's jacket. It was a small club concealed in the shirt and Jean Baptiste was momentarily stunned. Rushing forward, Butcher displayed his true character, kicking his victim about the head and face so that there was no chance of him rising again very soon. The fight was over and victory without honors went to the North West Company man. Jean Baptiste was carried back to his cell and left crumpled on the floor to recover.

It was dark when consciousness returned. His mouth was dry and he craved water. His face was bruised and swollen and one eye seemed to be permanently closed. The pain and illness were intense, but he lay quietly until morning when water and corn meal mush were shoved into his cell. The water he seized and gulped instantly. The food held no interest and he lay back on his blanket, wondering if he would ever see his wife and children again, and hoping the day might come when he would have the satisfaction of meeting Butcher on even terms.

For days Jean Baptiste was sore and sick and disfigured, but time brought recovery and by August he was beginning to feel much stronger. He longed to be on his way to Red River. The days remained long and dull, however, until a new excitement gripped the occupants of the fort.² Lord Selkirk and a body of armed men had arrived and were camping a short distance upstream from the fort. The North Westers were uneasy and Jean Baptiste was filled with curiosity and hope.

Selkirk's party had travelled by way of Lake Ontario, intending to avoid Fort William. But at Sault Ste. Marie the earl was intercepted by Miles Macdonell who came to deliver the sad news about the Battle of Seven Oaks and the second dispersal of the colony. The earl was enraged and resolved to go at once to Fort William to challenge the culprits.

Knowing that the earl and his men were within gunshot range, Jean Baptiste longed to join them and shoulder a gun. Next morning, William McGillivray, the Company's head man, answered Selkirk's warrant for his arrest. Before evening, all the other Company officers were served with similar warrants and Selkirk's soldiers had taken the big fort without firing a shot. Minutes after the seizure, the door of the butter vat prison cell was thrown open and Jean Baptiste walked out.

After hearing the details of his ordeal, the earl expressed regret for the suffering he'd had to endure, and told Jean Baptiste that he might wait to travel with the soldiers to Red River or go on in advance. He chose to start immediately, but there was something he wanted to attend to before leaving. Later that day he walked alone and unarmed to Butcher's cabin, but it was empty. He had been last seen a few hours earlier walking rapidly into the woods, carrying blankets as though he wouldn't be back for some time.

Jean Baptiste was not prepared to wait long for Butcher's return. He remained only until plans were made for the soldiers to start their march to Red River. Then, with a smile of anticipation and a joyful wave of farewell, he started away.

Now, after weeks of walking, he was back with his family. He had suffered both pain and indignity, but his health and vigor had returned. Except for his long hair and whiskers, his nose red from repeated freezing, and his tattered clothes and moccasins, he was the same Jean Baptiste who had marched away so fearlessly fourteen months earlier.

Marie Anne listened eagerly to the story, especially the information about the soldiers. As though the walls had ears, he whispered to his happy wife that the earl's soldiers were on their way and might be at Red River in days. Fort Douglas would then be retaken from the Nor' Westers and the settlers could feel safe in building again.

"Thank God," she said through her tears.

22

Over the walls

The secret concerning Lord Selkirk's small private army was well guarded. The only outsider allowed within the veil of secrecy was the reliable John MacLeod. Marie Anne, unable to forget the slaughter of the previous June, asked if the plan to recover Fort Douglas could be carried through without bloodshed. Jean Baptiste didn't know but assured her that the pedlars and their hired helpers from Qu'Appelle would not win this time. "Selkirk's men will knock hell out of them if they resist."

Jean Baptiste had confidence in the de Meurons. They had seen combat on the side of the British in the recent war with the United States. He had mingled with them at Fort William, wrestled with them, drank with them, and saw them as lazy fellows who would fight like demons when aroused. Captain Proteus D'Orsonnens and twenty-five of these mercenaries were travelling by way of Rainy Lake, where Miles Macdonell would overtake them and use his knowledge of the country to help them.

The Selkirk men seized the North West Company post at Rainy Lake and took possession of two oxen, two cows, a heifer, and a bull. Recalling Jean Baptiste's advice to obtain the services of John Tanner to show them the shortest route, the leaders found him eager for an excuse to get away from his nagging wife for awhile, and ready to join the snowshoe march across Minnesota. On the last day of the year—1816—the twenty-five former soldiers and a few civilians, with five cattle—one ox having been slaughtered for meat when it fell on ice and broke a leg—reached Red River near Pembina.

After a brief pause for a celebration at Pembina, they marched on happy in the realization that this was the last leg of the arduous trek. "Three more days," Miles Macdonell said, "will bring you to Fort Douglas. Then it's up to you."

The men and cattle—all growing tired of deep snow and January cold—pressed forward to within an hour's tramp from the fort, and then stopped to prepare for the assault against the stockade. The soldiers were impatient to strike, knowing that with success they would gain the comparatively comfortable quarters on the inside. But the captain wanted to know more about the defenders and their strength.

"We should find Lagimodière if possible," he said to John Tanner. "He'll be at home by now, unless he ran into trouble after leaving Fort William. Do you think you can find him and tell him to come here? You know your way around this part."

Looking more like a bedraggled trapper than a scout, he set out in a rising storm. But good fortune was with him; he met an Indian of his adopted tribe who gave him exact directions to the Lagimodière cabin on the far bank of the river.

It was midday when Tanner knocked at Jean Baptiste's cabin. After the two friends embraced, Jean Baptiste asked in a low voice, "Where are the soldiers? But come in and get warm and have some potatoes and turnips."

"What d' you mean? Turnips?" the visitor asked.

"I'll let Marie Anne tell you about them. She knows all about turnips."

Tanner entered, spoke to Marie Anne, and shrank back when he saw a stranger. She understood and said, "This is Mr. MacLeod. He's been a great help to us, and if I know your purpose, he'll be a big help to you too." She knew that Tanner was accompanying the armed men and added, "If you want to talk about attacking the fort, go ahead. Everybody here is on your side. As for Mr. MacLeod, he's been fighting the enemies of the colony for two years."

Relaxing with a plate of meat and boiled turnips, Tanner was ready to talk. He told about the long and chilly march from Rainy Lake, and then wanted information for the captain. "How many men holding Fort Douglas? Who's in charge? How high is the fence? Which side is best for attack?"

Being back only a few days, Jean Baptiste didn't know all the answers, but Marie Anne and MacLeod thought there might be forty men inside the walls. "And McLellan is the man in charge," Marie Anne reported, "Archibald McLellan. I'm sorry it's not that Alexander Macdonell wretch because he deserves a thrashing."

After further discussion, the men decided against leaving until after sundown. Better to guard against suspicion. In the meantime, they would smoke some of Tanner's kinnikinic, and John MacLeod would go to his cabin and get his warmest clothes and a gun.

It was still snowing when Marie Anne watched the three men cross the river ice and disappear into the gathering darkness. The wind was becoming more violent, and the walking, which would have been bad in daylight, was almost impossible at night as they couldn't see any trace of a trail. After almost two hours Tanner recognized the point of land where the de Meuron tents had been set up. Approaching more closely, they heard a sentry demand, "Who goes there?" John Tanner answered and at once the three were ushered into the captain's tent to discuss plans for the attack. Miles Macdonell joined them.

"That's good," the captain concluded after receiving the information he needed. "Tomorrow we'll make some ladders for the fence and attack. How about it, Lagimodière—and MacLeod—are you going with us?"

"Going with you?" MacLeod asked. "O' course we are. Why did ye ken we brought our guns? But take my advice, Mr. Captain. Make your ladders this vera night and gae over the walls early in the morning while the storm still rages. That would surprise the devils and ye might as well be sure o' yourselves."

The captain thought a moment, and running his fingers through his whiskers, asked, "Lagimodière, what do you think of that idea."

When both Jean Baptiste and Miles Macdonell agreed that it was a good plan, the captain called his soldiers and announced the final march starting at two hours before sunrise. Before retiring for a few hours' sleep in their draughty tents, the men made ladders by cutting some light poles and lashing steps to them—one ladder for every three soldiers.

It was not a pleasant task in the wind and stinging snow, but the job was eased by the thought that their operations could bring them closer to the warmth and comfort of the fort. And as in other posts occupied by North West Company men, there would be a good stock of rum. The men worked vigorously and then rolled into blankets to sleep for a few hours before facing the test for which they had paddled, walked, and snowshoed for nearly two thousand miles. John MacLeod and Jean Baptiste worked with John Tanner to make their ladder, and then settled down for a short sleep, but excitement denied them the slumber they wanted.

The storm raged on and in the morning the men were obliged to dig themselves out through fresh drifts. But that was what John MacLeod had hoped for, and he and Jean Baptiste led the way along the river at that early hour on January 10, 1817. When the outline of the fort became dimly visible, the captain called a halt for a final briefing: "Remember—advance elbow-to-elbow and place your ladders quietly against the walls. Climb to the top and drop in the snow on the inside. Remain quiet and inconspicuous until a door is opened from the inside. Then rush inside with your guns ready and cocked."

The plan was working perfectly. It was still dark. The stockade fence was hurdled without mishap and there was nobody on guard. A gentle knock at the door of each house brought a sleepy and unsuspecting occupant to open it, and from out of the darkness the armed men sprang to take possession. Archibald McLellan surrendered without a struggle and his men, knowing when they were beaten, did the same. Without a shot being fired, all the North Westers and their servants were placed under arrest. The attackers were jubilant. The de Meurons found the stores of food and rum; Tanner prepared to stay awhile before returning to his ill-tempered wife; John MacLeod shook his highland fist at each of the prisoners in turn; and Jean Baptiste announced that he was going to report to Marie Anne who had remained reluctantly at home. He would be back in an hour.

"Everything all right?" she asked anxiously when her husband entered with the first rays of the morning sun.

"All right," he replied. "Took the fort without even a bloody nose."

"How fortunate! I wonder if the settlers will have the heart to come back. I hope they do; it'll be better this time." She was clearly lost in thought for an instant and then said, "When you return to the fort, Ba'tiste, I'll go with you. Reine knows how to take care of the little ones, and I won't be long."

"What do you want to go there for?" he demanded.

"I have a few things to tell those North Westers, some things I couldn't say when they ruled Red River, and I have a few questions for them. I'll be ready as soon as you want to go back."

He knew it was pointless to argue. "All right," he said, "I'm ready."

The storm had abated only slightly as Jean Baptiste led the way to the fort. His wife followed him, taking the longest strides she could in order to walk in his footsteps. Addressing Captain D'Orsonnens, she said, "I'm Marie Anne Lagimodière, Jean Baptiste's wife. I'd like to talk with one or two of your prisoners."

"If you're Lagimodière's wife, I guess any request you make will be granted. Which one do you want to see first?"

"Archibald McLellan," she replied, "the man who was in charge here until today. I'd have enjoyed seeing Alexander Macdonell but he won't be here. He's too sharp to get caught. He's probably in flight back to Qu'Appelle now anyway."

"Oh," said the captain, "there's somebody talking to McLellan now—your neighbor MacLeod. Will you wait until he's through?"

"No," she answered. "I'll see him now. Mr. McLellan can listen to both of us."

As Marie Anne was escorted to where McLellan was under guard, she heard the familiar voice of John MacLeod bellowing, "I didna' come just to humiliate you further, McLellan, but there's a point or two aboot which you seem most damnably ignorant, you Nor' Westers. There's innocent blood on the hands o' every one o' you—Cameron, Macdonell, the lot o' you. May God forgive you, but that's a matter 'twixt him and yoursel's. What I want to know is this: Suppose you and your bloody tyrants get out o' this place alive; are you going to continue to persecute innocent folk? Yes, innocent folk, McLellan."

"Mr. MacLeod, you were here first," Marie Anne interjected, "but you won't mind if I enter into this discussion, I hope, because I was thinking of the same question. I don't know you, Mr. McLellan, but I've met up with Alex Macdonell—when I didn't want to see him—and some of the others. Now that you've had time to think it over, how can you justify your determination to prevent peaceful people from coming to farm along this river, if it's their choice? Does anybody suppose the North West Company has any exclusive claim to this country? You see, we think you have something to answer for, and you should be given a chance to tell us what you mean to do. I'm not speaking for anyone except myself but . . ."

"You're speaking for me too," John MacLeod blurted. "I'm tired o' these pedlar bodies who think they can make their own laws and stop decent folk from building homes and living in peace. Bullies—that's what your men are—bloody bullies."

"Before you answer, Mr. McLellan," Marie Anne said, "I should tell you that my Jean Baptiste and I are not settlers, but we'll fight against those injustices we've seen. I really came here to say that I think the settlers will return, and Mr. MacLeod and I want to know if there's enough honor left in your people to leave them alone."

McLellan responded in a subdued tone, his blue eyes under heavy eyebrows fixed in fascination upon the woman who had come to interrogate him. "I'm not about to argue except to point out that we traders were here first and to some of us—if prisoners be permitted to have opinions—farming will never amount to anything in this country. We honestly thought that we were doing the settlers a kindness by forcing them to quit before they wasted more of their time, yes, and their own lives. But things have taken a serious turn, I will allow; and while you wouldn't expect me to speak for all the rulers of our Company, I would be willing, personally, to leave the settlers alone if they are determined to prolong their suffering by trying to farm on this barren and godless ground. But tell me, if they're so determined to live here, why don't they trap and hunt like other people?"

"Very well, Mr. McLellan," Marie Anne replied. "That's your view. Some of us think differently. But regardless of personal opinions, if good people choose to try farming, why should fur traders be allowed to plague their lives by threats and cruelty? Don't tell me that the attackers who sent twenty of Red River's men to their graves weren't working for your Company. You and your friends have to be responsible for that killing, and I'm not sure that Selkirk's men should ever allow you your freedom. But if you do get out of jail, would we have your promise that you would use your influence to ensure that the settlers are left alone?"

"Yes, madam. I'm not admitting it will be good for the settlers but, yes, I'll give you my word."

John MacLeod was nodding approvingly. "They're coming back, I assure you, McLellan. You may be interested to ken that I'm one body who never left, and if we have to fight to live here where we have rights, I promise ye we'll fight. But I'm satisfied with what you say."

"You're walking back to your cabin, lass?" MacLeod asked, turning to Marie Anne. "Then I'll walk with you."

Days later, Jean Baptiste and his family abandoned the cramped and draughty cabin and moved into Fort Douglas to spend the remaining part of the winter. Word was sent to the settlers who had taken refuge in the north, informing them of the changing outlook at Red River, and with the coming of spring, they began to return, not confident but hopeful.

Then came the twenty-first of June, a day the settlers would not forget. In addition to being the summer solstice, it was the day after Lord Selkirk's forty-sixth birthday and, most important of all, it was the day of the earl's arrival at Red River. The settlers crowded around him to hear him speak and touch his fading tartan kilt. He was tired and, like his clothes, appearing worn, but he was gentle and kind and the people loved him. Shortly after his arrival, he enquired about Jean Baptiste and asked to see the family. The Lagimodières had just returned from an expedition into the buffalo country but were eager to accept the earl's invitation.

"We're going to see a great man," Marie Anne told Reine, now ten years old and alert. "He's the man your papa went all the way to Montreal to see." Wondering how a great man would appear beside an ordinary man, the child submitted more peacefully than usual as her mother scrubbed her face to a glistening cleanliness.

"What do we call him?" Marie Anne asked, but Jean Baptiste wasn't very helpful.

"Oh, I don't know," he replied. "Guess you can call him Mr.

Selkirk or Mr. Lord Selkirk. When I met him at Montreal, I didn't call him anything. It doesn't matter. He won't care."

The seven Lagimodières were ushered into Lord Selkirk's quarters at the fort and His Lordship arose to greet them. "I owe you all my gratitude," he said, "to you, Jean Baptiste, for your splendid service in accomplishing that remarkable trip to Montreal, and to you, Madame Lagimodière and the children, for letting him go on the dangerous journey. I want to do something for you. I propose to grant you a piece of land on the other side of the river, Lagimodière. How would you like that? And as for you, madame, I don't know what I can do, but if you think of some way in which I can help you, please let me know. Tomorrow, Lagimodière, if you agree, I will assign the land to you publicly."

Marie Anne gazed at the earl admiringly and thanked him. He looked the part of an aristocrat. His determination had been amply demonstrated, but his delicate skin and thin face seemed no match for the rigors of Red River. His health may have been failing at that time, but during the three months he spent in the settlement, public admiration and affection for him mounted. Acting with generosity and gentleness, he studied the needs of the people, confirmed land titles, and cancelled debts. He admitted the need for roads, bridges, and cattle, and he made a treaty with the Cree and Saulteaux Indians, whereby they yielded the land on both sides of the Red and Assiniboine Rivers, "as far back as a man can see under the belly of a horse"; in other words, about two miles.

With officers, soldiers, and settlers gathered together, the earl identified and set aside sites for a church and school and announced the grant of land to Jean Baptiste Lagimodière. It was a block bounded on one side by the Red River and on the other by the River La Seine, upon which an important section of the City of St. Boniface would someday be built.[1]

The earl had public praise for the courage and resourcefulness of both Jean Baptiste and his wife. Then, speaking of Marie Anne, he added, "She has a request which I invited her to make and which I shall be obliged to meet." The exact nature of her request was not disclosed at the time, but it was to be fulfilled in the next year.

23

Wintering
in a cellar
without windows

One with the instincts of a nomad would care little about a grant of land, but to Marie Anne it gave the prospect of a home with more permanency than she had known in the ten years of her life in the West. "You'll make us a house on it, Ba'tiste?" she asked, "a big house with two rooms and a cellar for turnips and potatoes!"

He wasn't ready for the question and side-stepped it with another. "Selkirk said you asked him for something. Sounded like a secret. What do you want from him?"

"Oh, Ba'tiste," she answered, "don't let it worry you. I won't tell you now because I might not get my wish. I'll tell you when you build our house. We have five children and we should have a house here on our Red River land where we can live without always moving. That little house we had on the other river is too small now and, besides, it has no place for turnips."

"Why do you want to live in one place all the time? Don't you like moving?"

"No," she snapped back, "not any more. Things are going to be different along this river, you know, and it'll be better if the children and I are settled—at least until we travel back to Maskinonge."

"Haven't you forgotten about that?"

"How could I forget? I'm not asking you to go back to live in the East. I might not like it either, but I'd like to see my mother and the dear old church. Wouldn't you?"

Jean Baptiste's silence indicated indifference and she gazed at him, wishing he was more sensitive to the things she cherished. But it was all right; in Rupert's Land, resourcefulness was more important than sentiment, and if Jean Baptiste had not been a practical fellow, she and her family would not have survived.

"By the way," she said at length, "Selkirk goes back today. He said he'll visit my mother if he's near Maskinonge. What a good man! I hope he doesn't have a lot of trouble in the courts back in Montreal. He looks worried and so pale."

Everybody living along the river came to the fort to bid farewell to the earl as he was about to start on his long journey. During his weeks at Red River he had captured the hearts of all the settlers, and now their moist eyes showed their sorrow. One by one, men and women shook the hand of the great and kindly earl whose sympathy for the unfortunate settlers was beyond question. He held shares in the Hudson's Bay Company but he cared nothing for the fur trade; his greater interest was in needy people. He looked frail and women gathering in clusters agreed that he was in poor physical condition for the two-thousand-mile journey ahead of him, not to mention the iniquitous charges and trials he would face. Even as he said farewell, he was under a court order and only free on bail. The formality of arrest had been made by Commissioner Coltman who came in June with warrants arising from Selkirk's seizure of Fort William. Perhaps the earl did exceed his authority at Fort William, but the sins of violence committed by the Nor' Westers made his misdeeds seem like boyish pranks.

Jean Baptiste, Marie Anne, and the children were there to say good-bye. She placed a parcel of bread and some wild honey in his hands for the trip. The earl thanked her warmly, commenting that he intended to travel by way of Kentucky in the hope of locating John Tanner's original family. Already he had sent the Falcon—as Tanner was widely known—back to Rainy Lake with a generous gift of money in recognition for his help in conducting the de Meurons to Red River. He admitted a special interest in this white-boy-turned-Indian.

"I hope you find his people," Marie Anne said to the earl. "Poor Falcon. I wonder what he'd be like if he'd been raised with white people. I guess we wouldn't like him any better than we already do."

"You probably wouldn't like him as well," the earl commented. "Unfortunately, I haven't much information to help me in searching for his family. He thinks the family name is Taylor but doesn't know much else. I'll see what can be done."

Marie Anne said Falcon had a recollection that his father was a tall man with some fingers missing from one hand. "Ah," said the earl, "that could help me. If I do obtain information for your friend, could I send it to Red River and ask you to have it delivered, Jean Baptiste?"

As Jean Baptiste nodded his agreement, Lord Selkirk waved his final greeting and stepped into a canoe at the river's edge. With his departure on the ninth of September, 1817, he would never see his colony again, and the unhappy settlers seemed to sense it.

Marie Anne's thoughts were still with the Falcon. Turning to her husband she said, "If the earl finds his family, do you think Falcon would quit the Indian life and go back?"

"Don't know why he would, unless to get away from that witch he married."

"I suppose we're all annoying at times," she said condescendingly. "But say, Ba'tiste, what about our house?"

"What house?" he mumbled. "Oh, yes. I figured we'd build a house, but are you sure you want a cellar? If you've got to have it, it'll take a lot longer."

He didn't mind cutting and fitting logs, but the thought of digging a cellar made him frown. A shovel was as foreign to a hunter as a powdered wig to a Sioux chief. But John MacLeod said he would help with the digging. Marie Anne had already selected a spot opposite Point Douglas and just north of where the Seine River fell into the Red. Marks on the ground showed the size she wanted and, reluctantly, Jean Baptiste began to dig. Every spadeful of that gumbo soil was like an insult to this man whose specialties were guns and axes. He wondered why Marie Anne wouldn't forget about potatoes and turnips and let him build a house without a cellar. He was sick of cellars even before he started to dig, but his eyes brightened when he remembered a promise to take Paquin's gun back to Pembina. Leaving his family in the tent beside the site of the new house, he was glad to be on his way. He left behind a cellar hole no bigger than a dog's grave.

Marie Anne was beginning to think that her request for a cellar had been an error. Nights were becoming cold and as the house must wait for the cellar, it looked as if the family might have to spend winter in the tent, or move back to the isolated one-room cabin on the Assiniboine. John MacLeod came along at mealtime, as he often did, and agreed that the house should have a cellar, but he looked worried as he gazed upon the small mound of earth and clay which told of nothing more clearly than Jean Baptiste's dislike for digging.

"I'll come wi' my spade on the morrow," MacLeod said before leaving. "I suppose if we could dig the whole o' it before your old man comes back, he'd be more likely to get on wi' the logs."

"I'd be embarrassed to see you doing it," she said, "but it's good of you to consider it."

MacLeod was momentarily lost in thought, wondering if his offer had been a mistake. What would Jean Baptiste think about it? He liked Marie Anne and her comfort and peace of mind were his concern. He had never tried to hide his admiration for her but he would never allow himself to even think about affection. At once, he relaxed. "Have you plenty o' meat and tatties if I should bring a friend or two with me?" he asked. Assured that food stocks were favorable, he waved and disappeared.

MacLeod made calls at the fort and the cabins on Point Douglas that evening. Before retiring for the night, he knew there were exactly eighteen shovels in the community—nineteen including the one at the Lagimodière tent. Early next morning nineteen men—half a dozen de Meurons among them— crossed the river and were led by the big-hearted MacLeod to the scene of their digging assignment beside the mouth of the Seine.

"There ye are lads," he commanded. "Do all your digging inside the wee stakes. We'll stop tae eat at midday and when we finish that hole, six feet deep, mind you, you can quit. And don't be forgetting that both Lagimodière and his wife did a big lot for Red River. Ah yes, and we'll throw the dirt weel back so there'll be no ugly pile." John MacLeod took the nineteenth shovel and the clay began to move. With the children around her, Marie Anne watched, and as tears of gratitude filled her eyes, she whispered, "May God reward you, John MacLeod."

By noon when hot potatoes and Red River fish were served, the job was more than half finished. It was heavy work and the gumbo was typically sticky and difficult. But late in the afternoon, the men climbed out of the biggest and best cellar along the river and began to spread the clay to make the site less ugly. At sundown, the scheme's instigator, like a highland chieftain after routing the MacDonalds in a Scottish glen, was striding triumphantly to the river, leading his tired but satisfied helpers toward their canoes while Marie Anne stood beside the big hole, gazing in silent wonder.

Jean Baptiste returned from Pembina and couldn't believe what he saw. When he learned how it happened, he was more puzzled than ever—not sure whether he should be pleased or embarrassed. But there it was, as symmetrical as the stockade fence around Fort Douglas, and the floor as level and smooth as the rawhide face of an Indian wardrum.

Now there was no excuse for not getting on with the logwork. The next morning he was leaving the home tent with an ax. He borrowed the ox that had been brought from Rainy Lake to drag the logs, one at a time, to the building site. It was a bigger job than he anticipated. Two rooms called for more logs and the cellar needed a log floor over it.

John MacLeod came again to help hew the logs for the floor and set them in place over the cellar. It was no small job and took as long as it would normally take to build an entire cabin with the time-honored dirt floor. Time was increasingly important; the nights were becoming cold and winter weather could descend upon the community with shocking suddenness. A day or two after the floor was finished, a north wind brought snow. Temperatures inside the tent were only slightly less frosty than outside, and the children shivered.

"What's to be done with us, Ba'tiste?" Marie Anne asked impatiently. "It's winter and this tent isn't good enough. Why, we'd be warmer living in the cellar than here."

Jean Baptiste seized upon the suggestion eagerly. "All right. Your idea. I'll fix up a fireplace with stones and your potatoes and turnips will have to stay in the tent." The move was made at once and the family took up residence underground. The entrance was a gap at one end of the logs, over which a buffalo skin could be drawn to keep in the heat. Certainly the clay walls would be draught-proof, no matter how hard the wind blew; and with snow on the logs overhead, the place might be satisfactory enough except for the dismal darkness which could be broken only by candle or the open fire. At least it would be better than the tent, and Jean Baptiste promised that with fair weather he would still get along with the log structure up above.

While the storm was still in progress, the Lagimodières had a visitor. "Falcon, it's you," Marie Anne exclaimed as John Tanner stumbled in, exhausted from facing the wind and snow. "How did you ever find us in this underground house?"

Jean Baptiste was glad to see his friend but puzzled. "What the hell brings you back so soon?" he asked. "Didn't think we'd see you till spring."

"Couldn't stand it at home," Falcon replied. "That woman! She'll kill me yet or make me crazy. Somebody shot me in the woods; I think she knows much about it. If she wants me more this winter, she'll have to come and get me. I'll stay here in this hole with you—if you let me. I'll help you build this house. When we need meat we'll hunt together."

That suited Jean Baptiste who knew Falcon as a handy fellow and one of the best with a gun. While Marie Anne wondered how another sleeper could be accommodated on the clay floor, she saw the advantage of having him to help with the logs. It was settled and an expression of relief came over the Falcon's face.

Marie Anne related Selkirk's hopes of locating John Tanner's family. "And if he finds them, he'll send a message to Jean Baptiste for delivery to you. If he does find your people, Falcon, would you return to them?"

"Don't know," was the reply. He'd thought about it many times, he admitted. "I'd like to see my father if he lives, but it might be a mistake to leave my Indians. They are good people. I will not find better ones to live with. If I was raised like a white man I would think differently, but I am satisfied to be an Indian. The only reason I might go back would be that damned woman. I had a good wife when Red Sky lived and then I married the wrong one. I don't want to leave my children; but don't worry. Selkirk will not find my people. Likely they moved many times since the Indians grabbed me from the woods."

During the days that followed, more logs were dragged to the building site and then, one by one, they were cut and fitted into the new walls. The work might have progressed more rapidly but there were interruptions. The building was halted when the men went for game, and there was a plea from Pembina where supplies were running low and experienced hunters were needed to avert a crisis. Jean Baptiste and Falcon dropped their axes and tramped south to help replenish the stores of meat. All Marie Anne's hopes of moving out of the dingy cellar and into the new log house during the winter were shattered, and she made up her mind to accept the hole in the ground until spring. She took comfort in the thought that it was at least an improvement over a tent in the winter, and with the two best hunters in the country living there most of the time, food supplies would not fail. She had much to be thankful for.

The men were back from Pembina only a short time when John MacLeod called to say there was a message at the fort for Jean Baptiste. It was from the earl of Selkirk, asking that the enclosed letter be conveyed to John Tanner. Delivery would be much easier than the earl might have anticipated and Jean Baptiste chuckled.

Falcon could read a little but—afraid of the nature of its contents—he didn't want to read this letter, and suggested burning it. But after carrying it for a day he handed it to Marie Anne, saying, "You read it if you like."

Written at Lexington, Kentucky, and dated November 17, 1817, the letter reported what the earl believed to be success. Proof would be difficult to establish, but Selkirk found a Taylor family whose young brother had been stolen by Indians many years ago, and whose father was tall, with two fingers missing on his right hand.

Marie Anne expected Falcon to be pleased, but he stared anxiously into space, clearly fearful of a decision he would have to make. The letter went on to assure Falcon that his return to Kentucky would fill his people with joy, and the earl would be glad to assist financially if that were important.

Excitedly, Marie Anne asked, "Do you think you'll go? Your family would be so happy."

"What good would it do?" Falcon asked. "They are white people you know and I am Indian. My brothers and sisters would be strangers to me. I would be a stranger to them. We would not understand each other. No, I won't go back, not now anyway."

Perhaps Falcon is right, she was reasoning. The sentiment that comes with years of close association would be missing. She caught herself wondering if Maskinonge would be a disappointment to her after the years of adventure in the West. She felt worried.

"I'll tell you something," Falcon offered, "I would like to take my children somewhere to go to school—maybe Kentucky—but I suppose the wife I have wouldn't let them go. We'll see. Think I will go back to Rainy Lake soon and see how things are. If her brother shoots me, I will have no more worries and if he doesn't, I'll have plenty of time to decide what I do."

Before Falcon was ready to go home, Chief Peguis and his medicine man Fox Tail stopped on their way back from a hunt, well supplied with meat. In a happy mood they invited Marie Anne to cook the best parts, and when they had eaten sumptuously, Peguis slouched on his blanket and went to sleep. Fox Tail, at the same time, became talkative and mystical. Gazing through half-closed eyes into the wood smoke as it curled upward, the old man believed he saw bad times ahead for prairie Indians. "The buffalo and beavers will be gone and the Indians will have to eat grass or seeds or starve. It is all because of the white man's folly and greed. He would rather be rich than happy; he would hunt for money instead of hunting for food; he's always in a hurry. He'll be in the same hurry to take this land from the Indians. White man a fool but he won't listen to the Indian."

The medicine man's words caught Falcon's full attention and he glanced at Marie Anne to see if he could read her thoughts. She knew what he was thinking but did not want to break Fox Tail's train of thought by speaking. She wasn't convinced that medicine men had prophetic powers, but she couldn't forget the old Indian on the banks of the Maskinonge River who foretold more dangers in her life than anybody would have had reason to suspect at the time.

Fox Tail mumbled on and turned his mysterious little eyes in the direction of Marie Anne. Pausing as if for inspiration, he said very slowly that as long as Red River flows to the north, Marie Anne Lagimodière's children—many of them—would live beside it. Again he paused, and staring into her eyes said in an Indian monotone, "You are a good woman. You should be Indian. For your children and yourself you want something. All right, six moons from now."

Jean Baptiste spoke up, "Six moons from now! Is it what Selkirk said he would get for you?"

"Maybe, Jean Baptiste; maybe," she answered teasingly. "We'll wait and see. I said I'd tell what the earl promised when the house was finished. It's not finished yet."

24

Rababoo,
roast beaver,
and Red River jig

Three moons after Fox Tail's incantations, when winter's cold had melted to nothing more than memories, Jean Baptiste surveyed the log structure and said, "Thank God, it's finished." He was as proud as a young fellow bringing down his first buffalo. At once the family moved from the cellar into the house, the best outside the fort. There was a fireplace at one end where the log walls extended beyond the edge of the cellar to allow the stones to rest on undisturbed sod. And there were bunks built against the walls so that nobody would be obliged to sleep on the floor.

Marie Anne gazed in admiration, still surprised that her hunter-husband had found the patience to finish the job with such little protest. "What a relief! A person must live underground awhile to appreciate being on top," she said, swinging the door on its leather hinges to assure herself it would really open and shut. Life in the cellar had spared them from the windy blasts, but it was an abode more befitting squirrels and badgers. Now their home would command the admiration of all the folk living on the Point Douglas side, those who had watched the building progress from a distance.

As the sun was setting on the evening after their move above ground, Jean Baptiste's sharp eyes caught a glimpse of canoes in midstream. Any strange brigade in the river posed questions. Before calling her children to the safety of the house, Marie Anne shaded her eyes and peered searchingly at the paddlers taking a direct course toward the new house. The canoes were full of men, women, and children. When they touched shore, she suddenly recognized the familiar faces of their friends from Point Douglas. And in command of the party was the redoubtable John MacLeod, coming to initiate the new house with a neighborly visit.

There was care-free conversation and a demand for Jean Baptiste's fiddle, unused for months. Then, in the dim light made by a piece of cloth burning in a dish of grease, settlers and soldiers danced awkwardly on the crowded new floor. As the evening wore on, drowsy children were tucked away one by one to sleep in the new bunks while elders continued to indulge in waltzes and reels.

At the height of the merriment, a young man came inside to report hearing the scraping sound of a canoe being pulled ashore. John MacLeod stalked out to investigate and came face to face with the newcomer, just a few rods from the door. From his clothes came the odor of fresh horse sweat and even in the moonlight it was possible to recognize his serious expression. He had ridden in from the west, and learning that most of the residents were at the Lagimodière home, he seized a canoe and crossed at once. When asked what he wanted, the visitor, knowing he was hated in those parts, hesitated, and before he was able to answer, MacLeod recognized him and roared, "Cuthbert Grant, ye bastard! What reason d' you have for being here? It's not a safe place for a bloody murderer, I'm warning you!"

"Hold yourself a minute," the Metis replied when he had a chance to speak. His voice was low and any emotion he might have felt was well hidden. "I know you blame me for the killing of two years back, but this is not a time to talk about that."

"Then what gi'es ye the nerve to come here this night when we want to enjoy oursel's? Nobody here wants tae see you and you must ken that fact damned weel."

"Sioux Indians, you fool," Grant answered. "I'm sorry if I interrupted your pleasure, but my boys report a war party on River Souris headed this way. I thought I should warn you. Now I'll leave and you can act as you think. Good night."

"God, man! Don't be going!" MacLeod replied excitedly. "D' you mean you rode in tae warn us of the danger? Well by the soul o' satan, I'd no expect the like o' that from Cuthbert Grant. But don't gae by till I talk wi' our own folk."

MacLeod left his visitor standing alone in the moonlight and hastened inside, holding his hands above his head to get attention. "Listen tae me, every one o' ye! 'Tis shocked ye'll be tae know that our visitor is that man Grant—yes Cuthbert Grant. But hold yer tongues till I tell ye all. I know you've sworn ye'd slaughter him if ye had the chance, but he's been tae tell us of danger—Sioux Indians on the warpath—riding this way from the southwest. Now, Grant is aboot tae leave, but if ye can let bygones be forgotten for a wee, no doubt he'll stop and advise us about defending ourselves. What d' ye say aboot it?''

There was an uneasy silence as shocked men and women wondered if they had heard correctly—that awful man here to warn the very settlers whose destruction he was believed to have plotted! Jean Baptiste laid aside his fiddle and moved instinctively to his gun hanging on a peg on the new wall. The fact that Grant was the bearer of the warning did not bother him especially because he had been slow to take sides in the Red River quarrels—at least until the Nor' Westers at Fort William made life so miserable for him. But he knew something about Sioux Indians, knew that nothing but bullets would discourage their lust for scalps.

Marie Anne spoke up: "Cuthbert Grant! Of course we hate him. But if he's earnest in bringing us a warning, we shouldn't let our dislike stand in the way of our own safety. Let's forget our quarrel and invite him in."

The uneasy settlers nodded without enthusiasm. They wondered if this might be another plot. John MacLeod, however, was in favor of bringing him in and turned at once to get him. As Grant entered, there was an icy silence. All eyes were on him. He was twenty-five years old and looked like a leader. Settlers had seen him before, but on this occasion he looked more mature and personable. His eyes were black and the hairline came low on his forehead; his shoulders were broad and he appeared a man of iron. Only Jean Baptiste had a friendly greeting for him.

Nobody wanted to be the first to speak, but Marie Anne raised her voice: "Mr. Grant, you will excuse the coolness. You will understand. If you've come to tell us of a danger, we're grateful to you. Now please tell us what we should do."

"Yes, I know how you feel about me," he replied, "and I would like, some day, to tell you my side of the story. But this is not the time. You are in danger. When the Sioux come this far you may be sure they come to kill. Now, they may change course and miss your settlement, but if they continue as they've been travelling, they'll reach the forks early tomorrow."

Grant's voice was clear and his manner was convincing. He didn't talk like a wicked man. His words were more like those of a friendly counsellor. "I suggest," he continued, as settlers closed in around him, "that you take your families to the fort. And you men should be ready to shoot first." With a faint twinkle in his eye he added, "If that MacLeod has his cannon and some links of chain, he'll no doubt end the fight for some of the warriors and their horses. But listen, about twenty of my men are north of the Assiniboine right now. If you'd feel better having them with you at the fort, I can have them there by the middle of the morning."

Forgetting momentarily about the last time the mounted halfbreeds rode into the settlement, men and women were nodding their willingness and John MacLeod, reading their thoughts, said, "Thank ye, thank ye! We should have your men and the gate'll be open."

"Very good," replied Grant. "I'll be on my way then; my horse is just across the river. I'll ride out tonight and be back early tomorrow. I'm sorry to spoil your party this way. I suppose you'll all be returning to the other side pretty soon."

"Before you go," Marie Anne said, directing her words to the settlers, "thank you for coming to our new house. Will you please come back and finish the party with us as soon as the trouble is over? Please, I want you all to come."

As Grant was leaving, he turned to Marie Anne and said, "You said 'all'. Does that include me?"

She looked puzzled. She wasn't expecting it and didn't know what to say. "Are you serious?" she asked. "Would you wish to come?"

"Yes, I would," he answered.

"Then come, by all means. I'd like to talk to you. Will you do it?"

"If I'm not too far away, I'll be here."

Excitedly, the settlers went to their canoes with Jean Baptiste and his wife following them to the water's edge. The Lagimodières were on the safe side of the river this time, but Jean Baptiste assured his friends he would join them at the fort in the morning. "And the children and I will be there too," Marie Anne added, waving good night.

Early next morning the Lagimodières crossed to Point Douglas. As the best marksman along the river, Jean Baptiste was made most welcome. There was no particular reason for Marie Anne and the children to go along except that she wanted to be with the settlers she was growing to enjoy so much. The small houses along the stream were being vacated as families made their way to the fort. At midmorning, just as he had promised, Cuthbert Grant, at the head of a column of mounted men, rode through the big stockade gate that was closed promptly after him.

"Any word about the Sioux?" Grant was asked.

"Yes, they're still bearing this way. If they come all the way, they'll make their surprise attack on the houses, expecting to find people in them. How many guns do we have?"

A count showed sixteen guns in the hands of Grant's men and at least twenty-four with the settlers and former de Meurons. Grant was taking charge without asking questions. "MacLeod will handle the cannon, I hope," he said, "and if any of the warriors come close enough, he can use it as freely as he likes and make all the noise and smoke possible."

MacLeod straightened himself with pride and said, "Mistress Lagimodière will stand wi' me and pass the stuff. Between us we'll keep the big gun hot."

Grant's estimate was good. Early in the afternoon, as he was surveying the defenses, he heard the piercing, blood-curdling war whoops, and saw half-naked Indians on spotted horses galloping toward the huts near the fort. The shrieks were enough to unnerve the stoutest heart, but the men at the fort rushed to their assigned gunslots and John MacLeod spoke tenderly to his cannon, "Ye'll no' fail me now, Maggie lass." Marie Anne's children were settled in the care of a settler woman while their mother took her place beside the Scot, ready to "pass the stuff."

"Don't shoot yet," Grant shouted to his men. "Hold your fire until the cannon has had a chance to scare hell out of both Indians and horses." He was counting on the unexpected noise to unhorse some of the attackers. His strategy was good. As the Indians bore down upon the empty cabins, the cannon boomed its unearthly roar. Mustangs bolted in terror, and a quarter of the riders were unseated and left to watch their mounts in frantic flight. The chain link shattered only a few aspen trees, but nothing more was needed to impress the attackers with the devastating resources in the settlement. The fire of flintlocks followed. A few horses fell and those Indians still left mounted circled toward the west and disappeared. The natives who lost their horses fled as fast as their legs would carry them. The battle was over except for removing some dead horses and burying one dead Sioux.

Among the defenders of the fort there was no injury more serious than John MacLeod's bloody knuckles, skinned when reloading the gun. As everyone relaxed, Cuthbert Grant dared to laugh and cracked that MacLeod's blood should be removed from the cannon before it dissolved the iron.

Good humor prevailed within the fort and for the moment at least, it was easy to forget the curses which the Red River settlers had once hurled at Grant. In the joy of victory, Grant was like one of themselves and they talked like friends.

As the next mealtime neared, settlers meandered toward their cabins, convinced that the Sioux would not return, and the Lagimodières prepared to cross the river. As she herded her family toward the fort gate, Marie Anne reminded everyone to come over the next evening to finish the party. She had a further message: "Jean Baptiste doesn't know it, but tomorrow is our anniversary—twelve years married—you must come." Then, looking straight at Cuthbert Grant, she smiled and said, "You'll join us? You said you'd come if you weren't far away. We'll talk and we want you to dance the native jig. Jean Baptiste will fiddle for you."

"I'd like to come," he replied, bowing like a French nobleman. "I suppose I still face the danger of being strangled, but even at such a risk, I'd like to come."

All next day Marie Anne was making her house ready for the party and preparing a mixture of pemmican and flour known as rababoo. Jean Baptiste went upstream on the Seine to get a fat beaver for roasting. It would be Red River's first house party, which Marie Anne hoped would bring new bonds of neighborliness. Suddenly Reine rushed in to say, "They're coming!"

Marie Anne went to the water's edge to greet her guests. They were all there except Cuthbert Grant who had left the fort with his men and had not returned. The settlers were not sure if they were glad or sorry, but Marie Anne's expression showed her plainly disappointed. MacLeod was philosophical, saying, "Ah weel, he deed us a good turn and he deed us a bad one. There's nae damned rush about wooing him."

She conceded that MacLeod might be right as she led her friends toward the cabin. But gaining the top of the bank, she glanced back to see a single canoe leaving the opposite shore. "There he is!" she gasped, showing unmistakable pleasure. They waited for Grant to join them on the way to the house. Clearly enough, there were still those who resented him, notwithstanding his gesture of the day before. But Marie Anne walked beside him, saying, "It seems unbelievable but I'm glad you came. We all thought we hated you and now most of us are wondering if we misjudged. I do want to hear your story. You said you'd tell me."

Jean Baptiste's fiddle was ready for the demands of a long evening. With no delay there was a waltz, then a strathspey, and with Grant's consent, a jig. It was an exhausting dance born with the Metis and gradually becoming known as the Red River jig. Most settlers had seen it at Pembina but no one had mastered it. Grant liked to dance and nobody could better him in doing the jig. Jean Baptiste struck a lively tune and without hesitation, Grant took the center of the floor and broke explosively into performance. It was soon evident that in this number endurance was just as important as skill, but Grant's moccasined feet moved swiftly and gracefully and the admiration of the spectators mounted. On and on he danced, while great drops of sweat rolled down his face and dribbled off his chin. Not until Jean Baptiste stopped fiddling did Grant relax, and then the other guests, pushing animosities further into the background, broke into a cheer for the man they had so recently feared and hated.

Marie Anne crossed the floor to speak her appreciation. "You do it well," she said. "I'd like to learn to do the jig. But don't forget, we are to talk."

"Yes," he answered, "I want to talk. It's more important than dancing."

Together they sat on a log beside the fireplace and she opened the conversation. "You talk well. Have you been to school?"

He nodded and explained that he was born at a post on the Upper Assiniboine. "When my father died nineteen years ago, it was arranged for me to go to school in Scotland. The pedlar people made the arrangements and believed they had a claim on me. I suppose they saw how they could use me as a tool. But that's all in the past. You still think I'm a murderer."

She nodded and he continued, "Well, Seven Oaks was an unfortunate affair and nobody regrets the outcome more than I. But you know, when there's strong feeling, trouble can easily start. Really, madam, I'm not trying to escape responsibility, but let me assure you, my men did not ride out that day for the purpose of killing anybody. They went to meet a brigade and see that it got through to the Assiniboine without interference, surely a pardonable purpose. But when Semple and his men strode out to intercept us, my people took offense and I suppose they cocked their guns."

"You mean you didn't plan to murder the settlers?"

"Alex Macdonell and some other Montreal men said we were going to kill, but we never said so. We were simply paid to do some police work for the Company and our bosses wanted to use us to scare the settlers. Sure, we were mad at Miles Macdonell for trying to stop us from hunting buffaloes with horses; and the other Macdonell was telling us the settlers were going to either run us out or crowd us out of the country. We were mad and made up our minds that we'd fight for our rights. But, believe me, we didn't ride in that day to kill anybody. There were guns on both sides, you know, and I can't tell you who fired the first shot. Once the shooting started, it was like paddling into a rapids; there was no turning back and no stopping until the battle stopped itself. When Semple was wounded, I tried to save his life, but an Indian who was with us became excited and finished him off. I was sorry about that. And then, when it was all over, it seemed only natural that the winners would take charge of the fort. It was too bad, but what happened suited Alex Macdonell and his friends perfectly. I can promise you, my men will do no more of that dirty work for the Nor' Westers. They pushed us into it but we're through with them. I hope that you'll understand our position."

"I don't know if I understand or not," she said, "but I know there are two sides to every conflict. I think I'm convinced that you're not a bad man." She paused and spoke again, "Why don't you come and live near here and help us all the time. This colony is going to succeed, you know."

"Do you think they'd ever accept me and my followers?" he asked.

"I'm not sure, but you've made a lot of progress in two days." Then, remembering her other guests, she said, "But excuse me; I almost forgot. I must put the roast beaver on the table."

The visitors ate and talked and sang Scottish and French songs. Grant joined in with the rest and everybody seemed happy. When it was time to go home John MacLeod had something to say. He stood on the roughly hewn table beside the remains of the beaver carcass and demanded order.

"Ye ken, folk, this is an anniversary. A dozen years this day the Lagimodières were joined together, and then the lass became the first white woman tae settle in this land. God knows there might be no settlement here today if it hadn't been for her and her old man. You'd hae me wish them weel and I'm instructed, mind ye, by the governor o' this colony tae present tae Mistress Lagimodière one coo, one of only four kye in the country; she's heavy wi' calf and should freshen before midsummer. I hope ye haven't forgotten how tae milk a coo. We'll see the bossie is swum across the river on the morrow. And it's damned near tomorrow right now, sae let's be away home."

25

After six moons

In the absence of calendars it was easy to become confused about days, weeks, and months, but except for the strict sabbath-observing settlers on the west side, errors were generally unimportant. In the early part of the new year—1818—however, Marie Anne Lagimodière was counting moons more meticulously than ever before. The good earl of Selkirk, although not of her religious faith, had promised to do what he could toward the realization of her most cherished dream, and Fox Tail said it would happen six moons from the time he took shelter in her cellar.

Four moons after the medicine man made his prophecy, the Lagimodière house was completed, and true to her promise, Marie Anne shared the secret of the earl's parting remarks with her husband. But he, instead of being excited about it as she had hoped, had no comment and dismissed it as though it were an observation about last winter's weather. Good man as he was, he could be provoking at times.

At five moons, spring was emerging resplendent and the new cow Molly celebrated in the manner of cows by disappearing. Marie Anne was worried. This cow was one of the few in the country and her loss would be serious. The children walked miles, searching through the river coulees and nearby wooded areas, but did not find her. They wondered if Indians had shot her and made off with the carcass, or if she had drowned in the river. Just as the search was about to be abandoned, Molly wandered back with a red bull calf walking awkwardly at her flank. Anxiety turned to rejoicing and Marie Anne told her children that they would now have milk and butter.

"What's butter?" Reine asked. "Is it something you eat?"

"Yes, you spread it on your bread and it tastes good." But before the children could taste it, somebody would have to master the technique of milking a cow. Nobody on the east side of the river had ever performed the task and Jean Baptiste, with a fine air of superiority, made it clear that he was still a hunter and would have no part in milking.

Marie Anne tried but without much success. She sent a message to John MacLeod to come at once. He had a fine store of experience in milking cows, feeding calves, and making butter in his native land. "Aye, I can show you weel," he said. "Where's your bucket? Now, follow me closely. You'll seat yoursel' on a block o' wood on this side o' the coo—not the ither side, mind ye."

Marie Anne and the children stood in silence to witness this exhibition of skill and MacLeod was inspired by their trust. "Ye'll hold yon bucket 'twixt yer knees. D'ye see? Noo, this is vera important: Ye'll seize two tits and press the milk frae top to bottom, one tit at a time. D'ye ken?"

"Yes," Marie Anne replied, "but I did all that and no milk came. I didn't want to hurt Molly by squeezing too hard."

"Aye, ye need no' be worried aboot the squeeze. Ye must make it a gude squeeze." To illustrate, MacLeod's powerful hands contracted more than necessary and the cow flinched, kicked, and upset pail, stool, and the Scot. It might have been embarrassing for the proud teacher, but while Marie Anne suppressed a smile of amusement, MacLeod gathered himself together and with no apparent loss of equanimity, returned to his place beside the cow, murmuring unconvincingly, "I wanted tae demonstrate what can happen. Noo, I'll continue."

With no further misadventure, the milking proceeded and Marie Anne said she would try again. This time she was more successful and completed the operation, stripping each teat as MacLeod directed. He then issued instructions about setting the milk in a pan to allow the cream to rise to the top, then placing the cream in a leather bag and shaking it to make butter. Somebody would have to teach the calf to drink skimmed milk from a pail, and if there was any difficulty, he would come again.

Marie Anne was busier than ever before. In addition to her five children, she had a cow and calf requiring her attention, and a bigger plot of turnips and potatoes. Whether she knew it or not she was, in a sense, the first mixed farmer on the east side of the river. But she was not too busy to remember that June would be "six moons" after Fox Tail's prophecies. She did not allow herself to accept the medicine man's forecast as something infallible, but there was fun in speculation and he might be right. She didn't talk about it because

Jean Baptiste would laugh, but on the sixteenth day of the month, when she was working in her turnip garden, John MacLeod paddled furiously to the east side to inform her that a runner had just arrived from the north with word of two canoes bearing French families and two priests. The party from the St. Lawrence would arrive in a couple of hours.

"Thank you, thank you, Mr. MacLeod. Will you wait a few minutes and the children and I will go back with you?"

The hoe was dropped between the rows and youthful faces were given a hurried scrubbing. Jean Baptiste was absent from home and it was just as well because MacLeod was more capable of matching Marie Anne's feelings at such a moment. He paced impatiently until the children were ready to be packed into the canoe, mumbling, "I canna' tell ye why but, Lord woman, I feel aboot as excited as if yon riverend gentlemen were o' the faith o' John Knox. I guess it's because I ken how much it means tae ye."

On the west side, men, women, and children were assembled, and when noonday shadows pointed straight north, two canoes flying HBC flags were seen making their way upstream. A cheer of welcome went up. At least one heart was beating furiously. This was the day for which Marie Anne had waited.

The two priests, Father Provencher and Father Dumoulin, were standing in the canoes, both invested in their church robes. Stepping ashore, the priests motioned to the people to sit on the grass and Father Provencher began speaking at once. He was a big man, and with his crucifix glistening in the sunlight against his priestly cassock, he talked in simple and kindly terms. The church had long hoped to extend its services to Red River, he explained, and the earl of Selkirk, returning to Montreal, had made a special request to the bishop of Quebec for a priest to be sent here. "He assured the bishop," Father Provencher continued, "that certain people at Red River would be a source of great help in establishing the church on the frontier."

Marie Anne understood. It was twelve years since she had seen and listened to a priest. "It is a good day for Red River," she was mumbling. "God bless the earl." She could not know that at that very moment, Selkirk, in failing health, was being caught up in a maze of court actions resulting from his efforts to bring relief to his Red River colonists.

Before retiring to their temporary living quarters at the fort, the priests moved about, greeting people, and asking names. When Father Provencher met Marie Anne he responded, "Ah, I recall. The earl of Selkirk spoke warmly of you. He's not well you know—consumption I fear, poor fellow. And the North West Company crowd is making life miserable for him. A good man, the earl. I recall clearly now; he made some remark about you but I'll not tell you at present. You are a close friend, I gather."

She blushed, not sure how she should reply. "Well Father," she answered finally, "the earl was very good to Red River and to me. His illness and troubles worry me. By the way, Father, I want you to meet Mr. MacLeod, a friend of my family."

MacLeod stepped forward and seized the priest's hand. Seeming to believe the occasion required explanation, he offered it: "A protestant MacLeod, Your Riverence."

There was a twinkle in the priest's eye as he enquired, "Is that a confession or a boast?"

"Aye, it's no' a confession, but if I can dae anything tae help ye here an' keep peace 'twixt the Church o' Scotland and Rome, I'll dae it gladly."

Father Provencher announced that church services would be held at the fort from time to time, and that a special service would be conducted immediately, to which parents could bring their children for baptism.

The governor escorted the priests to their quarters and Marie Anne hastened to tell her children that they'd be coming back to the fort on Sunday. "We're going to church and the priests will help us to be good."

John MacLeod seemed almost as happy as Marie Anne. "I'm glad for your sake. Ye've thought long on this and I must say I like the faces on yon priests, even though they are no' o' my faith. Maybe it'll no' be long before a real meenister o' Scotland's kirk'll be setting foot here. It'll be a gude day too. Ye'd agree wi' that lassie?"

"Yes, and I'll join with your Presbyterians to see him come ashore."

When MacLeod's canoe touched the other side the man with the paddle, thoughtful as always, had a parting message: "I'll be back for ye on sabbath morning in case Jean Baptiste has no' returned by that time."

On Sunday the Lagimodière household filed into the governor's residence inside the walls of Fort Douglas where half a hundred Roman Catholic children under the age of six were gathered for baptismal service. Marie Anne radiated the joy in her heart, saying, "Now I'm sure; someday people will agree that Red River really is a good place to live."

At the end of the service, she placed a package in the priest's hands, a parcel of butter from her own cow. The appreciation was clear; "We've not tasted butter since we left Montreal," one said.

But the sixth moon in the year of 1818 held disappointment as well as pleasure for Marie Anne and those around her. Even before the first church service ended, the region was showing its meaner side again. The air was suddenly full of insects—Rocky Mountain locusts. Their capacity for destruction was only partially understood by settlers, but their numbers were enough to darken the midday sky. Marie Anne told her children they were grasshoppers. "They eat crops, I think. I'm worried."

Local people had but a short time to wait before learning all about the destructiveness of locusts. The small fields of wheat, oats, and barley were attacked and cut down by the insect hordes, and settlers watched in helplessness. Even Marie Anne's turnip and potato tops suffered, but not as much as the grains.

Marie Anne knew the settlers would be discouraged. Once again some would conclude that Red River was not for farming. They would have to be reassured that grasshoppers would pass. But after six years in the country, they had lost more crops than they had recovered, and some would be considering going again to Pembina where they would be closer to the buffalo herds and meat. But those who were optimistic agreed that next year might be better on the little farms—provided, of course, that the necessary seed could be obtained.

One immediate need, Marie Anne noted, was a house for the priests. On her urging, Jean Baptiste cut logs and various people, including John MacLeod, came to help in the construction. It was built on the east side of the river, and the area later named St. Boniface, at the suggestion of Father Provencher. Marie Anne became an expert at peeling logs and by October, the house was completed. But the first use to which it was put was for the storage of seed grain for next year's planting, a small supply recovered by gleaning in the stricken fields.

The gleaners were a woman and three children. It was Marie Anne, of course, moving back and forth in the grasshopper-ravaged fields, recovering the few heads of grain missed by the insects. At the end of the day she had several armfuls of gleanings, good for, perhaps, a bushel of wheat. On successive days, other women joined her and then the two priests and a few men came. The results surprised everybody and thoughts turned to threshing; a dry floor was needed for the operation and the priests offered their new home, not yet occupied.

The priests also helped to flail the gleanings; the breezes carried away the chaff and the moderately clean grain was bagged and stored right there in the house which was to be Father Provencher's home, Father Dumoulin having decided to work at Pembina. No grain could be spared for bread making, but there was almost enough wheat to meet all local needs for seed.

Marie Anne's strategy had worked and the recent debate about future plantings ended. She spoke firmly: "Of course you'll plant wheat next year. And if it fails, you'll plant again the following year."

Father Provencher watched with growing admiration the woman who regularly brought butter to him. When he took up residence in the new house, sharing it with the colony's stock of seed wheat, he had a long talk with her.

"I can tell you now, Madame Lagimodière, if it were not for you, we priests would not be here. The earl of Selkirk admitted to the bishop that he was acting in part upon a promise to you. He did not minimize the service performed by your husband, but he believed the colony at this place might have collapsed if it hadn't been for your courage and influence. Now I want you to advise me on matters of public importance here."

She smiled modestly. "Yes, Father, gladly I'd do it for Red River as much as I would for you. Once I hated this place and would have left it if I could. But I grew to like it; it's like a baby boy whose mother believes he'll grow up to be a great man."

As she stood to leave the priest had another remark for her. "I didn't tell you before but I must tell you now. The earl of Selkirk said that if you were a man, he'd make you governor of Assiniboia. I know now why he said it."

26

Buffalo hunt
and bewilderment

Grasshoppers—countless millions—came again the next year (1820), ruining crops and the hope for bread. Patient women again gathered heads of wheat to furnish seed, but the conviction was growing that buffalo meat, upon which the prairie Indians depended almost entirely for food, offered the best security.

If local people could be assured of meat supplies, Marie Anne reasoned, the uncertainty of planting crops would be less frightening. "They'd be more ready to accept Red River as home. But why must all buffalo hunts start from Pembina? I know Jean Baptiste had his best hunting west of there," she told the priest, "but a party of our people could go directly from here with less inconvenience. We could make enough pemmican to do us for months right there in the field. I'd like to go."

There was endless discussion about the idea during the winter. Almost everyone thought it was a good idea but being cautious, they enquired, "What does Jean Baptiste think about it? He's the best hunter and knows the most about the buffalo."

Jean Baptiste was pleased to hear of his skill with a gun being recognized—the highest honor to which he aspired. The idea, he agreed, was a good one except for the inclusion of women and children in the party. "They'd be a nuisance on a hunt. Let the men make the pemmican and leave women and children at home."

But Jean Baptiste was ready to be a part of the hunt, even with the handicap of families on the trail and in the camp. He favored a joint hunt with the Pembina people. "We can meet in the hills southwest of here. My friend Paquin, he knows the place. He can lead the Pembina crowd."

A message was sent to Pembina and some days later, Paquin appeared at the Lagimodière house to report that his upriver friends were ready to meet the Point Douglas hunters wherever Jean Baptiste chose.

Marie Anne was expecting her seventh baby and Jean Baptiste was sure a woman in her position should stay at home in Red River with her family. But the idea of all the residents participating had come from her and she was determined to go and take the children with her. The family cow was dry and the garden would get along without her for a few weeks. It would be fun for everyone to take their places in the horse-drawn cart which would transport supplies to the field and bring meat and pemmican back.

As the morning for departure drew near, even the dogs seemed to sense adventure and barked excitedly. Twelve-year-old Reine was so moved by expectancy that she lost her appetite, and young Jean was already shooting buffaloes in every corner of the house.

Jean Baptiste borrowed a cart and pony from one of the de Meuron squatters on the west side. It was a shabby outfit and the harness seemed ready to fall apart, but it would serve the purpose and the owner would accept rental payment in pemmican. The Lagimodière parents and six children practically filled the cart, and Marie Anne enquired where they would pack the pemmican on the return. "Sit on it," was her husband's reply.

About a hundred outfits fell into line on that bright morning in June. The Assiniboine River had to be crossed and it was for Jean Baptiste, as leader, to select a suitable place and cross first, testing the firmness of the bottom and the depth of the water. The pony shied again and again at the chosen spot, but the driver held him firmly and swatted him with a willow switch to make him forget his equine nonsense. Timidly, the pony entered the shallow water at the shore and then plunged forward as he was struck again. The channel was deeper than Jean Baptiste anticipated and almost at once the pony was swimming and water was over the floorboards of the cart. The vehicle swerved in the current but the horse was making headway. Everybody except the baby on her mother's back had wet feet, and everybody except Jean Baptiste was nervous. "Are we safe, Ba'tiste?" his wife called.

"Just hang on; we're halfway," he answered.

She breathed a sigh of relief but it was too soon. The muddy bottom and the upward grade toward the opposite shore demanded the pony's best effort, and when Jean Baptiste made the mistake of striking the animal again, there was a tearing sound and the horse in broken harness plunged toward the bank, leaving the cart in three feet of water. Jean Baptiste had the presence of mind to hold firmly to the leather reins, and although drawn forward into the water, he retained control of the horse.

It was a bad beginning for the hunt, with the leader and his horse on one side of the river, his cart and family in midstream, and his followers in a hundred carts holding on the starting side.

The Lagimodière children were crying and Marie Anne was calling for assurance that her man was not injured. He acknowledged with a wave of his arm and moved quickly to tie the horse to a tree. Wading back to the stranded cart, he was mumbling that women and babies should never be allowed to travel on hunting expeditions. At once there was a distraction—a man swimming from the farther shore.

The two men reached the cart at the same time and Jean Baptiste was surprised to recognize none other than Cuthbert Grant, there to help him carry his family to land. He and some of his men had been camping nearby and rode to the crossing to see what was going on. After the second rescue trip, all the Lagimodières were safely on the south shore. And without the weight of its eight occupants, it was possible for the two men to pull the cart out of the water.

Advising that there was a better crossing point a short distance farther upstream, Grant offered to swim back and guide the other drivers to it. Jean Baptiste was slightly humiliated by his error but agreed to the proposal, and turning to repair the broken harness, left it to his wife to thank the famous native leader.

"You are most welcome, madame," the jovial Grant was saying. "If I could swim faster I might have reached the cart before your husband and had the pleasure of carrying you to the other side. But I'll have better luck another time."

Jean Baptiste completed some rough repairs to the rawhide harness and had the pony hitched by the time the first of the other carts reached the south side. Only one other cart encountered trouble. Its unusual and faulty construction caused the rack to separate from the wheels in deep water and float away, carrying a terrified woman a quarter of a mile before it lodged in shallow water beside the south shore.

Once the tearful woman and her cart were recovered, the cavalcade started again with the usual squealing of dry wooden hubs turning on dry wooden axles. A short time before sundown, Jean Baptiste gave the signal to halt and make camp for the night. Amid a babble of voices from tired children and impatient mothers, tents were erected, and the fire specialist with his flint, steel, and tinder set about to provide a campfire.

Jean Baptiste was bombarded with questions: "When will we meet the Pembina people?" "When will we see buffalo?" "Are we safe here tonight?"

"Two more days of travel and we'll meet the other hunters," he said. "Sure we're safe here—fairly safe. Better have two men on guard all night though. Who'll take that duty?"

A de Meuron and a Ross-shire man volunteered and Jean Baptiste instructed, "Keep your guns ready. If you see or hear anything, call me fast."

Weary men, women, and children bedded on the ground between robes and blankets and were soon asleep, comforted by Jean Baptiste's assurance that everybody would be safe. But about midnight the gun of a sentry sounded like a cannon, and Jean Baptiste and his wife bounded from their blankets. He reached for his gun and she inspected her children as well as possible in the darkness. Every adult in the camp made the same leap from bed with the same fear of Indian attack.

Jean Baptiste was the first to reach the men on guard and asked, "Indians? Where are they?"

The Scottish sentry spoke with embarrassment more than alarm. "Ye'll be killing me for this. We were talking aboot the buffalo hunt—trying to stay awake—an' I was telling Romeo what I wud do if a wounded bull charged me, and man, my gun went off—sort of accidentally. Forgive me. I don't want to be sent back alone."

At the end of the third day, precisely as Jean Baptiste estimated, they reached the hills north of the elbow in the Pembina River where the meeting was planned. And as darkness was falling, Paquin drove in with the Pembina party. He ordered his people to arrange the carts in a tight circle around the tents for use as a barricade in case of attack. Then the two seasoned hunters and old friends conferred, agreeing that a decision would have to be made soon about the leadership of the combined outfits.

In the morning everybody answered the call to gather on the grass. Jean Baptiste and Paquin were the acknowledged guides to this point, but neither made any claims to oratory, and neither was ready to present a way of organizing to obtain unified command. Even after everyone was assembled, Jean Baptiste and Paquin were still arguing about who would speak to the crowd. Suddenly Paquin had an idea: "Get Marie Anne to do it. She can do it well."

"All right," Jean Baptiste agreed, "if you can get her to do it. You ask her."

Paquin went to her at once. "We need you. Jean Baptiste and I can shoot but we can't talk. You ask the people who they want to be leader and make rules."

"That's a man's job," she answered. "You men say women shouldn't even be here."

"But no man will do it. You must." He was gently pushing her to a higher point on the hillside from which she could be heard.

Everyone cheered her when she faced them to ask, "Who do you want for your leader in the hunt?"

The answer came like a chorus: "We want Marie Anne Lagimodière."

She was not amused. Looking stern, she said, "You don't mean that. Be sensible. I'm not going to be your leader so tell me right now who you want."

Some of the Pembina people shouted, "Paquin for leader!" but the louder cry from all sides was, "Jean Baptiste!"

She turned to her husband, saying, "They want you. Now come and tell them what they must do."

He protested, mumbling, "I can't make a speech. Get a leader who can talk to them." But again they shouted for Jean Baptiste. He blushed and spoke quietly to his wife: "You tell them I won't make a speech, but if Paquin will help me and everybody promises to keep the rules, I will be leader."

Marie Anne relayed the message and immediately a voice asked, "What rules?"

"We've got to have rules!" Jean Baptiste said to his wife. "You tell them that Paquin and me, we make rules like nobody can shoot on Sunday and nobody can start to hunt before the leader says to do it. We must have rules and if anybody breaks them he has to be punished. Paquin and me, we got to be the bosses."

Marie Anne was relieved when the hillside assembly concluded, but Paquin and John MacLeod rushed to praise her for her performance. Said MacLeod, "Lassie, you're noo the moderator of this congregation."

Two days later she called the people together again to relay the message that scouts had located a big herd a few miles to the south. "First thing in the morning, you men be ready to ride behind your leaders. No forking off by yourselves; that's one of the rules. The leaders will tell you when to ride fast and start shooting. Paquin says to carry the extra lead balls in your mouthes and don't swallow them because there is none to spare. Now, what did I forget? Oh, yes, be careful not to shoot any horses or any of our men. And when you kill a buffalo, throw down your hat or some other marker so you'll know it's your meat, then ride after another. Is that clear?"

"Better tell the women what they're supposed to do," Jean Baptiste reminded her.

"Yes, the women will follow with the carts and be ready to skin and cut up the meat. What else do you want me to say, Ba'tiste?"

"That's all, except no fighting and no stealing. Anybody who breaks the rules and fights or steals is going to be sent home. Paquin and me, we decide."

At sunrise the next day, the men were in their saddles and the women, with the slower horses, were hitching to follow. Dogs were tied to carts to ensure against them frightening the herd. Mounted horses pawed the ground and reared in the excitement of the moment. Men watched Jean Baptiste and Paquin for the signal to start, and when the small flag was waved, they moved away.

They advanced slowly and quietly, hoping to get close to the wild cattle before disturbing them. Even after the herd came into view, quiet marching order was maintained. Cows and bulls grazed peacefully and calves lay still in the tall grass. The hearts of the hunters were beating faster and the horses were more difficult to control. The leaders were little more than two hundred yards from stragglers in the herd when an old bull sensed danger and bounded away, causing the entire herd to stampede. At that instant, Jean Baptiste waved his flag to signal a burst of speed. That was the last signal. Now it was every man for himself. Here was where a fast and surefooted horse was important. Jean Baptiste's horse was not fast—Paquin quickly passed him and shot a big bull—but his aim was always good, and on his first shot he dropped a young cow. Dust rose in clouds amid the thunderous pounding of thousands of wild feet. It was terrifying confusion as the animals dashed to escape and reckless hunters tried equally hard to cut them down.

The chase continued until horses and men were exhausted and the fleeing buffaloes were miles away. Hunters turned their mounts and faced the field of slaughter dotted with brown bodies in the grass, some still struggling. Not everyone escaped trouble; one man lost a few fingers from his left hand when his gun exploded; some were on foot after their horses stumbled on the rough ground; one was walking because his horse had been shot by a stray bullet.

As the dust settled, the cavalcade of carts driven by women and old men could be seen. The carts were stopped in the midst of the field of dead animals and wives sought their husbands to enquire, "Are you all right?" and, "How many did you get?" Most hunters could report at least one kill. A few could count up to five or six bodies bearing their identifying marks.

Marie Anne, her cart loaded with children, spotted Jean Baptiste and drove toward him, calling, "How many, Ba'tiste?"

"Four," he answered. "Paquin beat me by one."

"That's good. We'll be able to spare some meat for Father Provencher and the widow."

"Who do you mean by the widow?"

"You know, the widow Bruce. She lives alone north of the fort. Of course you know her. A pretty woman. She's riding with Murdochs; she just came for the fun, I guess."

Hours of skinning and cutting followed the hunt. The odor of fresh entrails was everywhere, and dogs ate until they could scarcely drag their bloated bodies. Marie Anne was becoming sick of the blood and warm stench long before the job was completed and the carts were loaded with fresh meat for drying.

Despite their fatigue the hunters sat around to indulge in some well-earned boasting about the day's success before retiring for the night. Jean Baptiste had to see certain people about the work of drying to begin the following morning, and when those duties were completed, he called at the Murdoch tent to tell the widow Bruce that he would have some meat for her needs. She was alone and he accepted her invitation to stay to tell her more about the hunt. She was pretty and did not try to hide her admiration for this man with the prestige of expedition leader. She was grateful for the meat and said that she would need advice from a strong man like Jean Baptiste. She hoped he would call again and with a boyish giggle, he said he would. As he walked away, he seemed to have forgotten he was tired.

The great pieces of buffalo flesh had to be cut in strips and hung on bushes, carts, and tentropes to dry. Once dry, it would keep a long time and be lighter to transport. But the drying and the making of pemmican took time. Hunters and their families had to live together for days before starting home. As boss of the camp, Jean Baptiste was getting along well. He was quiet but knew what should be done, and when instructions had to be delivered, Marie Anne continued to act for him.

But two days after the kill, Jean Baptiste had to face an ugly situation reported to him by Dan Murdoch. There had been a theft from his tent—three silver brooches belonging to Mrs. Murdoch, her dearest possessions which she had brought with her to prevent them from being stolen when she was away. Murdoch was impatient. "You said anyone who steals will be sent home. Now, what are you going to do about this?"

Jean Baptiste looked solemn. "What can I do? Are you sure they were stolen?"

"Dead sure. My wife was looking at them yesterday and today they're gone."

"Would you know them for sure if you saw them again?" Jean Baptiste asked.

"Yes, positively. They're all the same size and as big across as the eye of a buffalo. They have Jonathon Tyler's name on them; he made them. All very valuable."

"I don't know what we can do unless we search all the tents. Hell of a job."

"Doesn't matter about that," Murdoch answered. "You've got to find them. I'll help."

"Let's go see Paquin," Jean Baptiste said, leading the way to his tent.

Two of Paquin's friends agreed to conduct the search. Armed with authority from the two leaders, they moved from one tent to another, shaking out every blanket and article of clothing. After hours of searching, the two investigators came to the Lagimodiére tent. Members of the family were on the hillside working with the meat. When the searchers shook one of Marie Anne's spare stockings, two big silver brooches rolled out. The two men from Pembina were horrified, but it was their duty to report the discovery to both leaders. Neither Jean Baptiste nor Paquin could believe that Marie Anne had been the thief.

Paquin paced back and forth in anxiety. "This is bad, damn bad. Murdoch was there when they found the things. What do we do? Let's see what Marie Anne has to say."

Jean Baptiste took his wife aside to tell her the stolen silver brooches had been found in her stocking. "You'll have to explain it or take the blame."

"Is somebody playing tricks, trying to be funny?" she asked, denying any knowledge of the silver pieces. Her fears mounted. She had no explanation. Unless she could clear herself of the suspicion, there would be no alternative but to return home in disgrace.

"Jean Baptiste," she said with tears filling her eyes, "I didn't do it. You believe me? I don't mind going home, but I can't live with the disgrace of going as a thief."

"If it looks like you're guilty, I can't let you stay. I made the rule and you told the people. Guess you have to go. You and the children will have to go alone because I can't leave until the meat is dry."

"Ba'tiste, I'm sorry, but if we go, you must go too. I can drive the cart but you wouldn't let me and the six children cross the Assiniboine without you!"

Mrs. Murdoch had two of the three lost brooches back. She was shocked by the circumstances, and the story spread through the camp as fast as gossiping tongues could carry it. Jean Baptiste knew that his wife could not stay and at sunrise next morning, the Lagimodiére family was on its way home with a small amount of partially dried meat and some sad faces. Paquin was left in full command.

The trip was dreary. The woman whose talents had won the attention of all was now returning home as an alleged thief. The six days of travel on the homeward journey seemed endless, the worst she could remember. Jean Baptiste continued to grumble, not at the cloud of shame, but at having to forefeit his command. "Women on the hunt! Never again!"

It was unfortunate to be taking him away when he seemed to be at the peak of his career and she said so apologetically. But worse was that hideous stigma—a thief! Stole another woman's silver!

"I wonder if Father Provencher will believe me," she thought to herself.

She suffered silently as the cart bumped over prairie hummocks and across the Assiniboine without incident. She was glad to be at home, but at Point Douglas she received more unhappy news; an incoming brigade brought word of the death of the earl of Selkirk. With trouble weighing heavily upon him, he went to Scotland late in 1818, and early in 1820, died in the south of France.[1] Consumption, they said, and Marie Anne was further upset, if that were possible.

She was glad when Jean Baptiste left again for more hunting. She and the children would be better alone for awhile. But she miscalculated; sooner than expected, her baby arrived. Only the squaw of the old Saulteaux chief, ever loyal, was present to help. The new baby, seventh in the family, was a girl, and even before Jean Baptiste returned to see the little one, her mother called her Julie. Chief Peguis and Medicine Man Fox Tail came to inspect the baby. Rather grudgingly, as though it were her own, the Indian woman placed it on display. Gazing into the little black eyes, Fox Tail seemed to catch inspiration and mumbled, "Special papoose; be mother of special white chief."

The haunting sting of being accused of a crime eased only slightly and Marie Anne resolved to stay at home for the rest of her life—never again to cross to Point Douglas unless she had to. "I'm a thief, they say. I'd steal silver. An awful thing to have to live with! Why did I ever leave old Maskinonge? And to go back now with the name of thief clinging to me would be worse than staying here. Oh God, to think that my life at Red River would come to this!"

27

The wonder
of wedlock

Throughout the year ahead, pemmican more than bread would be the staff of life for Red River's people, and before winter's end, plans were being drawn for another summer hunt. In due course, a bigger cart train composed of settlers and Assiniboine River Metis moved by the same route to the grazing ground favored by the buffalo herds. Nearly everybody who attended the hunt in the previous year was going again except Marie Anne and the children. Cow, garden, and seven children were enough to occupy her time, and there was another reason. She had no desire to mingle with people whose glances seemed to shout thief, however unjust they might be. The passage of months helped but little, and her retirement from social life in the community tended to sharpen rather than dull the stigma.

But, thank God, the honorable and humble John MacLeod was still a trusting friend and he kept her informed about events of importance across the river. In absenting himself from the second community hunt, he was exercising a personal boycott both out of sympathy for Marie Anne's position and also because of the impulsive haste in which she had been condemned.

He was performing some morning chores near the fort when a canoe brigade from Fort William stopped at the landing. From its men came a story of unusual importance and without wasting a minute, MacLeod was paddling to the other side to share the news with Marie Anne. "News, Mrs. Lagimodière," he shouted across her garden.

She was interested in any news but, smiling, she interrupted to ask, "Must you always call me Mrs. Lagimodière? Why not call me Marie Anne like most of my friends do?"

"Na, na! I'll no' do that. I like you weel enough an' I'd no' trust myself wi' any such familiarity. Our friendship has not been marred by any irregularity and while it matters not aboot me, we'll not give pratting tongues any reason to gossip.

"As I was saying, Mistress Lagimodière, the canoes from Fort William bring strange tidings. You'd no' guess the word."

"No, I couldn't guess. I hope it's not more trouble for Red River."

"No, it's not trouble this time. It's wedlock—holy or unholy I canna' say but wedlock it is, and any kind of wedlock commands a woman's crowning interest. Fact is, the two old companies, the North West and Hudson's Bay, have become united."[1]

"Well, well, it did happen," she responded with evident satisfaction. "I knew there was talk about it ever since the earl's death, and it's not too soon when you think of the ruinous competition the companies were making for themselves. But I wonder if men like William and Simon McGillivray and Colin Robertson can work together after fighting so bitterly. Why, only three years ago, when Father Provencher came, the English company was going so far as to place a gunboat on Lake Winnipeg and take the pedlars prisoner as they came down the river. They wanted Jean Baptiste to be a sailor on the boat."

"Aye, it was real war, I allow."

"And to think of all the innocent blood that was lost right here. You call it wedlock. Well, I hope it'll be a peaceful marriage. By the way, any word from the buffalo hunt?"

He had no information about the hunt and soon departed, leaving Marie Anne to give Reine, Jean, Josette, and Benjamin their daily lessons in reading and writing. A usual reward for good behavior was a story and for this occasion, she told about the strife between the Selkirk people and the fur traders from Montreal. "Now," she explained, "the two big companies will work as one and there may be peace at Red River. Things are changing. When you grow to be men and women, you'll be proud of Red River."

When darkness fell and all the children were in bed, mother sat in candlelight, still dwelling upon the company union that MacLeod had called wedlock. Suddenly, the evening quiet was shattered by a loud thump at the door. It being more than a polite knock, she was frightened, but before she had time to collect herself, the door slammed open and a deep Irish voice filled the house. "Is this where Annie Lagimodière lives?" The voice was unmistakable. "Ah, bless my soul! We did catch you at home. And you're still worth riding a thousand miles to see."

"Well, Mr. Potlatch. You don't know how glad I am to see you. And who's with you?"

A young squaw followed closely behind, but in the dim candlelight, her face was shaded. "Meet Mrs. Potlatch—or Mrs. Patrick Dublin if you prefer," the Irishman roared.

Marie Anne replied, "Do you mean it?"

"Of course I mean it. I'd not be inviting you to put us down in one bed for the night if I didn't. Now, take a good look and tell me what you think of my choice."

Drawing closer, Marie Anne caught the outline of the face with its smile of unrestrained glee and recognized the bride.

"Mimmie!" she exclaimed, throwing her arms around the lady. "Mimmie, it's you! Dear, dear Mimmie! Do you mean? . . . Are you really . . . really married?"

"Confound it woman! I introduced her as my wife and she's not denying it. She's been cooking my pemmican for nearly a year, but she's still Mimmie to you."

Mimmie's command of the white man's language had improved only marginally since Marie Anne saw her, but she still had a way of communicating her feelings without saying much. She smiled, saying, "Glad, glad, glad!"

"It's wonderful to see you both," Marie Anne gasped, displaying an excitement she hadn't known for years. "I think it's twelve years since I saw you, Mimmie, and eleven since I saw Mr. Potlatch."

"Ten, lass, ten. Let's not yield to exaggeration. I know because your colt is ten years old."

"The colt! Then it did live? A boy or girl colt? What color was it? And the turnip seed I left with you? But let's not talk about turnips yet. Tell me about the colt."

"The colt? He was born one day after you were at my place. A boy colt it was, with a buckskin coat. You've got a good stallion this day—and no faster in the country."

"My buckskin stallion! Where is he now? I'd love to see him."

"We rode him down. He's stabled at Fort Douglas where we borrowed a canoe."

"Excuse me for being so excited. But I am excited—about you and Mimmie and the horse. I heard today that 'wedlock is a woman's eternal interest,' and perhaps it's correct. You really are married? No, I didn't mean to ask that again."

"Damn it, you did mean it. Just what kind of matrimonial evidence would you expect from a man and woman who live in the Stone Age? A houseful of halfbreed weans, I suppose. But what about yourself? I suppose there's a new Lagimodière baby every spring."

"No, we've just got seven. Reine, whose life Mimmie saved, and six more. You'll see them all tomorrow, right down to Julie who's a year old. But tell me, how long did you say you've been married?"

Mimmie raised one finger to indicate one year and with a laugh, tried to say "honeymoon."

"You'll not be satisfied until you get all the romantic details. You're a superior woman but a story about wedlock has the same fascination for you as for all the rest of your sex. It's a long story and I'm ready to relate every last detail when you want it."

"Right now," was Marie Anne's reply. "I'm honest. I can't wait."

"Very well, but before I begin, Mimmie has something she wants to deliver to you."

Mimmie reached into her leather bag and with pleasure written across her face, withdrew a small mirror and placed it in the white woman's hand. There was a moment of silence as Marie Anne studied the object and turned it over to see, scratched on the back, the words Trois Rivières. Her eyes flashed as astonishment struck. "It's the mirror I brought from home. Hawkfeather loved it so much I let her have it and she never came back. Is it possible? You found the mirror?"

Mimmie and her husband were chuckling. "You see, lady," the latter boomed, "it was this mirror that brought us together and you can decide for yoursel' if it brought fortune or misfortune. Now, are you ready for the mysterious story? After I've told it, you can point out a spot on your floor where we can spread our blankets."

Marie Anne was nodding her eagerness to get a full disclosure of the romance.

"'Twas like this. You won your way to the heart of my Mimmie long before I knew her. She told me all you did for her and how she lived with you until she discovered that her mother was still alive. All right; after that Mimmie married a warrior boy of her tribe and before long he was killed in a row with the Blackfoot. Of course you'd not expect a lovely lady like my Mimmie to escape the masculine eye, and another of her tribe wanted her. It was to encourage her affection that he presented her with this treasure he took as loot from a slain Sarcee. You know well how a woman likes a gift, but Mimmie recognized this one as the mirror she had seen in your tent years ago. Providence did some scheming to work this one out."

Marie Anne drew closer to ensure against missing a single word. Here was more joy than she had known since prior to her trouble at the hunt. "It's a sweet story. Don't stop."

"Ah, but that's only the beginning. God knows I can hardly believe it myself, to think I got such a prize out of it. Well, Mimmie couldn't forget what you did for her, and when she saw the wee mirror, she resolved to find you and return it. She's a true one, my Mimmie. I didn't think I could like any woman so well."

Marie Anne reached for Mimmie's hand and held it without interrupting the narrator.

"But how was Mimmie to find you after all these years? She didn't know if you stopped upriver or returned to the East, but she did know there was a white man—a social monstrosity—living in a log hut by the big river and not too far away. She would go there and hope to learn something of the woman she knew as Ningah."

Mimmie was following the story with as much interest as though it was new to her.

"And she did find you?" Marie Anne asked, hardly able to wait for the climax.

"Yes, she found me but not all right—found me with a hellish fever, and before she said anything about the mirror, she tried to make me comfortable, fetched me water, and made me think that heaven hadn't forsaken me. Well, when she produced the mirror, she found the words to explain that she wanted to return the thing to you. Could I help her to find you? I examined the mirror and recognized the name of Trois Rivières on its back. Long bye I heard of you saving an Indian girl from certain death and the story came back to my fever-stricken brain. I tell you, Annie, even through my swollen eyes, that girl looked like a bronze angel."

Marie Anne was chuckling and weeping and finding it impossible to be quiet. The suspense was too great and she bubbled again, "You'd have died if she hadn't come!"

"Yes, I'd have died and my house would have been my tomb. But she fixed me some food and made my bed feel like it wasn't a woodpile; I seemed to have a new interest in living. I told her all I knew about you, that you went back to Red River, and as far as I could judge, you were still there. And bless my soul, didn't the lass come back next day to feed a sick man, and then the next. Now, what do you think?"

"You proposed to Mimmie."

"Well, you might say I did. Perhaps the fever changed my senses some, but I began to see this little red angel as a permanent fixture in my house, and I told her I figured the wee place would be better with her in it. And so I just made her a proposition while I was still on my back and as helpless as a pussycat wi'out claws. I explained I was thinking of taking a buckskin stud to Red River in the hope of finding you. 'Now,' says I, 'if you'll become Mistress Patrick Potlatch, we'll go to Red River together as soon as I'm fit and able.' O' course, this Cree lass didn't know much about the English tongue, but, by the saints of Ireland, a woman doesn't need to know the language when a man's proposing to her. Mimmie knew exactly what I meant and she fancied the idea."

"Oh, what a lovely story!" Marie Anne was saying as she moved to kiss Mimmie and her man. "I only wish you were married by a priest or minister, that's all. There's a priest here at Red River now, in case you didn't know."

"Aye, I figured you'd be thinking that. True, we're not married by the church, but we're married according to the custom of the country and I've come to believe that's as good as you need to make it."

"We'll talk more about that tomorrow," Marie Anne was saying as she cleared a place on the floor for her guests' blankets. "It's a wonderful story and I'm bursting with more questions. But you must be tired. You can go right to bed. I hope you'll sleep well."

In the morning, the visitors were introduced to each of the seven children, from Reine, in whom Mimmie had reason for special interest, to baby Julie who induced her mother to quote the medicine man's prophecy. Then, Marie Anne's morning questions began with turnips. "What about the seed I left you? Did it grow, and what do you think of that crop in the fur country?"

"Oh, the roots did well, grew about as big as the best in Ireland. I had them for myself all that next winter and some for the mare and colt. Of course they'll grow."

A sympathetic audience was something she needed—and didn't often get—when she related her successes with potatoes and turnips. She told of the opposition from men in the fur trade, men who evidently did not want to concede that cultivated crops could be successful. They wanted no alternative to hunting and trapping, she contended, adding, "Our turnips and potatoes kept a lot of people from quitting here, and made me want to stay to see if Red River would become like the St. Lawrence country with farms and churches and happy people. I'm sure it's coming."

Patrick Potlatch was peering westward. "According to what I see from this side of the river, it's coming damn fast. You have the right idea. I thought so ten years ago, but I couldn't get more seed for turnips and potatoes so I made wild fruits and flowers grow in rows beside my cabin. Now Mimmie can pick berries right there to mix with our meat. Just give this country time and its crops will be worth far more than its furs.

"But where, Annie, are all the people? There aren't many about."

"They're on the buffalo hunt. Jean Baptiste is with them. It's the new idea to get the buffalo in the summer and dry the meat and make pemmican right in the field. Then if Point Douglas crops fail, the settlers have pemmican to fall back upon."

"I'm surprised you're not with the party."

"There's a reason, Mr. Potlatch." And she related the sad story, concluding, "Well, it just broke my heart, and until you came yesterday, it's been an unhappy year. I hardly ever cross the river anymore. I can't stand it when people look at me with an accusing expression."

"Where's the third of the stolen brooches? Has it never been found?"

"Not as far as I know."

"Did you or Jean Baptiste have any enemies in the camp?"

"Not that I know about. I thought everybody was my friend. There's just no reason. I suppose it'll remain a mystery—never be solved."

"I make no pretense to great wisdom but I think you blundered in removing yourself from the folk across the river. It was an unfortunate affair, but you should have gone about as though you knew you were innocent, instead of holing up like a self-conscious criminal. You're adding to your own punishment for a crime you didn't commit."

"Yes," she answered. "Father Provencher said the same. I guess I hurt myself."

"Now," said he, "if you've any respect for the wishes of Patrick Potlatch, you'll get back into the buffalo hunt and other affairs about here. Red River needs you, lass. When that other brooch is found and tells its own story, you'll not be standing like one self-condemned. We'd like to stay longer and help you, but we can't do it."

"You're going back so soon? I wish you could stay till Jean Baptiste returns."

"Na, we'll not do that. We have to pull grass to make hay for two horses. We've had three horses and we brought them all here so we'd have two for our return. Yes, there are hay and pemmican and berries to think about—and another reason for getting on the trail." He glanced mischievously at Mimmie who was laughing.

Marie Anne sensed what it was about and exclaimed, "A baby!"

"Yes, and if it's a lass, she's Annie Potlatch."

There was a tear in Marie Anne's eyes, but it was a tear of joy, something she'd almost forgotten. "And if it's a boy, will you let me name him?" When the two nodded agreement she said, "Thanks. He'll be Patrick. That's a good name. I hope it's a boy."

As everybody walked to the river, Mimmie promised she would come again when she had a baby to show. She and her man crossed the river in the borrowed canoe and Marie Anne followed in her own. On the west side, the visitors were taken to meet John MacLeod, and then there was the buckskin stallion—Marie Anne's personal property—to be inspected. He was stabled at the fort along with the other two the travellers would ride home.

"He's beautiful," Marie Anne repeated, stroking the animal's forehead. "He has a face like his mother, my little buffalo runner. What do you call him?"

"We call him Turnips because he was so fond of the roots from your seed. But has it occurred to you that his mother is still with us and stands right here?"

Marie Anne turned quickly. "Oh, the sweet thing. I thought she'd be dead and I didn't want to ask. I loved that little mare, even if she did give me a bad time. Our Jean was almost born on her back, and that wasn't funny."

Potlatch reckoned the mare was close to twenty years old, "but she can still shame a fast buffalo. She's Mimmie's mare now. There had to be a groom's gift to the bride, you know, and I figured you'd approve. And don't forget, you've got a good horse in my friend Turnips. Get Jean Baptiste to fix you a stall beside your cow and you'll get to fancy this horse. Give him lots of riding and I'll gamble there's no horse along Red River that can catch him."

"And now, my dear wifie, we'll be riding into the west and thankful we are that you weren't away on the buffalo hunt."

Marie Anne had a lump in her throat as she confessed, "I was feeling lonely and sorry for myself, but you drove the loneliness all away. I hardly recognize myself today. But before you leave, I want Mimmie to have something for a wedding present from me. Here's the little mirror. It's more than a mirror now and I want you to keep it. I think it's a token of luck; certainly it's done a lot for me."

Mimmie pressed it against her bosom and her smile spoke gratitude and happiness. She placed her cheek against her man's and held the mirror so both could see. As the woman laughed, he remarked dryly, "Created for each other, damned if I don't think so."

"One thing more before you go." Marie Anne didn't want them to leave before one point was reconsidered. "Red River has no protestant minister, but I could get the priest in a few minutes."

Potlatch hesitated momentarily, then continued to bit the horses, talking as he did so. "I understand your concern, but don't forget that Mimmie has a half interest in this marriage and it's in the way of her people. It suits her and I think it suits me. If it's a good wedlock or a poor one is going to depend on Mimmie and me." He paused again as if doubtful how his next observation would be received. "I've had lots of time to think there on my riverbank, and I've finally concluded that Mimmie and I have about the same faith. Her Indian Great Spirit and my Irish God are one and the same power. He witnessed our marriage back there on the river and knows we were serious. We don't think we need any more witnesses. The important thing is that we be true."

Marie Anne was impressed if not convinced, and knew that further urging would be a mistake. She watched them mount their horses and swing to the west. She mopped her eyes and threw a kiss.

Patrick Potlatch turned on his horse to have the last word. "Come and see us when you can; we'll have something to show— could be the brightest wee halfbreed in a' Rupert's Land." But it wasn't the last word yet. His horse made a few paces along the trail, was pulled again to a stop, and turned to let the rider shout, "Please don't forget the advice I offered you: for God's sake don't forget to stand as one who knows better than anybody that she's innocent of any crime. I know you're innocent, Mimmie knows you're innocent, and you know it. Now get back into the life of Red River. You owe it to the community and to your children. And say 'top of Old Ireland' to that buffalo hunting husband for us."

Marie Anne wandered back to look again at her stallion. His coat glistened. He was handsome. She pulled some grass for him and offered him water. But her mind was on many things—Mimmie, wedlock, the halfbreed baby, gratitude that she wasn't absent when these dear friends called, and Patrick Potlatch's parting instructions to get back into the life of Red River.

"He is convincing," she was thinking. "I wonder if I could get back into the life."

28

High water
and low spirits

Marie Anne shook her friendly finger at the buckskin stallion and told him he was about to be taken to his new home on the east side of the Red. He was familiar with rivers and didn't mind getting his feet wet, but he objected to the deep water and had to be given time to consider the necessity of swimming. Finally, with John MacLeod handling the canoe and Marie Anne holding the leather lead, the horse waded and swam his way to the far shore.

"A sensible fellow!" Marie Anne commented when the stallion came prancing from the river and whinnied as if in triumph. "Might have a stubborn streak, just like Potlatch."

Stubborn or not, Turnips was at once a favorite with the Lagimodière children and was showered with attention. Their mother rode him on local trails and into stretches of countryside she had not seen before.

But whether she worked about the home or rode the trails, Potlatch's instructions were nagging at her. "You owe it to your youngsters," he'd said. It was a point she'd overlooked; the children would be affected by her standing in the community. It would not be easy to return. There might still be some resentment, but if she should return, she'd do it.

Point Douglas had its first really bountiful crop in 1824. Marie Anne was in the nearby fields helping to tie sheaves and reveling in this proof of the goodness of Red River soil, no matter how fickle the weather. The vagaries of the seasons were obvious—sometimes adding discomfort, always adding interest. Extremes of heat in summer and cold in winter were symbols of the country's capacity for diversity.

That season—with sixty bushels of wheat to the acre—was a new experience, even for those who had been there from the beginning of the colony. The next year was unique as well with mice in unprecedented numbers appearing in the fields to devour the grain. And still nature's fund of tricks and tragedies was not exhausted. A severe winter with an early freeze-up and heavy snowfall followed the mouse epidemic.

On the bright side was the birth of Marie Anne's eighth baby, Joseph, a few days before Christmas (December 20, 1825); but on the darker side there was more for the record. Settlers were hard-pressed to provide firewood as fast as it was being consumed by their voracious fireplaces; and the supply of hay for Molly and Turnips was barely adequate. Buffalo herds remained far away and when pemmican supplies became depleted, some hunters perished in the chase. Even a few Red River dogs were said to have been consumed by settlers who had nothing else for their tables.

The winter was long as well as severe, and even in April when snow should have disappeared, drifts lingered and Red River remained fast in winter ice. But late that month, spring came with a mighty rush. Melting snow made rivulets to the bigger stream, and although the ice was firm in the river, Fox Tail advised residents to move to higher ground. The admonition went unheeded at the time, but on May 2, the incoming water caused the ice to heave and the river level to rise nine feet in one day. Settlers were startled but not worried because, they assured themselves, it wouldn't rise any more than that. But the river did rise until it overflowed its banks and inundated the settlement. The de Meuron homes were the first to be flooded and those at Point Douglas were next. Marie Anne could see people on the other side taking refuge on the roofs of their houses, until necessity forced them into the rescue canoes. As the water rose higher and higher, the little log houses began to disintegrate. Some floated away, one log at a time, while others stuck together to be carried away like packing boxes. Even as she watched, a big block of ice struck a riverside house and dashed it apart; the logs then floated away like pieces of firewood. One house was seen floating away with its terrified owner sitting on the roof—a most unenjoyable ride to a destination he could not anticipate. Nor was it possible for a spectator to help.

At the fort, things were only slightly better. The governor moved to the second floor of his house, but when the water reached a depth of ten feet on the outside, he was glad to move, too. Hurriedly, the settlers organized to leave and search for higher ground. Horse-drawn carts with men, women, and children on foot made their way northward toward that rise of ground known as Stony Mountain. On Marie Anne's side, the line of evacuation was northeasterly toward

Bird's Hill. It was in keeping with Fox Tail's advice and Jean Baptiste knew where it was.

Turnips was hitched to a de Meuron cart; Molly, the cow, was tied behind, and all the members of the Lagimodière family crowded into the vehicle. Molly protested and pulled back stubbornly until she discovered that Turnips could outpull her and it was easier to walk than resist.

Glancing back, Marie Anne could see the home of which she was proud set at the center of what seemed like a big lake. She wondered silently if it would be there when she returned. The thought of its loss pained her. For some of her friends it would be their third time fleeing from the colony. This time everybody was escaping, even John MacLeod whose stubborn spirit had defied the previous crisis.

Unpredictable and treacherous Red River! Marie Anne wrestled with questions for which there were no answers. She wondered if this would be the tragedy to break the settlers' spirits completely, if it would mark the end of the settlement for which the earl of Selkirk and others had struggled. Already some of the de Meuron men going to Bird's Hill announced with blasphemy that when the flood receded, they were leaving for good. They didn't know where they were going but they had seen enough of Red River.

At sundown the refugees from the east side were pitching tents amid the crocuses at Bird's Hill. Except for the flowers there was nothing very cheerful about the scene. The children were tired, the de Meurons were disgruntled, and Jean Baptiste was irritable. When the children were in their beds, no robes or blankets remained for the parents, and Marie Anne and Jean Baptiste stretched out on the sod with only a pile of dry grass for a pillow. Worried about this latest disaster and its impact upon the settlement, Marie Anne could not sleep. She seemed to spend the whole night squirming to find a position in which her tired body might fit the undulations of the ground.

Next day Jean Baptiste headed a small hunting party that went east from the hill to find meat, and returned with a deer. And on that and every succeeding day, somebody rode to the river to report back on the flood level. Day after day for three weeks the story was the same—high water and no improvement. The water level gradually began to fall, but before the residents were back at Point Douglas and nearby areas, there had been an absence of six dreary weeks. During that time there was no means of communication between the east and west side groups. It was good to be back. The Lagimodière house was one of the few to survive, but it was wet and smelly and had a thick layer of mud on the floor. Worse off, however, were the people on the Point Douglas side who had no homes. On Governor

George Simpson's invitation, the homeless people huddled together in buildings at the fort.

"What are we going to do now?" unhappy people were asking. It was mid-June and too late to be planting most crops. Perhaps it was too late for turnips and potatoes, but Marie Anne planted them in her garden anyway and urged her friends to do the same.

As soon as there was opportunity, she crossed to Point Douglas to see how the families had survived and who needed cheer. It was part of her adopted policy and she accepted the chance of rebuff. Most women seemed glad to see her. One proved unfriendly and told her that she was responsible for many of the woes of the settlers because she, more than any other, had urged the Point Douglas people to stay and try again. Marie Anne tried to speak but the woman continued, "Without you and your turnips and potatoes, my old man and I would have left years ago and escaped this last misery."

Marie Anne responded with sympathy. "Yes, you have suffered and I'm sorry. Perhaps I was wrong in trying to keep you. But isn't it possible that you are now better able to face the years ahead because of all these experiences? You can build your next house on higher ground and you may never see another flood like that. Peguis and Fox Tail have been around here all their lives and they never saw one like this. Don't give up. Please."

It wasn't easy for her to be optimistic. The fact was that her own faith had been shaken more than she was admitting. The continuation of farming had been one of her highest hopes and now she, too, needed encouragement. She turned to Governor George Simpson, even though she suspected there might be something superficial about his interest in the settlement. He was a relative newcomer but a fascinating little man with dynamic vigor and a patient interest in people, especially attractive women. But George Simpson's heart was in the fur trade and Marie Anne suspected that in giving encouragement to the settlers, he was motivated by the importance of cheap food supplies for his far-flung trading posts, more than a hope for a prospering and expanding farming community. But in spite of any hidden antipathy George Simpson may have had in his fur trader's heart, he did accept the colony as his responsibility, and outwardly at least, he was on Marie Anne's side in pleading with the settlers to stay and carry on.

As she continued to visit with the women taking refuge at the fort, she heard Mrs. Menzie's tale of woe. Her baby girl was ill, unable to keep any solid food in her sick little stomach, and there was no cow's milk at Point Douglas. Marie Anne's Molly was still giving milk, although the cow too had suffered during the flood and her output was considerably less than usual.

"I'll be back tomorrow with some milk," Mrs. Menzie was assured.

Molly co-operated by giving more milk that evening, and next day, leaving Reine in charge of the younger children, mother crossed the river with a pot of milk for the sick child. Mrs. Menzie was grateful and Marie Anne said that she would try to bring milk daily until the babe was better. There were times when her own children went short of milk, but she was doing something for a sick child and indirectly for her own young ones, as Potlatch had proposed.

The fort was being made ready for a big party. It was the governor's idea that a social gathering would help to make people forget their troubles. If more reason were needed, many of the de Meuron people were about to leave Red River to locate somewhere south of Pembina. Even though the de Meurons had never been fully accepted as neighbors, a farewell party seemed appropriate. The fort's food stocks were replenished and there was a promise of music and rum. People on both sides of the river were invited, and on the appointed evening late in June nearly all were present to eat, drink, and dance. Men and women who had been depressed for weeks found relaxation, and George Simpson was jovial. Outside, the night was clear and friendly, and those who were not dancing sat to converse or strolled about the fort premises. Marie Anne's movements showed that she had lost none of her dancing grace and none of her popularity as a dancing partner. When she wasn't dancing, she was showing Miss Reine—now eighteen years old—how to do some of the steps.

It was a good party. Everybody appeared to be enjoying it. Company officers were pleased. The de Meurons, who intended to quit the settlement, admitted to vacillation. When the rum was finished, the party came to an end and the folk who still had homes outside the fort walls went to them.

Late the next day, when Marie Anne made her regular trip with milk for the sick baby, she encountered an unexpected reaction. Mrs. Menzie accepted the gift but instructed that there be no more deliveries.

"Is the baby so much improved that you'll not need more milk?" she was asked.

"Ah well," came the reply, "we can get along well enough now." But the woman's voice revealed strain or fear and the expression on her face lacked its usual friendliness.

Marie Anne knew at once that there was some mysterious reason for her sudden refusal to accept more milk and asked, "Isn't the milk all right?"

"Yes, ma'am, nothing wrong with the milk."

"Then what's wrong?"

The woman was noticeably uncomfortable. She didn't want to say any more but Marie Anne, slightly on the defensive, was determined to know and pressed with more questions.

"Have I offended you in any way?"

"No, ma'am. Not that."

"Then what has occurred since yesterday to cause this change of attitude?"

Giving way to her emotions, Mrs. Menzie sobbed and said, "All right, I'll tell you, but remember, I didn't want to do it. They're saying things about you this morning, ma'am, and I thought it would be better if you weren't coming to my door every day. I'm not ungrateful for what you've done, mind you, but my old mother always said to have no truck or trade with people suspected of evil. That's all I can say."

"That's not all, Mrs. Menzie," Marie Anne replied. "We both know that's not all, and I must insist upon knowing the rest. Will you please tell me what they're saying about me and who is saying it."

"I don't know who all are saying it, ma'am; the widow Bruce told me and she said it would be better for me and my family if you weren't coming here. I'm sorry, ma'am, God knows, but each one of us must think about her own reputation. You know we lost everything in the flood, but we're honest people and we don't want to be mixed up with any dishonest dealings. I hope you'll understand."

"But, Mrs. Menzie, I don't understand! What do they suspect me of doing? Did I do something terribly wrong? You told me I was accused or suspected. You must tell me what they say I did."

"Well, ma'am, it's this way: Sometime during the party last night, the governor's snuffboxes made from polished rams' horns disappeared. They were from Scotland and nice ones. Somebody entered his private room, went through his chest, and took the snuffboxes — perhaps some other things."

"And do people suppose I did it?"

"Well, ma'am, they don't just say so, but they say that those who would steal silver brooches would steal snuffboxes."

"That's the widow Bruce's opinion, is it? What else does she say about me, now that her name has been mentioned."

"She thinks, ma'am, it would be better if you went back to the St. Lawrence."

"You don't suppose, Mrs. Menzie, that she has considered the possibility of the children and me going back and Jean Baptiste remaining here, do you?"

Still sobbing, the woman said she didn't know.

"In any case, Mrs. Menzie, I'll not worry you by calling with more milk. I hope your little girl will get better quickly. But before I leave, I should tell you I did not take the snuffboxes or anything else. You may tell any of your friends who are interested that I am one woman who can account for all her time while the party was in progress last night. When I wasn't with the people on the floor, I was attending to my children and never was I by myself. That, I believe, can be proven. I'm going now. I'm sorry this has caused you to be upset. You did nothing to deserve it."

Marie Anne spoke clearly, even calmly, but she was dazed as she hadn't been since she'd stood condemned for the theft of jewelry. Her efforts to regain a reputation for honesty and helpfulness seemed wasted. Her anger mounted and her impulse was to walk right to the quarters of the widow Bruce and ask her why she wasn't at the party. She walked briskly in the widow's direction, but before knocking at her door where the two women would have faced each other in bad temper, Marie Anne turned and went to find John MacLeod, always easy to locate when he was needed.

He'd believe her. He did believe her and admitted to something which on other occasions he would have kept to himself. "I admire ye, Mistress Lagimodière. Ye ken that. It's been a respectable admiration and ye'll ken that also. But I'm ready to testify that my eyes were following you for a' the time o' last night's party. Perhaps I should be ashamed to own up to it, but I know where ye were all the evening an' I'll swear ye were never at or near the governor's room. Noo, I'll gladly hold my hand on the King James version and repeat what I said."

A smile came over her anxious face. Marie Anne relaxed. "Bless you, John MacLeod. God knows ours has been the kind of friendship that makes me feel proud. It will be that way, always. I never wanted so much to kiss you as right now and I'm going to do it."

MacLeod blushed. "Lord, Marie Anne—I mean Mistress Lagimodière! What did ye do that for? Ye kissed me. Nobody ever did that since my ane mother did it. Ah weel, I'm no' sorry, mind ye. 'Twould be too bad tae die an' miss it."

Marie Anne laughed in spite of her distress. "Now," she said, "I really want your advice. I felt like going to the widow's room and talking to her, but it would have been difficult to remain calm. You know I've been trying to forget the circumstances that made me miserable a few years back, and I was progressing, but today I'm the thief of Red River again. What am I to do to clear myself and spare my children from cruel tongues?"

John MacLeod spoke more slowly than usual, "I'm no' a man of profound thought and I hesitate to give you advice, but if you should need my testimony about last night, I'll give it gladly. Matter o' fact,

I'll no' wait for instructions; I'll be telling it up and down these trails that somebody has started a black lie, a hellish black lie."

"You're so good. Thanks. Now I wonder if it's still better for me to try to ignore it all as something too ridiculous to be entertained seriously. That's what I'll do! I've been encouraging these dis-heartened people along the river to try again. I've coaxed them to try again. I suppose I shouldn't be giving up after a couple of failures." She laughed at the thought that flashed through her mind, then shared it, "I don't know if it's your strength or mine, but when I kissed you I felt immediately stronger. Now, I'm going down the trail and I'm going to smile at everybody I meet and prove to myself and them that gossip can hurt but it can't condemn."

"Aye lass, you're the paragon o' good sense."

"By the way, I suppose there'll be another buffalo hunt pretty soon. There's a lot of rebuilding work to be done along the river this summer, but the hunt is more important than ever because we know now there'll be no wheat—none planted. Some of us may have potatoes and turnips but we must have pemmican for next winter. Well, if there's a hunt, Jean Baptiste will be going—and I'm going too. That means all the Lagimodières will be going. It's a few years since I went with the crowd and I thought I'd never go again, but if I'm to insist I'm innocent, I'd better act like I'm convinced."

"Good sense, I figure. You'll no' enjoy it but you're a wise woman."

She was speaking again, "Some of the Red River people will be surprised, but I'm going, even if I have to walk. They'll have to accept me or find new reasons for condemning me. Are you going, Mr. MacLeod?"

"I hadn't intended to," he replied. "It doesn't take much meat to feed a bachelor body like me, but if you're going, lass, I figure these MacLeod eyes should be there—as they were last night."

Things looked brighter. Marie Anne was chuckling. "Take your old cannon and a few links of chain and show them all how to shoot. I wonder if I'll wish I hadn't gone. If somebody steals a horse or cart, I suppose I'll be the sinner. But truth should prevail ultimately—don't you agree, Mr. MacLeod?"

29

Without spot
or blemish

Log work became the order of the day. Wood chips flew like angry bees as rebuilding proceeded where riverbank homes had been brutally swept away by floodwater. What was supposed to be a summer buffalo hunt was, of necessity, pushed back to become an autumn event. Because no crops had been planted, the need for dried meat and pemmican was greater than ever and September, generally a friendly month across the plains, was seen as a good time for the great overland adventure.

Some of the best hunters from the Metis settlement beside the Assiniboine were going, and every able bodied citizen in the Red River community wanted to be included. This time, in spite of Jean Baptiste's protests, all the Lagimodières would be travelling with their own horse and cart. Molly, the cow, was temporarily dry, and with plenty of grass and water, could look after herself for a few weeks.

Reluctantly as usual, Turnips swam the river while the cart, with wheels removed and lashed to the underside of the frame, was floated across. On the west side, the Point Douglas and White Horse Plains carts united and moved away in a long cavalcade to ford the Assiniboine at the favored place and swing to the southwest to meet Paquin's carts from Pembina. Cuthbert Grant, who seemed to have gained a good measure of respect and forgiveness from the Red River people, was going and had two or three of the best and fastest horses. Grant and Jean Baptiste were on good terms and there would be no ill feeling regardless of which one was elected to the position of hunt leader.

The days were warm and the nights were cool and at each

evening camp Marie Anne moved about in her naturally easy way, enquiring about the comfort of mothers and babies, and sensing only a trace of the earlier resentment.

Three days of travel brought the Assiniboine and Pembina groups together with Cuthbert Grant being elected to the supreme command. Jean Baptiste and Paquin were named as his chief lieutenants. That was satisfactory with everybody, and the capable leader was one who could deliver his own orders in a voice ringing with fearlessness. As in other years, the united party drove deeper into the southwest until scouts reported a big buffalo herd in the vicinity of the Turtle Mountain.

"Hunters to be armed, mounted, and ready for the signal to ride at thirty minutes after sunrise on the morrow," was Cuthbert Grant's order.

Jean Baptiste had a problem. Turnips couldn't be both a buffalo runner and a cart horse at the same time. The stallion possessed speed and the first need was for runners. It was arranged, therefore, that a neighbor with a slow horse would haul two carts to the field and after the chase Turnips would take his place in cart harness.

Admiring women watched their men ride away with Cuthbert Grant in front flanked by Jean Baptiste and Paquin. It was an imposing sight and the mounted men felt proud to be the objects of so many feminine gazes aimed their way. Grant's strategy was good. Riding in against the wind, he and his followers were shooting only seconds after the horses were spurred to a hard gallop. Women, children, and old men coming on with the carts could hear the roar of pounding feet and gunfire sounding like a major battle.

The outcome was favorable and as Grant surveyed the carcasses strewn over a couple of square miles, he was sure there would be sufficient meat to fill all the carts. The remainder of the time in camp could be devoted to cutting and drying the meat and to such recreation as might be devised.

Evening found the men squatting beside the campfire, reenacting the hour of the slaughter with permissible exaggeration. It was conceded that Jean Baptiste riding Turnips had killed five buffaloes and that only one other hunter, a Pembina man known as Black Billy, had equalled that record. Both men were good hunters—no doubt about that—but much of their success, by campfire judgment, was due to their fast horses. Opinions differed about which was the faster horse and a race was inevitably promoted. Jean Baptiste was willing to put Turnips to the test, forgetting that the animal was really the property of his wife and untried in a race. The native owner, on the other hand, had seen his horse—Moose by name—win on many occasions at Pembina and was keen for the proposed match.

Camp sentiment was divided, with the natives from Pembina giving their undivided support to Black Billy's big gelding, while the Point Douglas crowd was ready to cheer for Turnips. Interest mounted. The race was on every tongue and arguments led to a few fights which Cuthbert Grant's policemen promptly stopped. The Metis were ready to bet everything they had—guns, carts, horses, and Hudson's Bay Company tokens. The Point Douglas Presbyterians were not given to the sin of betting on a horserace, but some of them could not resist small wagers. Paquin, although a member of the Pembina population, was inclined to stake his fortune on his friend's buckskin stallion. He made two gentlemanly bets, one in terms of Hudson's Bay Company tokens to the value of thirty beaver skins, and the other to the value of twenty skins. Those who didn't carry that much currency for paying their betting losses would be expected to settle with buckshot, horses, or leather clothing—satisfactory enough.

Such an important event as a horserace called for official supervision and Grant agreed to start the race and be ready to administer camp justice. A course of about one mile was stepped. The two contestants would start from a point beside the tents, race to a cart placed at the half-mile mark, turn, and race back to finish where they'd started. By remaining at the starting line, Grant could also declare the winner. No other rules were needed; if one horse refused to start, stumbled, or broke its neck, the other would be entitled to go on to win with ease.

The halfbreed was riding his own horse and the elder Lagimodière yielded to his son Jean who was eager to ride Turnips. The boy rode often beside the river and was at home on the stud's back, but he had never participated in a race. The crowd chatted and cheered as the horses came to the starting line. The experienced Pembina horse was undisturbed. Turnips, on the other hand, was puzzled and bothered. Neither rider had a saddle but both had green willow switches with which to urge their mounts to the limits of their speed.

Marie Anne, surrounded by her other children, was uneasy. This would be her son's first experience of the kind, and she said a prayer for his safety as he sped over ground made irregular by gopher holes and mole hills. But young Jean sat gracefully and Turnips, with beautifully proportioned body, a high head, and coat glistening like polished brass, was handsome. But will he run and give his best? she was asking herself. After all, he was a novice and might make a poor start.

Cuthbert Grant's gun roared the signal to start and Moose dashed away promptly. Turnips reared in confusion and Jean slid off over the horse's rump. For an instant, the stallion was loose, but somebody seized a rein and the boy's father made a mighty leap and was astride and ready to go. The other horse was fully twenty lengths ahead before Turnips appeared to get the idea of a buffalo chase and dashed away. The late beginning made a huge handicap. Spectators believed the race was already decided, and the Pembina people cheered loudly for Moose. Jean Baptiste, having no whip, pulled the belt from his trousers and used it to slap the stallion across the flank. Ever sensitive to a whip, the buckskin raced forward as if out of control.

Marie Anne turned to reassure herself that Jean was unhurt, and when her glance returned to the race, Turnips was back on the proper course, still far behind, but extending himself like a born racer.

"He's running well," Paquin told Marie Anne, "but he lost so much, he can't win now."

"I know," she answered, "just because he didn't know what to do. But he looks lovely."

It appeared that Turnips was beginning to recover some lost ground, and when Moose ran wide in making the turn at the cart, the stallion gained more. Paquin looked startled and shouted, "Holy heaven, that race isn't finished yet. Look at that buckskin devil go!"

Moose was tiring noticeably and his rider was pounding him furiously. Turnips seemed to have more wind. His ears were back and his head was low. At last he knew what he was supposed to do, and with Jean Baptiste no longer belting him, he was bearing down to reduce the other horse's lead. The animal was giving everything he possessed, and Jean Baptiste decided that it was better to leave the outcome entirely up to him. The Pembina crowd went silent and the Point Douglas folk began to shout their enthusiasm. If the course were longer, Turnips would win, but both horses were now nearing the finish and Moose was still ahead.

"What a race!" exclaimed Cuthbert Grant. "But the buckskin can't quite make it."

Marie Anne was saying nothing but her heart was pounding like Turnips' feet. She loved that horse just as she loved his stout little mother, but she never loved either more than now when Turnips was displaying his true mettle. While still breathing sorrow that her big horse had been so handicapped by a bad start, he bolted forward with a final reserve of energy. Like a prairie chicken coming in on a tail wind, he swept abreast and then ahead of the mighty Moose to beat him by two lengths of a flintlock.

Turnips was the winner and there was no doubt. Bedlam broke loose. Grant was thrilled to see such a display. Paquin, thinking of the bets he would collect, shouted boyishly. Marie Anne felt arms thrown around her and a kiss on her neck; it was John MacLeod who did not normally subscribe to the frivolities of horseracing and kissing. He was jumping up and down in youthful glee and at the same time stumbling through a halfhearted apology for what he'd done: "Damn it, Mistress Lagimodière," he was saying, "I didna' mean t' kiss ye but just forgot mysel'." It was difficult to tell if the man was laughing or crying but it didn't matter.

She was making her way to where her horse was standing, and pressing her face against his dilated nostrils, she whispered, "Turnips, boy, you've got the Potlatch spirit. Dear Turnips."

Men and women crowded around the sweating buckskin, touching his wet skin as if trying to catch some of his magic. Jean Baptiste showed his quiet satisfaction and retained a firm hold on the leather reins as if somebody might try to steal the winner. The widow Bruce sidled close to whisper words of congratulations—or something.

There was still the complicated business of settling bets. Jean Baptiste's one small wager involving a pouchful of gunpowder was relatively simple and easy to collect. With Paquin, whose bets were in terms of beaver-skin currency, settlement wasn't as simple. Black Billy, who rode the losing horse, was able to pay Paquin in the Hudson's Bay Company money to the full value of thirty "made beavers." But Porky MacTee, who bet twenty beavers on Moose, was obliged to confess that he didn't have the means. Paquin was angry. He knew Porky's reputation for slothfulness, but he expected him to pay a betting debt, especially after he had coaxed Paquin to make it.

"Porky," he shouted, "you're a damned crook. I should blacken your eyes. I'll report you to Cuthbert Grant and you'll pay up or he'll fix the penalty. He's tough."

Porky knew all about Grant and did not want a trial over which that man presided. He squirmed, and as Paquin turned to take the dispute to the camp boss, he called, "Wait a minute, Paquin. I make you a proposition. How much you give me for my silver treasure?" From an inside pocket in his shirt, Porky produced a tarnished ornament and continued to talk. "I should not sell this because I carry it long time and it brings me luck. But that Grant man not like me and you don't need to say anything to him. I tell you; I sell you this good thing for thirty made beavers, then I pay you and you pay me the difference. How about that?"

Paquin was fondling the ornament and trying to appear nonchalant. Actually he was studying it the way a detective might examine some crucial evidence.

"Where did you get this thing, Porky?" he asked.

"That thing? Oh, I get that years ago and always carry it for luck."

"You know it's not worth thirty beavers, nothing like it. I'll give you twenty-five for it."

"Only twenty-five? All right, I take that much."

Paquin pocketed the article, saying, "You owe me twenty beavers on the bet, and I'll give you tokens for five. Then we're even."

Porky nodded agreement and took the money, strolling away toward his tent.

The size and shape of the ornament held a striking familiarity for Paquin. He was trying to recall the circumstances of the stealing episode six years earlier. He hurried away to see Jean Baptiste.

"Hey, Jean Baptiste! What do you make of this thing? I just got it from Porky MacTee—paid him more than it's worth. Does it look like anything you ever saw before?"

Jean Baptiste examined the discolored piece, turned it over, and admitted that he hadn't seen anything like it. "Why did you want it? Something bothering you, Paquin?"

"You remember Mrs. Murdoch's brooches they said Marie Anne stole?"

"Yes, I remember them."

"Well, there were three stolen. Is that right? Two were found in Marie Anne's stocking and one was never found. Is that right, too?"

"That's right. You mean that might be the one? Wait a minute. I'll find Marie Anne."

"No, No!" Paquin was saying anxiously. "Not yet. I might be wrong and it would only upset her. I'll go alone to see Mrs. Murdoch. I'll let you know later."

With mounting excitement, Paquin went to the Murdoch tent. Mrs. Murdoch was there and Paquin was about to open the discussion when he noticed that she was not alone. In the shaded part of the tent sat the widow Bruce and the foxy Paquin merely asked for the loan of the Murdoch ax to cut some wood for the campfire. It seemed like an unusual request from Paquin, but it was granted and the Frenchman left. But while he chopped indifferently at some sticks near the center of the camp, he was watching the Murdoch tent. When the widow left, he hastened to return the ax.

Seating himself beside Mrs. Murdoch, he opened the serious question, "Those brooches. You remember? Two were found and one's still missing. I'm right?"

Mrs. Murdoch nodded. "We'll never see that one now, I feel sure."

"Where do you keep the two you got back?" Paquin asked.

"Keep them? Say, on a trip like this with Mrs. Lagimodière along again, I keep them right inside my blouse. They're valuable, you'll understand. Pure silver. Why do you want to know? First you want to borrow my ax and now you want to know where I keep my silver. Upon my soul, aren't you being cheeky? But you hunters do strange things."

"Now just a minute, Mrs. Murdoch. I have a thing that looks like one of your brooches—got it from a fellow who bet on the wrong horse and I'd like to compare it with yours."

That cast a different light upon things. The lady turned her back to her visitor momentarily, produced the two brooches, and placed them on a buffalo robe. Paquin laid his ornament beside them and Mrs. Murdoch looked startled. The tarnished article was identical in shape to the other two, and on its back was the maker's name: Jonathon Tyler.

"Heaven preserve us!" she exclaimed. "It is my other brooch. Where did it come from? Did Mrs. Lagimodière have it?"

The Frenchman hesitated; he didn't want to say too much. "I told you I got it from a fellow. I don't think Mrs. Lagimodière ever had anything to do with it. But look now, don't you say a word about this to anybody until I find out more. I'll let you know soon. In the meantime, you keep quiet."

Paquin wasn't sure where to go next, back to see Porky or call on Cuthbert Grant. He returned to Porky and said, "Look here, you— the brooch you sold me is one that was stolen right in this camp six years ago. I know that because the lady who lost it has identified it. Now how did you come to get it? Something damned odd about this."

"I didn't steal it," Porky protested. "I wouldn't steal anything."

"I wouldn't trust you with a rotten fish, you devil. Either you stole this brooch or somebody you know did. And by heaven, I'm going to find out. If you don't want to tell me, you can explain it to Cuthbert Grant."

Porky repeated that he didn't steal the brooch, and Paquin left directly to go to the captain's tent. Grant listened to the report. He knew that Marie Anne had been accused and readily agreed to order Porky, Mrs. Murdoch, and the Lagimodières to appear before him. Anybody guilty of theft would be sent home in disgrace—that order was unchanged and it seemed Porky might be going.

Paquin carried the order to the others promptly, stopping only long enough at Marie Anne's place to give her a hint of the development. "You'll hear more later."

Marie Anne's curiosity was almost more than she could endure. "You mean it might be the one? I'll be there. Would it be all right if Mr. MacLeod came too?"

Paquin thought it would be permissible for MacLeod to be present but made it clear that this was not to be seen as a public meeting. At the appointed hour, Grant faced the individuals named and John MacLeod was present as a privileged observer.

Grant, with many of the qualities of a good judge, directed his opening remarks to Porky. "The silver brooch you sold to Paquin today was stolen from Mrs. Murdoch six years ago. How did it happen to be in your possession?"

"I didn't do it," Porky said again. "If it was taken, it wasn't me."

"Very well," Grant continued. "If you didn't steal it, you had a stolen brooch and told Paquin you carried it for years. It was a stolen article and unless you can explain how it came to you, I must assume that you stole all three brooches."

Porky gazed at the ground in silence for a moment and then spoke up, "I didn't do it. A woman, she gave them to me."

"A woman?" asked Grant. "Why would she give them to you? Come now, tell the truth."

"All I know," he answered, "she said she had three silver things. If I will hide two of them in Mrs. Lagimodière's clothes in tent and keep quiet, I can have one."

Grant continued his questioning. "Who was this woman? Was she Mrs. Murdoch?"

Porky said no, and to a question about Mrs. Lagimodière's involvement, it was also no.

"Then what woman? Is she back with the hunters this year?"

"Yes," said Porky, "but I don't know her name. Jean Baptiste know her name; she often talk to him."

"Well, I'll be jiggered!" It was John MacLeod's voice. He could keep still no longer. "I ken who he means, Mr. Grant. Would ye have me go forthwith to her tent and invite her here so Porky can identify her?"

Grant approved and MacLeod was absent only a few minutes, returning with Mrs. Bruce. She appeared white and worried and MacLeod, without waiting for Grant to ask the first question, faced Porky and blurted, "Is this the woman?"

Porky looked and nodded and MacLeod mumbled, "Evil doer! I guessed it weel."

Grant, recovering his leadership from the effervescent MacLeod, said, "Mrs. Bruce, you may not know it, but the lost brooch that Mrs. Lagimodière was accused of stealing has been found today. This man, Porky, has been carrying it for six years, and he admits that you gave it to him for placing two brooches where they would make a thief of an innocent woman."

With mounting hysteria, the widow cried out, "I wouldn't do such a thing!"

"Just a minute now until I finish telling you what I know, and then you can explain. You have tried to win the interest of Mrs. Lagimodière's husband and your plot, so it seems, was to force her and her children out of the camp on that occasion six years ago. Everything suggests that you took the brooches from Mrs. Murdoch to split the Lagimodières."

"I can't go home alone!" the woman sobbed. "Are you going to send me? I was lonely when I did it and I wanted . . ." Her words failed and she swooned on the floor of the tent. Mrs. Murdoch and Marie Anne came to her side and fanned her face to cool it.

Relief and sympathy surged through Marie Anne's breast. She had trouble speaking: "Mr. Grant, I am the one who suffered most. For the sake of my children I'm so thankful the mystery has been solved. I wanted everybody to know that I didn't steal the brooches any more than I stole the snuffboxes that the governor found where he had mislaid them. But it's not my wish that this woman should suffer as I did. I don't want to see her sent home or obliged to stay in a tent where she's not wanted. If you will order it, Mr. Grant, I'll take charge of her. She can move into our tent tonight. And when we're going home, we can make room for her in our cart. Is that your order?"

"An order, Mrs. Lagimodière. One that makes me proud of my friends."

"And Mr. Grant, will you issue one more order?" It was John MacLeod. "Ye ken my mither was a Grant frae Inverness—'Stand Fast Craigellachie.' Ye'll do it for me, issue a command to John MacLeod to inform every man and woman in this camp that Madame Lagimodière's character is without spot or blemish, like new snow on the Grampians. God knows she'd no more steal a brooch than stand on her pretty heed in a kirk."

"That's an order too," Grant said, trying to suppress a chuckle.

Recovering from her faint, Mrs. Bruce was informed that she would not be sent home but would move instead into the tent of the woman who had been wronged and who had interceded on her behalf. "You will return to Point Douglas with the Lagimodières. I hope you'll appreciate what Mrs. Lagimodière is doing for you, and that you'll assist Mr. MacLeod—whose mother was a Grant—to inform all the people of the settlement that she is a better angel than Red River deserves."

Mrs. Murdoch was sorry she had been party to the injustices and said so. The widow didn't try to speak, but with gaze fixed upon the ground, she stood holding Marie Anne's hand. Jean Baptiste went back to the meat drying. Paquin had another question for the judge: "Who keeps the brooch I bought?"

"You deserve the medal, Paquin," Grant replied. "You paid twice what it was worth. You and Turnips earned the medals today."

"Let me polish the brooch for you, Paquin," Marie Anne offered, with a twinkle in her eyes. "You know tarnish will come off."

30

Julie's son

The fragrance of harvest filled the September air when a new grave at St. Boniface received the body of the seventy-eight-year-old frontiersman, Jean Baptiste Lagimodière. Had he lived a few months longer, he and Marie Anne could have looked back upon fifty years of married life—fifty years of adventure unmatched in the new West. Across the river at Fort Garry, built where hostile Fort Gibraltar had stood in other years, the Hudson's Bay Company flag fluttered at half-mast. At the graveside, hundreds of people for whom the valley had become home were present to pay respects to the great adventurer whose oratory was in deeds.[1]

"His gun spared this settlement from starvation," Bishop Taché said. "He was a man for whom no land was too far west."

For Marie Anne it was a sad moment; it couldn't be otherwise. Never again would she lean on the man she followed from the St. Lawrence to Red River and up the Saskatchewan where no white woman had ever travelled. Never again would she see him breaking kindling wood across his knee, or polishing his favorite gun with a rabbit skin. But she knew she had cause for gratitude—fifty years with the only man she had ever really loved was more than most women experienced—and he was healthy to the last and hungry for his pemmican to the day he died. Others along Red River might adopt diets of bread and fresh meat, but Jean Baptiste was loyal to pemmican.

The richest of Marie Anne's blessings, as she knew very well, was in being surrounded by her children. All were present on that funeral day except Reine who, with her husband, was living far away. And grandchildren? There were scores of them.

Not many of the friends from the earliest years survived. John MacLeod's grave was on the other side of the river, and most of those who had hunted with Jean Baptiste were buried at Pembina. Among those to grasp Marie Anne's hand and speak words of comfort was John Tanner, Jr., whose father had helped Jean Baptiste to build the log house. The elder Tanner's end had been a sad one. Living at Sault Ste. Marie, he married a white woman and was engaged as an interpreter for an Indian agent when he became angry at a young man paying unwanted attention to his daughter. The unwelcome fellow was shot and Tanner disappeared, never to be seen again until a skeleton was discovered in a swamp near Sault Ste. Marie. The rusted gun found beside it was identified as John Tanner's.

"Your father was a good friend," Marie Anne said to the young man. "We wanted to keep him at Red River but he wouldn't stay."

Following the funeral, Marie Anne and many members of her family went to Julie's home beside the mill on Seine River. There Julie placed the youngest of the grandchildren in Marie Anne's arms and a smile of pleasure came over the wrinkled face. Babies never became monotonous. The most recent arrival was as wonderful and full of interest as the first. Julie understood her mother better than her brothers and sisters did. She, more than the others, remained close to the older woman; not even matrimony had weakened the ties between mother and daughter. Julie was not the most beautiful of Marie Anne's girls, but she was the most serious and thoughtful —perhaps the most like the mother. For a time it seemed that she might be the only one of the children who would not marry, and Marie Anne felt a secret disappointment.

But romance is unpredictable and Julie found herself being admired by the young man who operated the mill on the Seine, just a short distance from the Lagimodière home. Riel was his name. His father was French and his mother Metis. An unusual fellow, this miller. His mind was as full of ideas as a summer hive is full of bees. He strongly resisted injustices and loudly protested the Company's trade monopoly. "Sooner or later," he contended, "the free men along Red River must take a stand against it."

Life with such a man would be trying at times, but it would never be dull, and Marie Anne liked him, liked his enterprise, liked his honest convictions, liked him because he was both French and Indian. It was a short courtship and Julie became Mrs. Riel. The first baby, as Marie Anne hoped, was a boy—Louis Riel, Jr., born October 22, 1844.

Never before had Marie Anne seen as many of her children and grandchildren assembled together as on that funeral afternoon, and as she gazed around her, every male face in the house seemed to look like that of Jean Baptiste.

"Mother," said Julie, "you'll not go back to your house anymore. You can live with us or you can live with Benjamin. He has a big house and it's warm in winter. You'll have your own room and privacy when you want it. But before you think about that, we have another proposal; we've been talking about your future and I think you'll like what we're going to tell you."

"I'm listening," she said with a smile.

"Well, it was really Joseph's idea but we're all in favor of it and if you agree we'll all help. You realize you've been here nearly fifty years. You used to talk a lot about going back to Maskinonge. Now we can manage to send you back there and you could live with your sister. It's a long trip, we know, but if it would make you happy, we can take care of the arrangements and Benjamin or Jean will accompany you."

"Go back to Maskinonge?" Marie Anne was gazing toward the west as though the answer might come out of the mouth of the Assiniboine. "Dear old Maskinonge! I can see the place so clearly. I can see my mother's pretty cabin beside the little river! I can hear her calling me, to braid my hair. Maskinonge! Isn't it a sweet word?"

Still holding the baby, she arose from her rocking chair and stood motionless as if she could think more clearly on her feet. Her gaze shifted to the east. Her eyes were wet but there was a smile. She was weighing the proposal and seemed almost in a trance, until she felt a tug at her skirt and heard a boy's voice sounding clearly and pleadingly, "Grand-mère, don't leave here! I don't want you to go to Maskinonge!"

The voice was that of Julie's eleven-year-old son. Marie Anne collected herself quickly and with a free hand she drew the lad close to her side, saying, "Louis, my boy, I was momentarily debating with myself, but now I know what I'm going to do. How did you know what I wanted you to say? I'm not going to leave. I guess I can talk about Maskinonge but your old grand-mère is not going."

Julie was listening in silence to the dialogue in which her son was proving more convincing than she had been. Marie Anne's words were now for everybody within the sound of her voice, "I have more to love and live for here at Red River than anywhere in the world. Do you think I'd leave here now? No! Besides, it's going to be exciting here. Maybe you haven't felt it yet, Louis, but you will."

"Mother, you sound as if you really mean that. We'll say no more about Maskinonge," Julie said, then let her mother resume.

"You might as well all know that when I married Jean Baptiste, I married Red River too, whether I realized it at the time or not. And so I'll just stay around and you can bury me beside my Ba'tiste."[2]

"I'm glad, gra'-mère," the boy whispered.

She smiled at him tenderly and added, "If I have my health, I'll see you grow up, Louis Riel, you dear scamp. You can go to see Maskinonge for me some day. It'll be better that way. Oh yes, you'll return here because Red River belongs to you and Red River will need you. Years ago, you know, Fox Tail said Julie's son would be a . . ."

She caught herself and stopped. She didn't really believe in sorcery. Anyway, she had never discussed Fox Tail's prophecy, even though she had on scores of occasions gazed at little Louis and speculated about the medicine man's words.

Notes

Chapter 1

1. André Nault's mother, Josette Lagimodière, was Marie Anne's third child, born somewhere near the Cypress Hills in what is now Alberta in 1810.
2. Julie, who married Louis Riel, Sr. in 1844, was Marie Anne's seventh child and fourth daughter, born at Red River in 1820.
3. The same sentiment and many of the same words were expressed editorially in the Toronto *Globe*. The editor, in the issue of October 24, 1871, said scornfully, "We already know how the ex-president (Riel) and lieutenant governor rushed into each other's arms and shook each other's hands, if they did not weep on each other's necks."

Chapter 2

1. Marie Anne's date of birth was confirmed from church records by Father Picton of St. Boniface.
2. Charles Gaboury died on December 17, 1792, at the age of forty-nine years. The date, as verified by church records, was furnished by Father Picton of Archbishop's House, St. Boniface, June 11, 1955.

Chapter 3

1. Information concerning their marriage on April 21, 1806, is from the register of baptisms, marriages, and burials for the Parish of St. Joseph, Maskinonge, 1806, and was obtained with the help of church officers at the Cathedral of St. Boniface. It translates as follows:

     After publication of one marriage ban delivered from the pulpit during parochial mass concerning Jean Baptiste Lagimodière, son of full age of Jean Baptiste Lagimodière and Josephte Beauregard, father and mother, voyageur, of this parish, of the first part, and Marie Anne Gaboury, daughter of full age of Charles Gaboury, deceased, and Marie Anne Tessier, her father and mother of this parish, of the second part, with both having obtained dispensation of the second and third bans from the Vicar

General of Trois Rivières and with no opposition, we, priest undersigned, have received their mutual consent and given the nuptial benediction according to the prescribed formula of the Holy Catholic Church, in the presence of witnesses . . . and many others of whom only one has signed with us, the others being declared unable to sign.

Louis Fiset

Ignace Vinet, Priest.

Chapter 5

1. The new North West Company fort soon to arise on the north bank of the Assiniboine River where it enters the Red would become well known as Fort Gibraltar. It was built in 1808 by the wintering partner, John McDonald of Garth. McDonald, writing rather apologetically about the choice of name, said "there was not a rock or stone within three miles." Located at the mouth of the river that drained the best buffalo country, Fort Gibraltar became especially important in the collection of pemmican for the support of the fur brigades.

Chapter 6

1. Alexander Henry, *New Light on the Early History of the Great Northwest, the Manuscript Journals of Alexander Henry and David Thompson*, ed. Elliott Coues (Minneapolis: Ross and Haines, Inc., 1897), p. 71.
2. The birth of a white baby to the Scottish girl who had lived disguised as a boy from the time of coming to Rupert's Land in 1805, was reported by Alexander Henry in his journal entry of December 29, 1807. The story is perpetuated in Alexander Henry, *New Light on the Early History of the Great Northwest*. p. 426.
3. For the basic historical information in this chapter and through most of the book, the principal credit must go to L'Abbé Dugast who spent twenty-two years at Red River and was the author of *The First Canadian Woman in the Northwest*, translated by Miss. J. M. Morice. The paper was presented as Transaction No. 62, December 12, 1901, to the Historical and Scientific Society of Manitoba, and was eventually published by the *Manitoba Free Press* in 1902.

Chapter 7

1. The post, situated north of present-day Melfort, on N.W. 18-49-17-W.2, was one of several posts called Prairie Post. It was known also as Isaac's House.
2. The scarred and blind Bouvier, according to L' Abbé Dugast in *The First Canadian Woman in the Northwest*, spent several years at the Fort of the Prairies and was then taken to St. Boniface where he devoted his last years to the making of crucifixes at the house of the archbishop.

Chapter 9

1. Dugast, in *The First Canadian Woman in the Northwest*, gives the name of the Frenchman-turned-Indian as Batoche Letendre.

Chapter 11

1. Dugast refers to this second child of Marie Anne as LaPrairie because of his

birth deep in prairie country. His real name, however, was Jean Baptiste and LaPrairie only a nickname. He ultimately farmed at Lorette, Manitoba, and died in 1886.

Chapter 12

1. Dugast, in telling of the massacre, ascribed it as an act of revenge by Sarcees who had recently suffered losses to the Crees.

Chapter 14

1. The second Fort Augustus was built on the north side of the North Saskatchewan, just below the location chosen ultimately for the Legislative Building in the City of Edmonton.
2. Reine was the first legitimate white child born in what was to become Manitoba, and the first born anywhere in the West to remain in the West. Jean Baptiste, Jr., if born at Isaac's House, which was one of several posts known as Fort of the Prairies, was the first white born in what is now Saskatchewan. And Josette, born at Fort Augustus, would be the first in what became Alberta.

Chapter 16

1. Scottish-born John McDonald of Garth came west in 1791 and became a wintering partner. Aggressive and pugnacious, his inclination was to settle an argument with pistols. John Wills came to the North West Company through the XY Company and was in charge of Gibraltar after McDonald's years.
2. Selkirk's "advance guard," consisting of twenty-two men, was already at York Factory on Hudson's Bay. They arrived there on September 24, 1811, after sixty days on an old sailing vessel and much distress from scurvy. Under the leadership of the big highlander Miles Macdonell, who had lived in Canada, the men were waiting for spring when they could travel the remaining seven hundred miles by canoe to Red River. Macdonell's instructions were to take possession of the allotted land at Red River and select a site for a settlement.

Chapter 17

1. It was on August 30, 1812, that Miles Macdonell, followed by members of the advance guard, arrived at the mouth of the Assiniboine to prepare for the settlers.
2. This, the first contingent of the genuine settlers, arrived at Point Douglas on October 27, 1812.

Chapter 18

1. John MacLeod's first appearance at Red River was as a member of Miles Macdonell's work force or advance guard that arrived at the confluence on August 30, 1812.

Chapter 19

1. In addressing the legal agents, Messrs. Maitland, Garden, and Auldjo, Robertson stated:
    The bearer of this express, Jean Bt. Lagimoneer, has undertaken this

voyage to Montreal on the following conditions — he has promised to take the packet of letters . . . and deliver the same safe into your hands on or before the first of March, 1816. As a recompense for this long and arduous journey, I promise him on the part of the Earl of Selkirk and the Honorable Hudson's Bay Company, whose interests I have in charge at this place, to pay or order to be paid by Messrs. M., G., and A., merchants of Montreal, to the said J. B. Lagimoneer, the sum of fifty pounds Halifax currency, two suits of clothes consisting of capots, two shirts, two neckcloths, two pairs of pantaloons, two pairs of stockings, two pairs of shoes, and one pound per week from the time of his arrival in Montreal until the navigation is open, so as to enable him to return to this place. . . . Permit me to recommend Lagimoneer as a man worthy of any trust you may repose in him. . . . He is a real honest man but hard in his dealings and highly worthy of the confidence I have reposed in him. . . . I have also promised that should any unforseen accident happen to this man while in charge of the express that the Earl of Selkirk and the Honorable Hudson's Bay Company allow his wife seven pounds per annum for ten years. I have also agreed to keep his wife and family at our Establishment here until his arrival at Red River.

Chapter 20

1. Fort Gibraltar was seized on March 13, 1816.
2. Colin Robertson's departure with his prisoner was on June 11, 1816. He intended to take Cameron to London to face trial.

Chapter 21

1. Jean Baptiste's arrival at York was on March 1, 1816, and at Montreal on March 10.
2. Lord Selkirk and a hundred hired soldiers arrived at Fort William on August 12, 1816.

Chapter 22

1. Mayor Joseph G. Van Belleghem of St. Boniface, in a letter to the author on November 3, 1955, confirmed the Lagimodière land grant as consisting of three parcels, numbered 681, 682, and 683 of "Register R" of the Hudson's Bay Company land records, and 73, 74, and 75 of the Dominion Survey. This would place the southern boundary of the land on Mission Street, extending from the mouth of the Seine River eastward 100 chains and northward to the C.P.R. highline, 16 chains. The grant would thus comprise more than 160 acres.

Chapter 26

1. Lord Selkirk's death on April 8, 1820, was at Pau, France, whence he had gone in the hope of recovering his health. He was forty-eight years old.

Chapter 27

1. The union of the Hudson's Bay Company and the North West Company carried the date of March 26, 1821.

Chapter 30

1. Jean Baptiste's death was on September 7, 1855, and burial was in the cemetery of St. Boniface Cathedral.
2. For the last years of her life Marie Anne Lagimodière made her home with her son Benjamin at St. Boniface. They were peaceful and comfortable years, ending with her death on December 14, 1875. Thus, she lived to see the creation of the Province of Manitoba, the coming of the North West Mounted Police, the beginning of homesteading, mass immigration, and the acknowledgment of the Northwest as a good land for agriculture — all expressions of the hopes and ideals for which she once stood almost alone.